Education for
CHILD REARING

By
ORVILLE G. BRIM, Jr.
Sociologist, Russell Sage Foundation

RUSSELL SAGE FOUNDATION
NEW YORK . . . 1959

© 1959
RUSSELL SAGE FOUNDATION
Printed in the United States
of America

Library of Congress
Catalog Card Number: 59–14553

WM. F. FELL CO., PRINTERS
PHILADELPHIA, PA.

Contents

3

PART TWO. PROCEDURES AND RESULTS

Foreword

THE FOUNDATION presents this addition to its list of publications with a special sense of the appropriateness of its sponsorship and of its timeliness and significance to the field to which the book is addressed.

The Child Study Association of America is, as Dr. Brim points out in the historical section of his report, "the oldest organization in the United States having a continuous parent education program, and today is the only national agency exclusively devoted to parent education."

Russell Sage Foundation throughout its fifty-two years has had as a central theme the development of ways and means for effective utilization of social science knowledge in the various fields of practice concerned with the welfare of the American people.

It was, therefore, singularly fitting that Dr. Gunnar Dybwad, then executive director of the Child Study Association, should propose that the Foundation support a study of the field of parent education from the point of view of social science. It was hoped that such a study would provide a useful organization of what is recognized as a field that has little or no generally accepted theoretical framework; and would point to ways in which social science knowledge and ideas could be efficiently applied to problems of practice in the field and to problems on which basic research was needed.

The appropriateness of the joint sponsorship of this undertaking was matched by the fortunate availability of Dr. Orville G. Brim, Jr. In providing those responsible for the conduct of parent education a look at the field from the perspective of a social scientist, he has laid the basis for a clarification of the working assumptions and explicit formulation of objectives in a field where these things have been largely implicit, diffuse and frequently contradictory. He has pointed the way to a more rational choice of available methods of operation and to the development of new, more suitable ones in the light of clarified assumptions and objectives and scientific knowledge of the relevant social processes involved.

One of the most significant sections of the book is addressed to the problems of evaluation. It is when this problem is seriously attacked that one comes to the full realization of the necessity for specifying assumptions and objectives and for identifying in explicit and manageable terms the component processes and variables that make up the operations or "method" of training parents toward greater competence in their roles as parents. Here, too, is seen the value of a high degree of sophistication in research method if evaluation efforts are to produce reliable results. But beyond these important points Dr. Brim's analysis of the problems of evaluation makes clear the need for a reexamination of theory and practice that should affect the whole range of activities in this field.

While this book is written for practitioners in parent education, it must be clear that it has a high degree of significance for child development research workers and sociologists concerned with the family. The book leaves no question as to the necessity for these scientists to devote serious and systematic attention to the problems of this field, and it is worth adding here that such attention will be productive for the sciences as well as for the practice. It was early discovered in the conduct of this study that the results of social science research could not simply be imported directly into the field of parent education. Rather a social science approach served to identify problems and significant variables which must be studied in the field of parent education itself.

Finally, it is clear that problems identified in the field here under discussion have much in common with those in other fields. Actually the problems in parent education are similar to those that plague other efforts in preventive mental health programs. The whole range of activities directed to child guidance, marriage and family counseling, the development of community competence to handle such problems as juvenile delinquency, and many other similar activities have many of the same basic problems. The present report points to the possibility that the future may well see a concerted attack on common problems of theory and method.

LEONARD S. COTTRELL, JR.
Russell Sage Foundation

July, 1959

Preface

OVER THE PAST SIXTY-FIVE YEARS this country has witnessed an ever-increasing interest in efforts designed to develop in parents a greater competence in the task of rearing their children. Today millions of parents are reached through such efforts and millions of dollars are spent in developing and maintaining such programs. For thirty years the term "parent education" has been in general use to refer to this work.

Aside from notable beginnings during the 1920's and 1930's supported by the Laura Spelman Rockefeller Memorial and spurred on by the White House Conference on Child Health and Protection, there has been a gross lack of systematic research in the field of parent education. Moreover, in spite of its position in modern American society parent education has no clear status. Claimed by some as a movement, by others as a profession, it is ill defined both as to content and method, and cannot claim a firm basis from which it can proceed in orderly development. It has borrowed liberally from psychiatry, psychology, education, sociology, social work, anthropology, and more lately, from the fields of group dynamics and mass communications. However, from all these disciplines it has taken its materials and procedures often much more from the ill-defined fringe areas than from the solid core of tested scientific knowledge. Hence, there is missing a solid frame of reference with regard both to theory and to practice against which the soundness of these activities could be measured.

From the viewpoint of the sociologist, the effort in the United States to educate parents is seen as a systematic attempt to change the social requirements and performance of one of the major roles in modern society, namely, that of the parent. It follows that programs seeking to educate parents for child rearing must involve the theory and research data of the social scientist at many points in the program. These include the assumptions of parent educators concerning the basis of human social behavior, and their assumptions about the methods which are effective in changing such social behavior.

This volume seeks to explore and clarify the contributions which social science theory and research already have made, and potentially could make to the successful planning and execution of educational efforts directed to parents. Of equal importance, an attempt is made to discover and analyze other issues in parent education to which the social sciences cannot contribute significantly at this time. The purpose of this volume is, therefore, to describe the contributions of the social sciences to parent education theory and practice, and also to call attention to areas of research which have been neglected.

This book is organized around those issues in the education of parents which are common to all programs. It does not contain successive chapters simply describing parent education programs in the United States. Data on specific programs in this country are used to exemplify the points made in the sociological analysis of the issues, and to provide the basis for generalizations about parent education.

One theme occurs frequently throughout these pages and serves as the unifying theme to the extent that one is suitable in such a work. This theme is the probable success of parent education in achieving its primary objective. The primary objective of those parent education programs generally acknowledged as successful and outstanding in quality is to make the parent more conscious of his role performance, to make him more autonomous and creative, to improve his independent judgment, to increase the rationality of the parent's role performance. One can fairly say that the effort of such programs is to improve the decision processes of parents, both in the parent's choice of ends in child rearing and in his selection of actual child-training practices.

This objective is sought by providing the parent with information both on children and on parents, and by providing educational settings in which parents are able to discuss, or individually to think through, and hence to formulate with conscious deliberateness, the ends they will seek and the means they will employ. The recurrent question one must face in the pursuit of this aim is the degree to which it is possible to increase the conscious and rational aspects of role performance by the modern American parent.

The author's knowledge of the field of parent education has been gained by reviewing the available literature on parent education programs, as well as by reading much of the material directed to parents themselves which has been published by parent education organizations. This information has been augmented by frequent consultation with the personnel of some two dozen widely regarded organizations conducting parent education programs. These organizations were selected to represent varying points of view, localities, and program emphases, as well as auspices under which the programs are carried out.

I am much indebted to many persons for valuable help in the conception and execution of this volume. The Child Study Association of America which acted as co-sponsor of the project with Russell Sage Foundation is the only organization of national scope exclusively concerned with parent education in all its various media. At the same time it is the oldest such organization in existence, with authorities dating the development of parent education from the organization of the Child Study Association's corporate predecessor, the Society for the Study of Child Nature in 1888. Thus, the Association reflects in its present activities much of the status of parent education today. Its historical files, its published reports, studies, books, and pamphlets for parents, and the development of its various experimental and demonstration programs provide both a broad and deep representation of parent education from its earliest beginnings.

During the course of this project I had the benefit of almost daily consultation with the professional staff of the Child Study Association, and it is just to say that this volume could not have been written without their continuous help. Dr. Gunnar Dybwad, the executive director until 1957, had the vision and leadership to initiate this study. During the course of the project, he gave much of his valuable time in assisting me with every detail, both professional and mundane, and graciously introduced me to personnel in other parent education organizations in the United States. In the past year A. D. Buchmueller, the current executive director, and Mrs. Clarence K. Whitehill, president of the Association, were of significant help in the completion of the project. The long and frequent discussions of critical issues with Aline Auerbach, Gertrude Goller, Salvatore Ambrosino, and other members of the professional staff were invaluable.

The Child Study Association of America is known to have its own point of view regarding the education of parents and is sometimes challenged by various other organizations in the country. Throughout the more than two-year period in which the professional staff of the Association acted as my primary resource, they consistently were able to distinguish their own point of view from that of others, and to present the assumptions and theory underlying other programs with care and honesty no less than that which they gave to their own. On the points where I still disagree with this staff, I trust that I have been able to present in this volume the basis for my conclusions as clearly as they were able to present theirs.

I am indebted also to many leaders in the field of parent education who read various chapters of this book in either published or working draft form and were kind enough to give their detailed criticisms.

Finally, the contributions of Mary J. Fleischman, Arla McMillan, and Merle Fried of the project staff, and of Margaret R. Dunne, editor for Russell Sage Foundation, are acknowledged with deep gratitude. This has truly been a joint venture with them.

During the course of this study several parts of this book were presented as lectures or articles. Chapter II was presented in the University of Texas lecture series, "Personality Development in Children," in 1958. Chapter III was presented in abridged form at the Twelfth Annual Institute for Workers in Parent Education, sponsored by Child Study Association of America in 1958. It was published by the Association as "The Sources of Parent Behavior" in the *Proceedings* of the Institute, and also appeared as "Sources of Parent Behavior" in *Children*, volume 5, 1958. Chapters II, III, and V all include portions of an address, "Some Basic Research Problems in Parent Education with Implications for the Field of Child Development," given at the conference commemorating the Fourth Anniversary of the Child Welfare Research Station, State University of Iowa in 1957; this is published in *Monographs of the Society for Research in Child Development*, volume 24 (No. 5), 1959. Chapter IX is based on two reports first presented at professional meetings and subsequently published: "Evaluating the Effects of Parent Education" was prepared for the Elizabeth McCormick Memorial Fund Family Research Conference, and appeared in shorter form in *Marriage and Family Living*, volume 19, 1957; "Recent Research on Effects of Education in Human Development" was presented at the First Institute on Preventive Psychiatry, State University of Iowa, in 1957, and appeared the same year in *Four Basic Aspects of Preventive Psychiatry*, edited by Ralph H. Ojemann and published by the University.

ORVILLE G. BRIM, JR.

PART ONE. ASSUMPTIONS AND OBJECTIVES

CHAPTER ONE:

The Nature of Parent Education

EDUCATIONAL PROGRAMS for parents have existed in this country for as long as we have records. During the past three generations, from about 1880 on, there has been an uninterrupted expansion of these programs. At present many organizations, both public and private, commercial and nonprofit, at the national, state, and local levels are engaged in educating parents about child rearing. Parents are counseled by physicians, clergymen, teachers, and nurses. They participate in groups discussing child rearing which meet under the auspices of mental health, parent-teacher, and other associations; read books, pamphlets, magazines, or news-paper columns; view films, plays, and television programs; and listen to lectures and radio programs, all concerned with educating them in child care.

In this first chapter we analyze the basis for parent education and clarify the distinction between it and other related endeavors.

THE SOCIAL CONTEXT

The development of the broad social movement to educate the American parent in child rearing had two fundamental causes. The first was the breakdown of cultural traditions in child-rearing practices, which in turn was a result of still other anteced-ent social changes. The latter include the change in the status of women in our society toward increased autonomy in both their family and nonfamily roles; the decline in frequency of inter-generational family relations, arising from the fact that now in our society most newly married couples establish residence apart from their parental homes; the increased contact through immigration and social mobility between members of different ethnic backgrounds and social classes who have contrasting cultural traditions of child care. All of these have contributed either to the isolation of the new parent from his own cultural traditions of child training, or to his exposure to different ways of rearing children which present a challenge to him.

The consequent breakdown in tradition forces the modern parent into greater consciousness of his child-rearing practices and demands that he develop many aspects of his roles as a parent *de novo*, either from his own resources or with the assistance of persons outside his family group, whether they be neighbors, physicians, ministers, or professional parent educators. One surmises, therefore, that organized parent education programs were a response to this situation, developed to fill the need for guidance caused by the decline of traditional child-rearing practices.

However, it would be a mistake to conclude that parent education arose only in response to the needs of parents. The second fundamental cause of this social movement was the growing belief on the part of many persons that there existed better ways of rearing children than those prescribed by traditions. This belief was nurtured by the research on child development in both Europe and the United States, which began just after the turn of the century, and gave promise of providing a new body of scientific knowledge of the desirable ways to rear children.

Those holding this belief sought to teach to all parents the findings of child development research, so that they could consciously and deliberately select those child-rearing practices consonant with their own aims, and proved by science to be superior to their own cultural traditions. The zeal of some proponents was extreme; for example, through parent education "many of the stresses of our culture would be reduced and even the relationships of nations might move toward a more peaceful, cooperative, productive basis" (1, p. 9), or through parent education "more profound changes in human life might result than have occurred since mankind emerged from the cave." (17)

The development of parent education from this source served to challenge further the cultural traditions of parent role performance by presenting both theory and research data contradictory to long-held beliefs about child development. Thus, this second independent cause of the parent education movement made the first loom even larger as a contributing factor to the development of parent education. The result has been to create a national situation in which research on child development and parent-child relations continues to increase in volume, with an accompanying increase in the sensitivity to, and the demand for, the results of such research on the part of the American parent.

In this context one can view parent education as a movement aimed at altering the role performance of parents on a massive scale, endeavoring to move the modern parent away from his cultural traditions toward a greater conscious and rational role performance and also to supply, in response to parental demand, the guidance he seeks instead of following his own traditions. It is true that certain parent education programs may seek to substitute the beliefs of the parent educators themselves for the traditional beliefs of the parents. The parent faced with the crumbling of his traditional culture turns quite naturally to seek some new authority rather than accepting the burden of autonomy and conscious role determination. It has been the task of parent education to avoid meeting the demand placed upon it to serve as a new authority and instead to help the parent become more competent and independent in his role. The fact that certain segments of the parent education movement are either unable or do not wish to face this challenge, but instead are gratified to find the parent treating them as a new authority, does not lessen the importance of the fact that parent education on the whole, and especially the programs recognized as outstanding, are concerned with engineering a unique and fundamental change in a major role in our society; namely, with transforming the parental role from one guided by cultural tradition and internalized values to one in which the parent must become, in part, his own judge of good and evil, and seek to develop a highly conscious, rationally determined role performance.

A DEFINITION OF PARENT EDUCATION

Parent education can be defined as an activity using educational techniques in order to effect change in parent role performance. Nothing is implied about this activity being directed to a specific end such as physical health of the child; on the contrary, parent education is customarily employed in the pursuit of a variety of ends.

This definition leaves several points which require amplification. These concern: (1) the relation between education and other techniques of personal influence; (2) the relation between educational efforts directed to influencing the role behavior of parents in contrast to role behavior in other situations; and (3) the distinction between the ends of parent education and the ends of other programs of influence. We will consider these points in order.

Education and Therapy

The distinction between education and therapy is difficult to make, and the problem has beset parent educators for a long time. Lindeman and Thurston (11, p. 13) in 1935 pointed out that "parent educators are now searching for that new line of demarcation which reveals where education leaves off and psychotherapy begins." We need simply add that twenty years later they are still searching. Nor is the confusion one-sided. Therapists also wrestle unsuccessfully with the problem, as seen in the various attempts to define therapy for the purposes of licensing or certification. In some instances the definitions presented of therapy are such as to have rendered illegal, except for licensed medical personnel, many activities commonly held to be educational (18). The distinction between education and therapy may be much like the legal distinction between sanity and insanity in that in any specific case it is very hard to apply. Indeed, future research may show that it is invalid, but that current practices are based on the distinction and demand that one recognize it.

The working distinction which we will employ throughout this analysis is the following: educational techniques are those directed to the conscious (and near-conscious) aspects of the individual personality, and exposure to educational programs ideally should arouse only conscious beliefs and conscious motives. In contrast, therapeutic techniques are directed to unconscious motives, expectations, and attitudes, and the instrumental goal of therapy is to make the individual ready to profit from subsequent educational experiences. In this sense, therapy is a kind of interaction designed to dissipate the individual's defenses and to render him educable, that is, susceptible to change from various educational procedures.

Several points follow from this basic differentiation. The first is that education avoids pressing forward where the person is resistant, on the assumption that the resistance arises from strong defenses which in turn arise from unconscious motives. As Auerbach (2) has pointed out, the distinction between a group educational experience and group therapy is that the former does not "expose, explore and work through the pathology of its members."

However, and secondly, there is no implication that education does not examine why a person feels as he does. To the extent that the "why" is under conscious control it is suitable subject matter for the educational procedure. Only when the reasons are unconscious should education avoid examination of the causes of a person's feeling and behavior (5).

Third, it follows that the changes resulting from education will comprise minor changes in the person's character, when compared to the major personality reorganization held to result from successful therapy. This is satisfactory, of course, in view of the assumption that most parents neither want nor need a major reorganization of their personality.

Fourth, note that both education and therapy can give information of a personal, specific kind. It is not satisfactory to attempt to differentiate education from therapy on the grounds that the former gives just general information, whereas the latter relates it specifically to the given individual in therapy. Indeed, the whole emphasis of modern educational theory, stemming from John Dewey and William H. Kilpatrick, is that education is most successful when the materials to be learned are related directly to the specific personal interests and experience of the student.

Fifth, distinctions have been offered on the basis of working with healthy aspects of the individual's personality in contrast to the pathologic aspects. For example, as Neubauer (16) says, "Therapy directs itself to the deviant aspects of personality, the symptoms or the character disturbance, with a view toward effecting change in individual pathology. Making use of a specific technique consciously applied, it approaches conflicts in order to free the energies bound within them, thus making these energies available for healthy growth.

"Education is aimed at those faculties of the ego which are undisturbed by conflict. It is oriented toward the healthy factors of the personality and appeals to the ability to judge, to gain understanding, to learn to use one's experience for new and different [experiences and] situations, to plan, to make choices, to adapt to changing circumstance, to add new experiences." This distinction is useful if one also recognizes that individuals may have serious conflicts which arise from consciously and accurately recognized sources, and in this sense are potentially under conscious control. That is to say simply that some of the major conflicts experienced by persons would be solvable by educational techniques.

Sixth, we must recognize that both the educator and the therapist can establish an affective, warm, and personal relation with the pupil or patient as the case might be. Indeed, one would suppose that such warmth would be every bit as conducive to the success of education as it is to that of therapy.

Finally, we note that the aim of therapy is the emotional health of the individual, and that this end is not restricted to any particular role. Although the specific problem leading the individual to the therapist usually arises in some specific role area such as in the family or in one's work, it is misleading to hold that therapeutic methods are directed to shifts in performance of any particular role, even though they may initially begin in a specific area. Therapeutic efforts are directed toward influencing the individual in a general way, that is, in terms of characteristics which customarily are not specifically related to any role. They pertain to what Linton (12) has called the "core personality" which contributes in part to every role performance. Thus, we conclude that therapeutic methods of influence are directed to changes in the individual which are not role specific. Whether there really are such general or "core" personality characteristics, or whether all personality traits are specific to some certain role, is at present a matter of contention. In any case, education contrasts with therapy in that while education is in fact general, much of it is specifically focused on some given role as in one's occupation, family, or community.

In sum, education is the attempt to influence a person by appeal to those motives and beliefs which are under conscious control, whereas therapy is an attempt to influence one by working with unconscious motives or beliefs which interfere with the individual's learning from educational techniques. While this distinction may leave several issues unresolved, we have found it helpful in differentiating between educational and therapeutic programs and we use it henceforth as our working distinction.

The Parental Role

Parenthood represents a particular status in our society, and associated with this, as with every social status, is a particular role which it is expected the parent will perform in interaction with the child. This status and role of the parent differ from others which the individual holds, for example, those of wife or husband or other adult statuses; and this provides a basis for a distinction between parent education and other educational efforts. The point has been made by others such as Lindeman (10) and Kotinsky (9) that parent education must be distinguished from other kinds of education in terms of the area of life to which it is directed.

First, in considering the relation between parent education and adult education one sees that parent education refers to efforts directed toward influencing a specific role, and adult education refers to educational efforts directed toward influencing *any adult* role, whether it be as community members, as American citizens, as parents, or whatever. Logically, therefore, parent education is a part of adult education, and the former educates persons in but one of their many adult roles. This point of view is not new, for it was recognized twenty or more years ago (4) that parent education was a subdivision of the growing adult education movement. In current discussions of adult education and in surveys of the extent of adult education (e.g., 15) programs which are clearly and purely parent education in nature are often included. Moreover, major national organizations, such as the Adult Education Association, which are composed of persons seeking to educate adults for whatever role performance, regularly include a number of persons specifically concerned with parent education.

A second point in differentiation involves the relation between parent education and the broader activity of family life education. Family life education should, and customarily does, refer to those educational programs which are directed to influencing the performance of specific roles within the family context. Such roles include those of the child, the sib, the parent, and the husband and wife. Logically, therefore, parent education constitutes one-fourth of those activities designated as family life education (which, of course, in part belongs to adult education). Certainly there are distinctions between the education of junior high school or high school students as children, the education of individuals for their better performance of husband or wife roles as with marriage counseling, and the education of adults as parents. While it is true that the parental and marital roles are closely related, so that educational efforts which influence the performance of one frequently have their effects spill over into the other, the problem is primarily empirical and not definitional. We point out here only that it is possible and necessary, too, to distinguish between educational programs which have as their primary target change in parent role performance and other family life education programs which have as their primary target changes in performance as a husband or wife. It may well be that the future will see an increasingly close relation between the two types of family educational programs which more fully recognizes the integration of the parent and the spouse role.

At present, even though there are some separate organizations within the area of family life education for marriage counselors, for parent educators, and for others, the more broadly organized professional groups, such as the National Council on Family Relations, customarily include persons involved in both marriage and parent education programs. The programs of meetings of these organizations include materials on both parent education and marriage counseling.

A third distinction remains to be made, namely, between parental and preparental roles. Many educational programs try to influence the parent role performance, although they are in fact directed to individuals who are not yet parents. Such programs include formal courses in the field of "human development," which are given in colleges and universities, high schools, and even elementary schools (3). Included also are the many classes for prospective mothers and fathers, and the individual counseling given by physicians and others during the pregnancy period.

Here we must make an arbitrary distinction in our definition. The term "parent education" is assigned to those programs concerned with educational efforts directed to people already in the parent role, while the term "preparental education" will be used to refer to those activities involving individuals prior to their entrance in the parent role but designed to educate them for later role performance. If we do not make this distinction, parent education becomes synonymous with all activities directed to parents whether prospective or actual; programs directed to actual parents disappear into this broad educational effort of our culture and our problem of assessment becomes unmanageable. While we believe that many aspects of our analysis of parent education will be relevant to preparental educational programs, we do not systematically consider such programs.

The Objectives of Parent Education

It is important to stress that the use of parent education is not limited to the pursuit of some single objective. We have said so far that parent education is an activity employing educational techniques and designed to influence parent role performance. But the influence upon the parent may serve many ends, and the fact is that parent education *has* been employed as a method of achieving various ends. In 1930 at the third White House Conference, considerable attention was given parent education, and it is noteworthy that in addition to the report (19) of the Committee on the Family and Parent Education, many of the committees on other aspects of child welfare indicated that their recommendations for children could not be implemented without changing the parent, and that parent education should be used for this. Numerous publications (e.g., 8, 13, 14) attest to the variety of ends for which the education of parents has been used; for example, training for good citizenship, choosing a dentist, preventing blindness, improving diet, selecting clothing, procuring baby sitters, training in the use of money, teaching good manners, and so forth, as well as the major current emphasis on promoting the mental health of the child.

It is this variety of ends which permits a working distinction between the general concept of mental health education and that of parent education. First, we recognize that most parent education programs are primarily concerned with improving the mental health of the child. While for practical purposes in this volume we stress analysis of these particular programs, it is important to point out that parent education is *not* used only for mental health ends. In contrast, "mental health education" *is* directed to a single end, but seeks to achieve its objective through educating persons in *many* roles. Ginsberg (6) and Gruenberg (7) have noted that special educational activities in the service of mental health ends are directed at different groups of persons, including "parents, children, teachers, doctors, pastors, lawyers, policemen, welfare workers, administrators, newsmen, and others." (7)

In sum, we might say that parent education differs from mental health education in that the former focuses on a specific role but is directed to a variety of ends, whereas mental health education focuses on a specific end but is directed to changes in a variety of roles. But parent education and mental health education overlap to a significant degree in the effort to influence parent role performance for the purpose of mental health. Indeed, in such instances parent education and mental health education are virtually identical, and, therefore, while we analyze parent education in this volume, the analysis must of necessity apply to an important segment of mental health education.

REFERENCES

1. Allen, Winifred Y., and Doris Campbell, *The Creative Nursery Center:* A Unified Service to Children and Parents. Family Service Association of America, New York, 1948.

2. Auerbach, Aline B., "Parent Discussion Groups: Their Role in Parent Education," *Parent Group Education and Leadership Training.* Child Study Association of America, New York, 1953, pp. 1–8.

3. Brim, Orville G., Jr., "Recent Research on Effects of Education in Human Development" in *Four Basic Aspects of Preventive Psychiatry:* Report of the First Institute on Preventive Psychiatry, edited by Ralph H. Ojemann. State University of Iowa, Iowa City, 1957, chap. 4.

4. Brunner, Edmund de S., "Some Problems in Parent Education from the Standpoint of the General Field of Adult Education," *Parent Education,* vol. 2, 1935, pp. 5–8.

5. Dybwad, Gunnar, and Gertrude Goller, "Goals and Techniques of Parent Education," *Casework Papers.* Family Service Association of America, New York, 1955.

6. Ginsberg, Sol W., "The Mental Health Movement: Its Theoretical Assumptions" in *Community Programs for Mental Health,* edited by Ruth Kotinsky and Helen Witmer. Harvard University Press, Cambridge, Mass., 1955, pp. 1–29.

7. Gruenberg, Ernest M., "The Prevention of Mental Disease," *Annals of the American Academy of Political and Social Science,* vol. 286, 1953, pp. 158–166.

8. Kawin, Ethel, *Parenthood in a Free Nation.* Parent Education Project, University of Chicago Press, Chicago, 1954.

9. Kotinsky, Ruth, "Parent Education: An Attempt at Delimitation," *Parent Education,* vol. 2, 1935, pp. 9–13.

10. Lindeman, Eduard C., "A Philosophy for Parent Education" in *Parent Education:* Types, Content and Method. White House Conference on Child Health and Protection, Section III: Education and Training, Committee on the Family and Parent Education. Century Co., New York, 1932, pp. 22–35.

11. Lindeman, Eduard C., and Flora M. Thurston, *Problems for Parent Educators.* National Council of Parent Education, New York, 1931.

12. Linton, Ralph, *The Cultural Background of Personality.* Appleton-Century-Croft, Inc., New York, 1945.

13. McGinnis, Esther, and Marie Pfeiffer, *Family Centered Education:* Annotated Bibliography. American Home Economics Association, Washington, 1953.

14. National Congress of Parents and Teachers, *Parent Education:* The First *Yearbook.* The National Congress, Washington, 1930.

15. National Education Association, Division of Adult Education Service, *A Study of Urban Public School Adult Education Programs of the United States.* The Association, Washington, 1952.

16. Neubauer, Peter B., "The Technique of Parent Group Education: Some Basic Concepts," *Parent Group Education and Leadership Training.* Child Study Association of America, New York, 1953, pp. 9–15.

17. Rogers, Maria L., *A Contribution to the Theory and Practice of Parents Associations:* A Discussion Based on a Five-Year Experiment Made by the United Parents Associations of New York City, 1925–1931. United Parents Associations of New York City, New York, 1931.

18. Sanford, Fillmore H., "Psychology, Psychiatry, and Legislation in New York," *American Psychologist*, vol. 9, 1954, pp. 160–164.

19. White House Conference on Child Health and Protection, Section III: Education and Training, Committee on the Family and Parent Education, *Parent Education:* Types, Content and Method. Century Co., New York, 1932.

CHAPTER TWO:

The Influence of Parent on Child

IN THIS CHAPTER and the two that follow we consider some of the fundamental assumptions in parent education. One must recognize in parent education that underlying program planning, the selection of content for parents, the setting of aims for parent education programs, and the selection of techniques of education are several basic assumptions about the kind of people that parents are, why they behave as they do, and the effects they have upon their children.

It is this latter assumption about the effects of parents on their children which we consider in this chapter. It gains importance when we recognize that parent education is in the last analysis designed to influence parent behavior in a way which is beneficial to the child. This effort to benefit the child through education of his parents is justified only on the assumption that the parent is an important influence on the child's life. Our discussion of this basic question has three major parts. The first considers the kinds of information available to parent education on this question; the second considers several critical issues pertaining to the effects of parents on children, such as which aspect of parent behavior may in fact have the greatest effect, whether such effects are subject to change, and so on; the third gives some indication of the actual use made of the available information by parent education.

INFORMATION ON THE EFFECTS OF PARENTS ON CHILDREN

The scientific findings on the effects of parents on children are of three kinds. There is the information from clinical studies, from studies of child development itself, and from studies made in the social sciences such as sociology and social psychology. Each of these three kinds of scientific information has important values but also some recognized defects which are not yet fully corrected. Thus, the clinical material (that is, the information drawn from studies in psychoanalysis, psychiatry, and other such fields) is rich in theories and ideas about the effects of parents on children. Yet this information is not generally applicable because it is drawn frequently from single case histories. Even where a number of cases are used they are obtained in such a way that they do not represent the general population. In addition, the ideas developed concerning the effects of parents on children from the examination of these clinical materials are rarely tested in families whose members are free from emotional disturbance. We do not know whether or not many of the ideas discovered are true for the average, healthy person.

The descriptive and experimental child development studies begin about 1920. These are carried out by child psychologists, educators, research pediatricians, home economists, and others. They provide a great amount of information on characteristics of children, especially on the stages of development in children's growth. However, these scientific materials until quite recently have suffered from the fact that the child was viewed almost as if he had no parents, which is to say that parents were rarely included in these studies. It has been pointed out recently (34) that in the revised edition of Carmichael's *Manual of Child Psychology* (15) out of some 1,200 pages of text fewer than 25 pages scattered throughout the book pertain to parent-child relationships. Thus, we gain little insight from these studies into the role of parents in such matters as stimulating or retarding the child's development.

The materials from sociology and social psychology which describe the family provide information on the behavior of the adults both as husbands and wives and as parents, but much more on the former than on the latter. This research deals very little with children or with the effects of parents on children. Indeed, in contrast to the child development research, it has in large measure viewed the adults in the family as if they had no children. Even though some of the very earliest research and thinking on personality development in children in this country was carried out by sociologists, somehow it did not become a major area of interest, and very little more was done until about ten years ago.

Since World War II there has been some convergence among clinicians, child development researchers, and sociologists in their studies of the effects of parents on children. This is true both in the research techniques which are used and in the theories which guide and support the research. A psychiatrist doing research may now consider sampling problems, that is, obtaining cases representative of a given group; and he may use a research design involving experimental and control subjects. The student of child development would now consider the influence of parents in forcing the child through maturational or developmental stages, and at the same time would enrich his explanations of child development with ideas from the clinical field. Sociologists have moved in number into programs of research upon the family as a whole and bring with them ideas from studies of small groups of other kinds to integrate with the traditional child development theories and with the theories of psychiatrists and other clinicians. The results of this convergence of interest are apparent. An increasing number of important studies of the effects of parents upon children now appear in the professional journals of all three of these areas of science. Often the studies are quite similar with respect to basic ideas and research techniques.

From these three professional groups there has accumulated during the last half-century a very large body of data on the family and child development. Much of this material, as we have pointed out, is not concerned with the effects of parents on their children. But even after subtraction of the research which is not relevant, the amassed scientific data with which parent education should be familiar in formulating its assumptions about the effects of parents are nearly overwhelming. Anderson in a recent paper (4) has summarized trends in the publication of research from all sources in this field of child development, pointing out the continuing increase and the fact that at the present time nearly 5,000 research studies have been reported. The *Manual of Child Psychology*, mentioned previously, includes over 1,200 pages of terse summaries of research studies. At present those who would keep informed on current thinking about the effects of parents on the child must turn regularly to the *Child Development Abstracts*, which appears bi-monthly and which in the course of a year summarizes over 1,000 studies in this area. To keep informed on research in progress which is not yet published, one needs to consult regularly *Research Relating to Children:* An Inventory of Studies in Progress, a Children's Bureau publication issued periodically.

SIX BASIC QUESTIONS

The available research leaves in doubt the answers to many important questions regarding the effects of parents on children's personalities. Six of these have been selected from a much larger number which could have been dealt with because they seem to have special relevance to parent education planning.

Effect of the Parent Versus Other Forces

This first issue really has two aspects. One concerns the effect of the parent upon the child in contrast to the effects of the child's inheritance or genetic determinants. It is clear that parent education as well as other educational movements must assume that the experience of the child is a powerful determinant of his behavior in contrast to genetic factors. If not, then programs for improvement of mankind should emphasize eugenics rather than education.

With regard to the influence of heredity versus environment upon the child's personality, the controversy continues today as it has for some three generations. The belief prevalent in the late nineteenth century that variations in individual personalities were primarily inherited gave way to the opposite viewpoint: that differences in character came from differences in experience. The latter drew its strength from conditioning and learning experiments in psychology and from research in cultural anthropology, demonstrating that variations in personality were correlated with variations in cultures. In particular, the work of Margaret Mead (28) was highly influential, suggesting as it did that even such basic characteristics as masculinity and femininity differ in different cultures, and that their expression is determined by modes of child rearing and later social norms.

One characteristic after another of the person was transferred, so to speak, from the domain of inheritance to the territory of environment. During the extreme phase of this change even intelligence became suspect as to its major determination by inheritance. This new viewpoint reached an extreme around 1920 and during the decade which followed, and is given perhaps its most famous expression in this quotation from the writing of the psychologist John B. Watson. "Give me a dozen healthy infants, and my own world to bring them up in, and I'll guarantee to train any one of them to become any kind of specialist I might select—doctor, lawyer, artist, merchant, chief, and even beggar man or thief." (45) One should note that with the exception of intelligence very little scientific research actually was done on the comparative influence of heredity versus environment.

A reaction to this extreme position set in some years ago. It is apparent in several ways. One is the growing recognition (e.g., 7) that certain kinds of behavior, for example, nail biting or enuresis, are common enough to suggest they are characteristics of normal development for many children, and not the result of "mismanagement"; that before these behaviors are viewed as symptomatic of abnormality one must know their frequency, multiplicity, and duration, and the age at which they occur. Another example is the growth of scientific research on the influence of heredity on personality traits. The recent research has dealt with the effects of heredity upon schizophrenia (e.g., 23), and the effects of different body types upon such personal characteristics as introversion and extroversion (e.g., 40). A third instance is the way that medical practice now emphasizes biochemical determinants of personality traits and the biochemical treatment of mental illness. A fourth is a reinterpretation of the cultural anthropological data pointing out that while culture may overcome the influence of genetic factors such as sex, that it does so at some cost; that, as someone has put it, it remains easier to make a man out of a man than it is to make a man out of a woman.

Thus, the conception of how plastic and changeable human nature is seems to move from one extreme to another. It leaves us still in the dark as to the relative effects of parents upon the child's character with respect to many important traits, such as desire for achievement, level of activity, aggression, dependency, and many others. It seems hardly a coincidence that the major development of parent education took place when environmental determinism was at its highest point. To the degree that new research shows important limits to the influence of parents upon children, it follows that parent education may seek more limited objectives. While "nature versus nurture" research continues to be contradictory, albeit at a higher level of knowledge, the data do demand the continuing attention of parent educators. For example, in a recent research study Cattell and his colleagues (16) report that the "authoritarian rigidity" syndrome of the personality appears more genetically than experimentally determined. This study is unique but cannot be ignored for that reason. The parent educator is challenged to examine his assumptions about the influence of parents in producing authoritarianism in children and to appraise his own program as to its rationale.

The second aspect of this question of the effects of the parent in contrast to other forces deals not with heredity versus environment but rather considers only the relative influence of differing environmental effects, namely, the parent in contrast to other persons and groups. It is clear that the parent educator must assume that the parent is a powerful influence in specific contrast to the child's siblings, peer groups, teachers, and the like. Otherwise the educational program is more profitably directed to these other groups than it is to the parent.

Ojemann (30) has pointed out that in the decade of the 1930's, in contrast to the optimistic beginnings of parent education, there was considerable discussion of whether or not the home had any important influence on the child. Even among those who believed that it did, many held that it was relatively minor. (In the Appendix it is noted that the decline of parent education during the half-dozen years following 1938 is attributed by some to this sentiment.) It is not that greater influence was attributed to inheritance but rather that the child's neighborhood, housing, schools, and the like were viewed as the prime determinants of the child's character.

However, since that brief interlude the parent once again has taken his place as the primary influence on the child. Beginning with the influential studies by Hartshorne and May (22) research (e.g., 19, 35) has continued to show that the correlations between attitudes and beliefs of the child and those of his parents are greater than are correlations with those of his friends, club leaders, schoolteachers, and so on. The theories and research of clinicians have contributed to this shift of opinion back to giving greater influence to the parent. The changing outlook is illustrated with respect to the alleged causes of juvenile delinquency. For the period about the middle 1930's and some years thereafter, the accepted cause of delinquency was that individuals learned it from their friends (39). However, the increasing interest of psychiatrists in delinquency, together with the research of the Gluecks (20) and others, now seems to have shifted the explanation in vogue to the "unhealthy influence of parents." Indeed, some have made the humorous observation that children appearing earlier before a juvenile court explained their behavior to the judge in terms of "bad companions," but now explain it by saying that their mothers did not love them.

One suspects that the reaffirmation of the great influence of the parents in contrast to other interpersonal experiences has reached an extreme and that reaction to this extreme is again under way. As instances: Blatz (12) stresses the influence of the teacher upon the child; Bossard (13) calls attention to the influence of other members of the household, for example, siblings, maids, and the like; recent research (14) concretely shows the influence of the siblings on the child's personality in regard to sex typing. It would seem that most parent education programs view the parent as such a powerful influence upon the child that they neglect consideration of the peer group, the school, and other comparable influences. One notable exception is the National Congress of Parents and Teachers (17, p. 17) which holds that "nothing in the child's environment at home, in school, in the community . . . is without bearing in the child's development." It follows logically that parent-teacher association activities include not only parent education, but also citizenship, current events, and neighborhood improvement.

Indeed, the problem is still more complex than we have indicated because the relative importance of parents and other people in their effects upon the child may vary according to certain other factors in the environment. For example, where the family is large and the younger child is taken care of by his older brothers and sisters, it follows that the influence of the parent is to some degree diminished. Where the child grows up with only his parents on an isolated farm, parental influence will be greater than in a crowded urban environment such as New York City's Harlem in which the bulk of the child's time is spent not with his parents, but with friends his own age. Much more research is needed on this point. In some cases, undoubtedly too much influence has been ascribed to the parent. In other cases his role has been minimized. In sum, at this stage of our knowledge, it is impossible to say concretely how influential are the different persons in the child's life with respect to the development of most of his personality characteristics. Recognition by parent educators that there is much ignorance in this area and that they themselves must make some assumptions about parent influence may guard them from making thoughtless assumptions.

Effect of the Mother Versus the Father

Programs in parent education from the beginning have been designed on the assumption that the mother is the primary influence upon the child. In this, parent education is similar to other programs pertaining to the family. For example, Pollak (33, p. 38) points out that mothers are interviewed before fathers in child guidance clinics, and in fact such clinics often do not ask to see the father even when he was the one who made the initial referral of the child. To some unknown extent this position has been forced upon parent education, because it is the mothers who are more available and who express interest in parent education. However, this position has long been bolstered by folklore, for example, "the hand that rocks the cradle rules the world"; by psychoanalytic thought, which stresses the durable effects of infant experience which is largely derived from the mother; by studies such as those of Hartshorne and May (22) and Forer (19), which show that the correlations between the child's beliefs, attitudes, and values run higher with his mother than with his father; by research such as that of Barker and Wright (9), which points out that interaction episodes between mother and child are three times as common as are those between father and child; and by research (36) on the patterns of authority in New England families, which shows the mother to play a much larger role in making child-rearing decisions.

Granted that the influence of the mother is possibly greater, it should be noted, however, that this idea is based on two hidden assumptions. One is that it is the early life experiences which are most influential. Evidence showing that experiences in later life, say during adolescence, were equally important would thus increase our estimate of the father's effect upon the child, since in the later life experiences the father plays a larger role than earlier. We return to this point later. Hidden also is the assumption that parent influence can be dealt with in some general, vague way. The real question, however, may not be who has the greater influence in general, but rather which parent has the greater influence in certain areas of the child's development. For example, in a child's learning how to behave as a man, it certainly could be argued that the role of the father in acting as a model for his son equals or surpasses in importance the influence of the mother.

Since there has been little challenging scientific study of this topic, it follows that our knowledge is somewhat vague and unformulated. There seems to have been a tendency to settle the issue by assuming that the mother is the primary influence, and that it is good for the father to assist her in child care even to the degree that he comes to share many of the duties traditionally the mother's in our society. The extreme view is that the mother and father are in a sense interchangeable in providing child care, with each being suited to take on the responsibilities of the basic mother role in rearing children. But we do not know how desirable it is to maintain a clear separation of the roles of the parents, since the child may acquire different parts of his personality from exposure to different roles in the family. Various hypotheses exist with respect to this problem and whichever is correct will have far-reaching implications for parent education programs. Recently Parsons (32) has made a distinction between what he calls instrumental or task-oriented roles, which involve personality traits such as aggression, initiative, and planfulness, and expressive or social-emotional roles, which involve traits such as cooperation, appreciativeness, and cheerfulness. He goes on to suggest that every child must acquire the ability to act both ways, to play both roles as it were at different times; and suggests that the child learns the former task-oriented role through interaction with the father, and the other through interaction with the mother. If this is true, then failure to stress the importance of both mother and father roles may result in their dilution, one by the other, with a resultant ambiguity in the child's personality development.

To generalize, it is clear that the question of the mother versus the father as the primary influence needs careful examination and considerable thought, particularly with reference to the areas of primary influence of the mother and father. To operate simply on the assumption that the mother is the primary influence and, therefore, the suitable target for parent education is to operate at the surface level. It appears that parent education programing requires some basic rethinking in terms of conceptions of appropriate maternal and paternal roles in the parent-child system, since confusion here may deprive the child of necessary models and render him incompetent in later life. Consideration of this problem may lead to specialized kinds of programs directed to fathers and to other implications for parent education activities.

The Aspect of Parent Behavior Most Effective

The third question regarding parent influence concerns the aspect of parent behavior that is most conducive to the child's mental health. Does the child's mental health depend upon the care with which parents, in their training of the child, follow carefully the prescribed pattern based on psychological principles, for example, in "training him for the toilet"? As long as they follow such a systematic program, does their emotional attitude toward the child make any difference? Is love necessary? On the other hand, if parents evidence constantly warm affection, may they disregard "desirable practices" of child rearing and yet do no harm to the child's mental health? Is love enough?

Difference of opinion as to which is the better method of child personality development can be found in another phase of the problem—the effect of type of early treatment upon achievement motivation.

Studies by McClelland and his colleagues (27) suggest that early independence training is productive of high achievement motivation, while the work of Ausubel and his colleagues (5) suggests that the important determinant of this high achievement motivation is not the training for independence but rather loving the child for what he does in contrast to what he is; that is, valuing the child in terms of his performance, rather than in terms of his qualities. Now the former studies emphasize an overt behavior practice; the latter indicates that a feeling or motivational factor is involved. If one is interested in developing in his child a high desire for achievement, to which should he give priority: training him early for independence or loving him only for what he does?

The position of parent education with respect to this question has moved from a belief in the dominant effect of overt behavior to a belief in the dominant effects of parental motives and feelings. These changes parallel the shifts in parent education from reliance predominantly on Watson and behavioristic psychology to reliance predominantly on Freud and psychoanalytic psychology. The current sentiment is expressed by Woodward (47) in the following quotation: "If there is genuine affection, mutual respect, true pleasure in the person and personality of the other, and something approximating equality in the sharing of privileges and responsibilities, an interpersonal atmosphere is created in the home in which the budding personalities of children can thrive. If, instead of understanding and mutual regard and pleasure, there are friction, tension, and animosity, children suffer no matter how systematically the mother and father may try to observe psychological principles." Also, in 1950 the Mid-Century White House Conference on Children and Youth drew several fundamental conclusions from the reports of the various workshops. Among them was the important statement that "the feelings for children on the part of parents and professional people are more important than the techniques they use." (13)

This is a critical problem for research because its answer indicates where students of child development should look for the most important influences upon the child's character. It is also a critical problem for parent education, for if the answer is that the parents' feelings are the important factor it leads one into an aspect of the parents' personalities which many believe less subject to change by education. We discuss this problem in detail in the following chapter, and mention it here only to underscore its importance in studying parent effects upon the child.

What do the scientific findings show? There are only a few research studies which were set up specifically to test the relative importance of these two aspects of parent behavior. These studies seem to point in quite opposite directions. Thus, one (e.g., 11) indicates that it is indeed the parents' feelings or covert attitudes which are the most important determinants of the child's personality. Another study, in progress at the Merrill-Palmer School, finds that what the parent actually does, that is, overt acts which observers can actually see, are the most closely related to certain aspects of the child's character. Thus, in spite of the arguments pro and con, the question goes unanswered. Perhaps in the years ahead research will show that parents' feelings are more important with regard to some parts of the child's personality, whereas the parents' overt behavior is the primary influence on other parts. Perhaps the research will indicate that the influential aspects of parent behavior depend upon the child's age. For example, it may be that the older child is more sensitive to his parents' feelings than their overt behavior, because he has reached the age where he is better able to perceive and discriminate subtle cues, or is able to work with a concept of motivation and recognizes that there is a difference between his parents' actual behavior and the intent which they may have.

Potency of the Single Event

The fourth point which we raise is another on which the available research points to no clear conclusion and, thus, the parent educator must carry the burden of the decision as to the position he takes. We find at one extreme the belief that certain child-rearing acts may have great potency, great influence upon the child. This belief is associated in the main with psychoanalytic theory, which suggests that single events may be traumatic, that is, deeply shocking and with immense and long-lasting effects. Bakwin (6) pointed out that much of the literature on mental health represents the child as a helpless creature, threatened by disaster, to whom irreparable harm can be done by a few parental mistakes. Such psychiatric literature has a note of urgency in it, a take-it-or-else quality that is frightening to the parent. Parent education, making this assumption and transmitting this view to the parent, gives the parent the feeling that some single child-rearing act may have an influence far greater than that of a long sequence of acts of an opposite kind. Thus, the parent who has once beaten his child in anger may feel that the many situations in which their relationship is friendly and rewarding cannot outweigh this single past event. The arguments against this theory include the one that much of the clinical material on which the belief about the potency of the single event is based, does not constitute sound research data. It is especially suspect because of the absence of comparisons of normal with emotionally disturbed people. Thus, the case of a neurotic person who reports an unusual and seemingly shocking childhood experience with great clarity and feeling, still gives no basis for concluding that it was this childhood event which produced the neurosis. The reason is that we do not know how frequent such an experience may have been among those people whom we do not call neurotic. Perhaps they could, and indeed do, recall such experiences with equal ease and clarity. If this were true, then the effects of such incidents upon the character structure are ruled out and they become simply interesting examples of what people can remember of their childhood.

Another argument against the theory, and favoring a directly contrary theory, is that there is a tremendous body of scientific research on learning which shows the powerful effects of repetitive experience. Thus, the extreme opposite in theory is (e.g., 18) that the learning process for children is one in which the long repetition of systematic rewards and punishments far outweighs any isolated event in its effect upon the child's personality. Here, as Bakwin puts it, children may be viewed as hearty creatures who can take a great deal of pushing around, who have a strong urge toward normal growth and development. This view, like the other, appears in parent education materials; for example, Wall (44) states that parents may make many mistakes in handling their children without lasting damage to them if they remain affectionate, supporting, and consistent. And Sebald (37) writes that mistakes with a normal child may be relatively harmless because of the child's strong drive toward normality and because of his flexibility in learning, unlearning, and relearning.

An integrative theory seems in the process of development. The modern clinical view is that the effect of the single event depends on when it occurs in the child's development, and in what series of events, as well as the meaning given to it by the culture. The view of the experimentalist is becoming one in which he sees the possibility of certain "pivotal" or direction-determining events, which can change the meaning of the daily repetitive rewards and punishments so that what is learned from the repetition is different. Just what such events may be, however, remains to be determined, and in absence of this the available evidence should lead the parent educator to favor the position that no single parental act has a very marked effect; but that the greatest influence of the parent upon the child comes from those actions which are repetitive and consistent in nature.

Permanence of the Effect of Early Childhood Training

The fifth problem to be considered is closely related to the foregoing. It is that of the permanence or durability of the effects of parents upon the child's personality. The position the parent educator takes here can influence many aspects of his program. For example, if one assumes that the effects of early childhood training are permanent there will be little interest in programs directed to parents of adolescents, since any changes in their behavior would be superfluous because they are too late.

As Lemkau and others (26) have pointed out, the "psychogenic" hypothesis is fundamental in American psychiatric thought, namely, that early life experiences are causally related to later life disorders. This idea is manifested in many hypotheses about the effects of early infant experience. It is carried over into parent education programs which draw heavily upon clinical material, with the implication to parents that child rearing is irrevocable in its consequences, and that at any age whatever bad characteristics the child or the adult shows can be laid at the doorstep of earlier mistakes made by parents.

There are two categories of scientific findings which one should consider with regard to this issue. The first of these concerns the effects of early experiences upon the child's personality. The second concerns the relation between early childhood experiences and the adult personality. Let us now consider the first.

Most of the work in the first category deals with the general hypothesis, derived from psychoanalytic theory, that the way in which the parent handles the weaning of the infant, and his early toilet training and feeding, will have powerful effects upon the child's character. In support of the hypothesis are numerous clinical studies, although their results have limited generality because of sampling problems referred to above. There are also several well-designed studies which validate this hypothesis. The report on many different cultures by Whiting and Child (46) attempts to relate specific child-rearing practices to the locus of adult anxiety. In certain cultures, for example, where weaning is severe, illness tends to be attributed to eating food which has been poisoned in a magic fashion. (Customary adult explanations of illness are assumed to indicate the particular area of anxiety.) The conclusion emerges that severity of training of a bodily function, elimination, for example, tends to be positively related to explanations of illness in terms of a disturbance in a particular area. The authors' general view is that this supports the principle of fixation in psychoanalytic theory. In other less extensive studies, it has been shown that early age or severe toilet training is associated with less tolerance for getting dirty and staying dirty (2); that severity of early childhood training is positively related to adult preference for complex art forms (10); that the variables of age of completion of weaning and age of bowel training are related to intensity of guilt over hostile thoughts (1).

In contradiction to the foregoing a series of recent important studies finds no systematic relation between early infant training practices and later personality. In studies of American society, Sewell (38), Thurston and Mussen (43), Stendler (41), and Behrens (11) all find no relation between such parent behavior as early and strict toilet training and subsequent personality, whether personality is measured by standard paper and pencil tests, or by projective tests such as the Rorschach and the Thematic Aperception Test. Orlansky's general survey (31) of the influence of infant-training practices on personality in many cultures finds no systematic relation. Straus (42) in a careful study of the Sinhalese tested the relation between infant feeding and toilet-training practices, and subsequent personality characteristics. In this study he used both the California Test of Personality and the Rorschach as personality tests. The former revealed no reliable findings of any kind. The Rorschach findings suggested five relations, but all five had a pattern of association opposite to that postulated on the basis of psychoanalytic theory.

The second aspect of the problem of durability of parent influence concerns the consequences for personality in later life. As was true for the above problem, much of the evidence of parental influence is derived from clinical case histories in which adult characteristics are related to early childhood experiences. We have already noted the scientific defects in some of these materials. The experimental research, in contrast, reports very little about the durable effects of early experience on adult personality. Authors such as Murphy (29) have called attention to this as an important neglected area of research in personality development. One thing which has been demonstrated (e.g., 24) is that the adult personality continues to change. Indeed, common sense would argue that there would be transformations of personality following such critical events as marriage, the birth of children, divorce, death of parents, major changes in work, and many others which could be thought of as important influences on one's character.

The absence of firm evidence indicating the durable effect of early childhood experiences and the more recent evidence indicating changes in personality over time has influenced parent education assumptions on this topic. It is important to note that one of the major conclusions resulting from the 1950 White House Conference mentioned earlier was that a generally healthy personality is not definitely established once and for all at a given age period, but can be strengthened or weakened at any time (13). However, it is valid to say that parent education, in general, stresses the permanence of the effects of parental behavior during early years and gives less than deserved consideration to possible effects of later-life events.

Multiple Causation in the Effect of the Parent on the Child

Our sixth and last issue pertaining to assumptions about the effect of the parent on the child is the complexity of the cause-and-effect relation. The question is the degree to which there is a one-to-one relation between some type of parent behavior and some resulting characteristic in the child. Note that we do not speak here of the potency of a single act, as before, but rather of the potency of the "type" of action or class of acts of the parents.

In one sense the position a person takes on this issue is dictated by his position on certain of the earlier issues, namely, the genetic versus experiential issue, the effects of parents versus other persons, and, indeed, the effects of the mother versus the father. Thus, where one recognizes that genetic factors play a role in the child's personality, that the parental effect is mixed with that of other persons, that both mother and father share with each other their influence upon the child, it must follow that the development of any particular characteristic in the child's personality, such as honesty, aggression, or desire for achievement, is the result of these several forces rather than any one alone.

To give an example, one might assume that if a son is rejected, that is, disliked and rebuffed by the mother, he would develop feelings of inadequacy and worthlessness. Yet one could hardly doubt that the effects of such rejection are diluted, and could be almost negated, in instances where the son is strong, healthy, and intelligent, is loved by his father and his brothers and sisters, is respected and honored by his friends and by the neighbors, and is highly prized by his teachers. This is to illustrate the point that some given mode or pattern of parent behavior is not itself the sole determinant of the child's character traits, but that multiple causation in personality development is the rule.

There is a second and different aspect of multiple causation which should concern us. This involves not the role of the parent as one of several causes; but rather the question of whether one or many types of parental acts produce a certain personality trait in a child. To use the preceding example again, it may not be the mother's act of rejection alone which contributes to the child's feelings of insecurity, but rejection combined with other types of actions by this mother. The fact is that we know very little about the interaction of different kinds of parent behavior and their effects upon the child's personality. In one stimulating study, which points the way to further research in this area, Baldwin (8) has shown how the effects of rejection upon children are quite different, depending on whether the parent is *in addition* hateful to the child, or simply neutral and indifferent to him.

What of the evidence? Regarding either aspect of this multiple causation question, whether it be a type of parent behavior in conjunction with other outside influences or a type of parent behavior in connection with other types of his behavior, one fundamental fact exists. It is that the relation shown in scientific studies between a given type of parent behavior and a particular characteristic of the child's personality is always low. The relation is not strong in any study. True, one could argue that this does not mean the influence of any type of behavior is as weak as it seems, but rather that our ideas and research procedures are inadequate. To some extent this must be true. But it hardly permits us to ignore the probability that the relation between any given act of a parent, and a given personality characteristic of a child will *always* be low; no matter how purely conceived or measured, because the characteristic involved is a product of more than just one cause.

The multiple causation assumption has been strongest in those parent education programs which have a link with experimental child development. This is true because the data on which such programs are based have consistently shown low correlations, thus forcing one toward the multiple causation assumption. In addition, they were not involved, as were parent education programs drawing on clinical theory, in the effort to isolate the traumatic event in the production of neurosis and, therefore, did not develop the practice of the clinician of singling out some event reported by the patient. Lasswell (25) has pointed out that a major impact of the behavior sciences upon child-rearing theory has been to emphasize multiple causation, since such sciences through their research point out new sources of a child's behavior. This point of view is seen in the following statement: "One further idea which it is important for the physician to get across to the parents is a concept of the multiple, nonspecific character of etiological factors in emotional disturbances." (3, p. 65) However, it is probable that the conception of multiple causation has influenced thinking only with respect to the production of undesirable or neurotic traits and has yet to be extended to assumptions about the origins of valued traits such as honesty or personal security.

It follows that if no given type of parent behavior alone has a simple and direct effect upon the child, but rather that such behavior is combined with many other factors in complex ways which together produce an effect, then parent educators should tailor their educational programs accordingly. In the contrasting position, where one assumes that a given type of parent behavior is the sole determinant of some desirable characteristic of the child, it follows that the parent educator must strongly emphasize the importance of this behavior and stress that the parent must assume the great responsibility (as well as guilt over failure) of performing this type of action correctly.

HOW DOES PARENT EDUCATION UTILIZE AVAILABLE INFORMATION?

When faced with this large accumulation of data on parent-child relations, unintegrated and conflicting in its implications, what can the parent educator assume about the effect of the parent on the child? Like the parent faced with the problem of what to do, and whom to consult, when the experts disagree, so too, the parent educator must decide what materials to study and how to integrate them so as to make intelligent program assumptions.

He will find no generally accepted view of personality development which unifies available research findings through some master theory. To read the excellent book by Hall and Lindzey (21), which presents detailed reviews of more than 15 leading personality theories, is to realize that there are some vast differences in these theories, that each may have a piece of the truth, but that none does justice to all the available facts. Moreover, such a general theory, even were it to exist, would soon be obsolete as the social sciences advance. No answer for the parent educator lies in this direction. He must instead recognize and squarely face the fact that our knowledge of parent-child relations will always, because of its continued growth, have unintegrated and even contradictory segments; that these segments may endure side by side for decades; and that he, the educator, must learn to live with this situation and neither seek a single master theory nor reject science because it cannot provide that theory.

The easiest and most common solution has been for parent education programs to draw upon a limited but fairly distinct and integrated area of theory and data and to exclude conflicting information from other sources. The major differentiation occurs along the lines of clinical as contrasted with experimental child development materials. In large part also the one or the other orientation seems determined by the actual housing arrangement, so to speak, of the parent educator and his differential access to the various kinds of information. Thus, one finds that parent education programs associated with child development centers (notably in universities with parent education extension programs) draw primarily, and almost to the exclusion of other sources, from experimental child development research. It is not unusual for the research staff in such a situation to prepare summaries of their research for the parent education staff, to consult with them, and to acquaint them with relevant research literature. In contrast, many other parent education programs are attached to hospitals, therapeutic clinics, mental health associations, or are simply independent in nature. All of these seem more frequently to draw on psychoanalytic and other clinical sources for their theory and information. It is of interest that some of these parent education organizations, such as the Child Study Association of America, were established earlier than the child study centers in this country and developed their orientation to psychoanalytic theory because they found it the only pertinent professional source material available on the effects of parents on children.

The more difficult but more honest solution involves the effort to be intelligently eclectic and to draw upon all sources of relevant information. This effort is made by some organizations both in establishing the working assumptions of the programs and in preparing materials for parents, notably the United States Children's Bureau, the Louisiana Society for Mental Health, and the National Congress of Parents and Teachers. This course demands that the parent educator himself learn to be critical, to weigh the evidence where he can, to consider theories and research findings on their merits. Perhaps most important of all it means that he must be willing to shift allegiance from one idea to another as our knowledge of personality development in children grows. This is perhaps the most difficult; but one's attitude toward knowledge must be such that at any given time he uses the most valid information available, although he knows that it will soon be replaced by something still more valid.

REFERENCES

1. Allinsmith, Wesley, *The Learning of Moral Standards*. Unpublished doctoral dissertation, University of Michigan, 1954.

2. Alper, Thelma G., Howard T. Blane, and Barbara K. Abrams, "Reactions of Middle and Lower Class Children to Finger Paints as a Function of Class Differences in Child-Training Practices," *Journal of Abnormal and Social Psychology*, vol. 51, 1955, pp. 439–448.

3. American Public Health Association, *Health Supervision of Young Children*. The Association, New York, 1955.

4. Anderson, John E., "Child Development: An Historical Perspective," *Child Development*, vol. 27, 1956, pp. 181–196.

5. Ausubel, David P., Earl E. Balthazar, Irene Rosenthal, Leonard S. Blackman, Seymour H. Schpoont, and Joan Welkowitz, "Perceived Parent Attitudes as Determinants of Children's Ego Structure," *Child Development*, vol. 25, 1954, pp. 173–183.

6. Bakwin, Harry, "The Aims of Child Rearing," *New England Journal of Medicine*, vol. 248, 1953, pp. 227–231.

7. Bakwin, Harry, "Etiology of Behavior Disorders in Children," *Postgraduate Medicine*, vol. 9, 1951, pp. 260–265.

8. Baldwin, Alfred L., *Behavior and Development in Childhood*. The Dryden Press, New York, 1955.

9. Barker, Roger G., and Herbert F. Wright, *Midwest and Its Children:* The Psychological Ecology of an American Town. Row, Peterson and Co., Evanston, Ill., 1954.

10. Barry, Herbert, III, "Relationships Between Child Training and the Pictorial Arts," *Journal of Abnormal and Social Psychology*, vol. 54, 1957, pp. 380–383.

11. Behrens, Marjorie L., "Child Rearing and the Character Structure of the Mother," *Child Development*, vol. 25, 1954, pp. 225–238.

12. Blatz, William E., "Insight into Parenthood," *Bulletin of the Institute of Child Study*, University of Toronto, Canada, vol. 19, 1957, pp. 12–16.

13. Bossard, James H. S., *The Sociology of Child Development*. Harper and Bros., New York, 1954.

14. Brim, Orville G., Jr., "Family Structure and Sex Role Learning by Children: A Further Analysis of Helen Koch's Data," *Sociometry*, vol. 21, 1958, pp. 1–16.

15. Carmichael, Leonard, *Manual of Child Psychology*. 2d ed. John Wiley and Sons, New York, 1954.

16. Cattell, Raymond B., Glen F. Stice, and Norton F. Kristy, "A First Approximation to Nature-Nurture Ratios for Eleven Primary Personality Factors in Objective Tests," *Journal of Abnormal and Social Psychology*, vol. 54, 1957, pp. 143–159.

17. Dale, Edgar "Achievements That Blaze a Trail," *The Parent-Teacher Organization*. National Congress of Parents and Teachers, Chicago, 1944, chap. 2.

18. Dollard, John and Neal E. Miller, *Personality and Psychotherapy*: An Analysis in Terms of Learning, Thinking, and Culture. McGraw-Hill Book Co., New York, 1950.

19. Forer, Raymond, "The Impact of a Radio Program on Adolescents," *Public Opinion Quarterly*, vol. 19, 1955, pp. 184–194.

20. Glueck, Sheldon and Eleanor, *Unraveling Juvenile Delinquency*. Harvard University Press, Cambridge, Mass., 1950.

21. Hall, Calvin S., and Gardner Lindzey, *Theories of Personality*. John Wiley and Sons, New York, 1957.

22. Hartshorne, Hugh, and Mark A. May, *Studies in Deceit:* Book I. General Methods and Results; Book II. Statistical Methods and Results. Macmillan Co., New York, 1928.

23. Kallmann, Franz J., "The Genetic Theory of Schizophrenia" in *Personality in Nature, Society, and Culture*, edited by Clyde Kluckhohn and Henry A. Murray. 2d ed. Alfred A. Knopf, New York, 1953, pp. 80–99.

24. Kelly, E. Lowell, "Consistency of the Adult Personality," *American Psychologist*, vol. 10, 1955, pp. 659–681.

25. Lasswell, Harold D., "The Normative Impact of the Behavioral Sciences," *Ethics*, vol. 67, part II, 1957, pp. 1–42.

26. Lemkau, Paul V., Benjamin Pasamanick, and Marcia Cooper, *The Implications of the Psychogenetic Hypothesis for Mental Hygiene*. Paper presented at the 1953 Annual Meeting of the American Psychiatric Association.

27. McClelland, David C., A. Rindlisbacher, and Richard de Charms, "Religious and Other Sources of Parental Attitudes Toward Independence Training" in *Studies in Motivation*, edited by David C. McClelland. Appleton-Century-Crofts, Inc., New York, 1955, pp. 389–397.

28. Mead, Margaret, *From the South Seas:* Studies of Adolescence and Sex in Primitive Societies. William Morrow and Co., New York, 1939.

29. Murphy, Gardner, *Personality:* A Biosocial Approach to Origins and Structure. Harper and Bros., New York, 1947, chaps. 30 and 31.

30. Ojemann, Ralph H., "Parent Education and the Citizens of Tomorrow," *Proceedings of the Eighth Annual Convention* of the National Congress of Parents and Teachers, Chicago, 1944, pp. 103–120.

31. Orlansky, Harold, "Infant Care and Personality," *Psychological Bulletin*, vol. 46, 1949, pp. 1–48.

32. Parsons, Talcott, "The American Family: Its Relation to Personality and to the Social Structure" in *Family, Socialization and Interaction Process*, by Talcott Parsons and Robert F. Bales, in collaboration with James Olds, Morris Zelditch, Jr., and Philip E. Slater. The Free Press, Glencoe, Ill., 1955.

33. Pollak, Otto, and collaborators, *Social Science and Psychotherapy for Children*. Russell Sage Foundation, New York, 1952.

34. Radke-Yarrow, Marion, and Leon J. Yarrow, "Child Psychology," *Annual Review of Psychology*, vol. 6, 1955, pp. 1–28.

35. Remmers, H. H., and Naomi Weltman, "Attitude Inter-relationships of Youth, Their Parents, and Their Teachers," *Journal of Social Psychology*, vol. 26, 1947, pp. 61–68.

36. Sears, Robert R., Eleanor E. Maccoby, and Harry Levin, *Patterns of Child Rearing*. Row, Peterson and Co., Evanston, Ill., 1957.

37. Sebald, Dorothy D., "The Importance of Education for the Parents of Exceptional Children," *Education for the Parents of Exceptional Children*. Porter Sargent, Publisher, Boston, 1956, pp. 2–8.

38. Sewell, William H., "Infant Training and the Personality of the Child," *American Journal of Sociology*, vol. 58, 1952, pp. 150–159.

39. Shaw, Clifford R., and others, *Brothers in Crime;* with Special Chapters by H. B. Hanson and E. W. Burgess. University of Chicago Press, Chicago, 1938.

40. Sheldon, William H., and S. S. Stevens, *The Varieties of Temperament:* A Psychology of Constitutional Differences. Harper and Bros., New York, 1944.

41. Stendler, Celia B., "Possible Causes of Overdependency in Young Children," *Child Development*, vol. 25, 1954, pp. 125–146.

42. Straus, Murray A., "Anal and Oral Frustration in Relation to Sinhalese Personality," *Sociometry*, vol. 20, 1957, pp. 21–31.

43. Thurston, John R., and Paul H. Mussen, "Infant Feeding Gratification and Adult Personality," *Journal of Personality*, vol. 19, 1951, pp. 449–458.

44. Wall, William D., *Education and Mental Health:* A Report Based Upon the Work of a European Conference Called by UNESCO at the Musée Pedagogique in Paris, Nov.–Dec., 1952. UNESCO, Paris, 1955.

45. Watson, John B., *Behaviorism*. W. W. Norton and Co., New York, 1928.

46. Whiting, John W. M., and Irvin L. Child, *Child Training and Personality:* A Cross-Cultural Study. Yale University Press, New Haven, 1953.

47. Woodward, Luther E., "Fostering Mental Health Through the Church Program" in *The Church and Mental Health*, edited by Paul B. Maves. Charles Scribner's Sons, New York, 1953, pp. 129–157.

CHAPTER THREE:

Causes of Parent Behavior

WHERE EFFORTS ARE MADE to influence the behavior of parents, some assumptions are necessary about the causes of parent behavior. Parent education programs, seeking to increase the rational performance of parents in their role, must take a view of human behavior in which some share of the individual's action is under conscious volitional control; where the individual is able to set goals for himself, to evaluate, and then select means of reaching these goals; and, finally, to put such means into practice. Educational programs for parents not only must assume that there are rational aspects of the parent's role performance, but must also take the position that these can be increased through educational programs. On this basis, education appeals directly to the individual's conscious concerns, supplying him with information, suggesting new values he can pursue from the great range of values open to man, providing him with numerous elements of rational problem-solving skills which better equip him to make his individual decisions.

This model, of course, is not fully descriptive of the behavior of men or of parents specifically. There are many segments of human behavior which are not the simple expression of goal seeking in which the individual consciously selects the best means at his disposal and exercises such means. There are other determinants of human behavior which limit his rational autonomy in role performance, and, hence, which place limits on the possible achievements of education in increasing the parent's rationality. It is not our aim to imply that the pursuit of greater competence and rationality in parents is foolish. Rather, we seek to appraise other determinants of parent behavior in the belief that a conscious recognition of the limitations they place on the success of education must eventually lead to wiser and more fruitful parent education programs. Each of the causes of parent behavior discussed here has implications for the aims which parent education pursues, and for the methods it employs. In this chapter we suggest these by way of example, saving for the next and subsequent chapters a more detailed analysis of these implications.

There are a number of ways in which one could classify the different contributing causes of parent behavior. We have taken the customary broad categories of personality, cultural, and social situational factors, and have indicated types of causes within each of these. No important theoretical organization is implicit in the categories we have chosen; rather the organization used makes easier the portrayal of the different views of parent behavior. We speak of six types of causes of parent behavior in addition to the rational, self-controlled elements implicit in educational programs. These six types of causes can be identified in the following way: ability factors, unconscious factors, cultural values, interpersonal and social controls, group structural determinants, and ecological or physical factors.

Note that we have omitted any serious consideration of instincts as determinants of parent role performance. Not many years ago we would have had to consider, for example, a "maternal instinct" and its implication for the educability of parents in their role performance. However, the decline of instinct theory in general from 1915 on, the data of cultural anthropology showing the vast differences in maternal role performance in various cultures, and various research studies (e.g., 19, 21) all indicate that maternal affection is acquired. It may be that physiological differences between women, in the endocrine system, for example, may strongly influence how much maternal affection will be learned, but at present this is not known. For our purposes here we have assumed that biological determinants of parent role performance place few limitations on the educability of the parent.

With respect to the six types of causes of parent behavior considered here, one recognizes that the individual operates or behaves in his parent role as part of a social system. The parent engages in behavior vis-à-vis the child in interaction situations which are regulated by social norms or rules as to what is appropriate and inappropriate. As an individual, the parent is also restricted by repressed and unconscious motives which work to determine his behavior in parent role performance in ways unknown to him. Moreover, the pressures of time and the demands of the conflicting social situations involved in a large family as well as restrictions placed upon behavior by the absence of certain economic goods, whether these be living space, the absence of toys, or more generally, the simple absence of money, all work to limit the rational and self-controlled performance of the role.

The critical issue regarding the several causes of parent behavior is the degree to which these restricting factors do in fact cut down on the influence of education in changing the parent's role performance. Thus, it may not be sufficient to supply factual information or to discuss the range of values to be selected by the parent and anticipate that the parent will utilize these educational data in his role performance where his intelligence is limited, or he has unconscious motives which cause him to distort, or indeed, not even to remember the information he received. Nor is it useful to adopt this procedure where, say, the mother is given information leading her to select a new course of child rearing, but is unable to put it into action because her husband does not believe that this is appropriate and forbids her to behave in this way. It would seem of little value also and, indeed, even punishing, to discuss the merits of establishing a nurturant and intimate relation with children in the family where the mother has more than a half-dozen children and is obliged to work outside the home in order to provide for them. Thus, it is important to place the assumption of the educability of the parents, and the parent education programs which result from this, in perspective with other assumptions about the determinants of parent role performance and the possible modes of influence which issue from these other assumptions. For it is clear that different assumptions about the prime cause of parents' behavior will lead to quite different programs of influence designed to change parent behavior.

In general, parent education has been clearest and most sensitive to the limitation of the educability of parents attributable to unconscious motives and the issue of education versus therapy as methods of influence has long been raised in parent education. Indeed, a generation ago, one complete issue of the then current professional magazine in parent education was devoted to parent education and psychoanalysis. To some extent, parent education has been sensitive also to the limitations imposed by economic and environmental factors, although this has not been stressed sufficiently. Virtually no attention has been paid to the intellectual abilities of parents, to the problems of power relations or of social control in the family, or to the limitations placed on performance by internalized cultural values which the parent himself may not recognize. And, regarding the category we refer to as group structural determinants, we believe that this also has been overlooked. We now turn to these determinants in order.

PHYSICAL ABILITY FACTORS

The first of six types of determinants of parent behavior comprises three factors: the parent's intelligence; his general health including things such as physical disabilities and levels of energy; and his physical strength and size. These factors contrast with others (discussed later) which refer to personality characteristics of a different sort: the parent's beliefs, attitudes, and motives.

These causes of parent behavior have received little attention from parent educators in considering the effectiveness of their program. If attention has been given, it usually has occurred in programs carried on under medical auspices, because the personnel in such programs are more aware of the powerful influence upon behavior of an individual's state of health. Since there is no research, and little theory, we do little more here than to call attention to this class of determinants of parent role performance, and offer examples of how differences between parents in various physical abilities can influence their responses to parent education.

We begin with what is probably the least important, the size and strength of the parent. This becomes important in connection with the parent's disciplinary control of deviant behavior by the child. The parent is charged with the responsibility for teaching his child conformity to commonly shared standards of behavior; he is authorized to control the child's behavior, as necessary, by any of a wide variety of techniques, including appeal to others, physical punishment, deprivation of privileges, and threatened and actual withdrawal of affection. The effective use of physical punishment in contrast to other influence techniques obviously depends on the degree of superior strength and/or size which the parent has with respect to his child. With younger children the issue of superiority does not occur. However, as children, and especially male children, reach the age of eleven or twelve and thereafter, the child's physical strength begins to equal that of his mother's. Even with younger sons it is a frequent statement by mothers that their sons are too active for them to discipline through physical punishment. The mother confronted with the fact that the child is her equal in strength will find it necessary to engage in something else besides physical punishment to control him. The significant effects upon a child's personality of the use of physical punishment, in contrast to withdrawal of love, as an influence technique (19) leaves no doubt that changes in disciplinary techniques must be important events in the parent-child relation.

With respect to parental health characteristics, consider the parent whose level of energy is low, from such causes as dietary deficiencies or a debilitating infection. It requires little insight to recognize that this parent when faced with active children, or with a large family, or with frequent occurrences of interpersonal conflict between children, may not have the stamina to maintain good parental control over the situation. The course of her child-rearing practices often will move in the direction of enforced restrictions upon the children's activity with the objective of reducing the children's demands upon her. Requiring the child to stay in his room, separating siblings, or withdrawing herself from the child while permitting him freedom to roam so long as he does not intrude upon her, all are familiar as techniques employed to reduce demands upon the parent.

A third and most important ability factor is, of course, that of intelligence. We find no studies which correlate parent intelligence with understanding of child development, or with actual child-rearing practices. However, the absence of research on parents notwithstanding, it is instructive to generalize from other studies of the effects of intelligence. Probably a fundamental effect of differences in intelligence of parents is upon their ability to derive specific child-rearing practices from general ethical and moral principles, in contrast to the need to rely upon *ad hoc*, situationally specific, "rules of thumb." It is made clear in subsequent chapters that parent education programs range in content and method from discussions of general philosophical principles of child care to the presentation of specific child-training rules. Discussions of the merits of one or the other procedure appear in large number. These discussions fail to consider the now obvious point that it takes more than a moderate level of intelligence to discuss child rearing profitably and pleasantly in terms of broad and general principles. For parents who do not have this level of ability the effective educational program, as well as the one which the parents prefer and demand, probably involves a more specific and pragmatic emphasis. For example, in one program (13) the idea is implicit that in individual counseling of mothers about jealousy in the older sibling, some mothers cannot be helped by providing a general understanding of the topic of jealousy, or of the need for affection in human beings in general and eldest children in particular; rather, the counselor asks of the mother whether she could arrange to spend a half hour of her time per day alone with the older sib; little or no theory, little or no consideration of principles from which specific applications are derived; simply the situational solution.

To conclude, parent education programs to be realistic must take into account the varying abilities of parents and should not assume, for example, that all modes of supervision and discipline are available to a parent to choose between, regardless of the parent's size, strength, and physical stamina. And it seems an inescapable conclusion that in planning parent education programs the intelligence of the parents who are expected as clientele must strongly influence decisions about certain aspects of the program planning, such as the generality of the materials and the method of instruction.

UNCONSCIOUS FACTORS

The second of the types of causes to be discussed consists of unconscious determinants of parent behavior. Consider the example where a parent has been forced as a child to learn to repress his aggressive feelings and is frightened and shocked when aggression occurs between children in his family. His alarm comes from his own anxiety about the possible expression of his own repressed aggression, but he does not know this is the reason. In this instance, it seems of little value to discuss sibling relations and to advocate the permission of a moderate display of aggression between siblings when the parent does not understand the origin of his own feelings about aggression in children and is unable to change them simply by exposure to education. To influence the parent in this area requires procedures more therapeutic in nature, to create understanding on his part concerning the source of such feelings, thus making them amenable to educational influence.

There can be no doubt that every parent exhibits in his behavior the influence of unconscious factors. The rich clinical data on parent behavior (e.g., 17) continually portray in case histories the expression of unconscious factors by the parent. The fact that these cases are based on clinical subjects mitigates against their general applicability in normal parents. However, there is much research using samples of normal parents which could be cited as supporting the same point. For example, in the recent work of Sears, Maccoby, and Levin (19) the authors report a significant positive relation between sex anxiety in mothers and a refusal to breast feed, thus suggesting that the latter is an expression of a general anxiety over matters pertaining to sex. The authors point out that education directed to the performance of breast feeding is likely to be unsuccessful and discomforting for the mother who resists the practice because of unconscious factors producing sex anxiety. Another example (10) of a study of the relation of child-rearing practices and authoritarianism in personality (as measured by several tests) shows that parents scoring high in authoritarianism consistently use more "nonlove-oriented" techniques in child rearing. Given the additional data from *The Authoritarian Personality* (1) that authoritarianism is caused in part by repressed hostility and other unconscious factors, this study indicates the link between one aspect of child rearing and such unconscious factors.

Many parent education programs have been naive about the role of unconscious factors in parent education, and have not seriously considered the limitations such factors place on their own efforts, or the additions required to their conception of the parent as a consciously self-determining actor. All parents to some degree, and perhaps some parents to a great degree, are influenced by unconscious factors. It follows that there will be parental feelings and behavior which will be little influenced by education.

Ideally the parent educator would tailor his program to those persons and child-rearing areas open to education. In the program under the direction of David Levy (13), for example, an effort is being made to find a series of observational items that permit the pediatrician or nurse to differentiate mothers as being high, average, or low "maternal," so that different types of recommendations can be made in the counseling situation to the different types of mothers. Education is not attempted with the "low maternal" mother; rather, she is encouraged to plan her work so that she can be away from her children a few hours a day, or even to take a job if she desires.

Had we prior information as to such people and areas, this would be relatively easy. Lacking such information, it follows that the educator should be able to recognize in a given parent those areas of child rearing which are protected from educational influence by the unconscious, and to limit his educational program accordingly. This further suggests that the competent educator must receive special training, which is a matter we consider in a later chapter.

While some parent educators have underestimated the role of the unconscious, others have been too heavily influenced by clinical theory stressing the unconscious, to the extent that they do not fulfill their possibilities as educators and even go to the extreme of asking themselves whether educational efforts are justified at all. Clinical writings are very persuasive on this matter. One of the most extreme statements of this point of view presented by Kubie (14) occurs not with reference to parent-child interaction but to marital interaction, in which almost all segments of marital role performance are analyzed and attributed to the expression of unconscious desires. Similar analyses of maternal behavior can be found in clinical writings (e.g., 17) which imply that there is very little in parent role performance other than the playing out of unconscious factors acquired in one's own childhood. Some authors paint the dismal picture of childhood training patterns being perpetuated from one generation to the next, the same unconscious parent-child drama being played again with only the actors changed.

As we pointed out previously, there has been an increasing tendency to consider the attitudinal and emotional, in contrast to the behavioral, characteristics of the parent as having the greatest influence upon the child. This presents a critical problem for parent education, since one feels that the overt behavior of parents—toilet training at a given age, scheduling versus self-demand feeding, even such things as permitting the child to show aggression toward the parent—are learnable through education; hence, if it is this behavior that most influences the child, parent education has its rationale. If, on the other hand, it is the parent's feelings which really matter, if it is such fundamental motives as love of the child or esteem for one's self which are crucial, then parent education is challenged. These are felt to be personal characteristics not influenceable by simple educational procedures, but which require therapeutic measures. As Barbara Biber puts it (2), if parent education contends that it is not what the parent does but what he is that is important, then the parent asks, "But what do I do with what I am?"

This has led directly to questioning of the justification of parent education. For example, Gruenberg (8, pp. 160–161) has said, "As knowledge of personality development has increased, the specific behavior of parents has taken on less significance, and the general family atmosphere, the attitude of parents toward children and toward each other, become more important. The extent to which educational programs can modify these attitudes is currently a matter of controversy." At least one prominent parent educator (20) has expressed the view that the proper role of the parent educator is to be supportive, comforting to the parent, and that attempts to change parents through education result in the production of anxiety and in poorer child rearing.

In view of this tendency of some to reject educational procedures, it is appropriate to call attention to the fact that major studies (12, 18) have shown that deep-seated personality changes occur over time in individuals, entirely apart from the effects of therapy. Kelly, cited in the previous chapter as the author of one of these studies, reported the correlations between scores on many personality measures by some 300 married couples tested at the time of their marriage and again twenty years later. The results show quite marked shifts in such things as masculinity, femininity, dominance and submission, the nature of one's interests, the values which one holds, and many others, thus indicating substantial changes over the twenty-year period. He summarizes these results as follows: "Our findings indicate that significant changes in human personality may continue to occur during the years of adulthood. Such changes, while neither so large nor sudden as to threaten the continuity of the self-percept or impair one's day-to-day interpersonal relations, are potentially of sufficient magnitude to offer a basis of fact for those who dare to hope for continual psychological growth during the adult years." (12, p. 681)

The evidence argues for the presence of both conscious and unconscious determinants of parent role performance; but in spite of the long duration of interest in this problem and the amount of argument it has generated, no one can say how much of the variability of parent behavior is determined by unconscious as contrasted to conscious factors, or designate areas of child rearing or the kinds of parents where unconscious influences are greatest. One can ask the simple question: Is it 10 per cent, 50 per cent, or 90 per cent?—without being able to bring to bear on the question any research data at all.

Clearly more work is needed here. Studies of the unconscious determination of behavior in the parent role may indicate that such determinants are idiosyncratic and distributed among people and among areas of child rearing in unsystematic ways, rather than being exhibited by individuals generally in the same way and in the same place in a given society. If research shows this to be true, then the parent educator must acquire the skills to recognize, in his educational efforts, when he is confronted with a parent for whom some area of child-care practice is not under conscious control. Thus, in the training program mentioned earlier (13) the pediatrician and nurse are first trained to distinguish among three groups of mothers. First, there are mothers who are not seeking information, but simply come for a routine examination and reassurance. At the other extreme are mothers with severe pathology. The third group is mothers who fall within the normal range and who want and can accept help from the physician in the area of developmental, emotional, and relationship problems with children. The two extreme categories are not ignored: in the first, where there is objective evidence of a problem, the pediatrician speaks, and in the latter, referral may be necessary. However, counseling efforts are to be directed primarily to the more promising middle group.

On the other hand, studies of the degree of unconscious determination may show that such unconscious factors are systematically related to certain kinds of parents and to certain aspects of child rearing so that educational programs can be tailored in advance to fit those other areas of the parent role which are under his conscious control. It may be, for example, that in the area of sex education of the child the outlook for a successful educational program for parents with respect to such training is relatively poor compared with child-rearing areas involving, for example, teaching the child the use of money. It may be found that certain groups of parents because of characteristics of their unconscious are unsuitable, or at least unpromising, as clientele for parent education programs.

In either case, we need to find out how unconscious determinants of the parent role are distributed among individuals, and to avoid either a blanket rejection of educational efforts on the grounds that feelings are the important consideration and that all feelings are under the control of the unconscious, or the reverse position in which even the existence of the unconscious is ridiculed, and it is naively assumed that individuals could behave at all times in a fully conscious and rational manner. Appropriate research on this aspect of the causes of parent behavior would seem to be imperative as a foundation for planning a satisfactory educational program.

CULTURAL VALUES

A third assumption pertaining to the causes of parent behavior is that much parent behavior springs from what can be referred to as "internalized" cultural norms. This is to say that parents perform their role on a habitual basis, pursuing ends held desirable by the general society in which they live, and which they acquired in growing up.

The existence of cultural values which regulate parent behavior presents an obstacle to the success of many parent education programs. A large amount of research (4, 11, 15) has shown that new ideas and practices are accepted by individuals to the degree that they "fit in" with existing cultural patterns. It is likely that some of the content presented in a parent education program will be compatible with the existing internalized culture patterns of the parent, and thus no resistance will be encountered. But some of the content will not fit the existing patterns; indeed, it will be a challenge to them. What is the educator to do then? He cannot retreat, change his objectives, since it is likely that the transmission of the challenging or controversial material is the major purpose of his program. Instead he must try to bring out into the open the parent's cultural values, where they can be reexamined as part of the educative process.

A research study exemplifies both of these aspects of the influence of cultural values. This study (5) of the child-feeding practices of mothers from different subcultures in our society shows a clear demarcation between those mothers who are concerned about their children's eating because they wish them to have an adequate diet in order to obtain good health, and those mothers who are concerned about their children's eating because they want them to be large. Italian and Jewish mothers far more frequently fall into the latter group, whereas Negro and northern European white groups are mothers of the former type. This study shows that when such parents are exposed to an educational program emphasizing permissive feeding of children, the permissive actions are adopted by mothers concerned about their children's health, since it can be demonstrated to them that children's selection of diet is adequate to produce good nutrition. In theoretical terms it fits their existing value system. In contrast, the educational program is comparatively unsuccessful with the mothers who are concerned about the size of their children, since self-selection of diet does not normally produce an especially large child. In the latter case, if the parent educator wishes to further the value of permissive feeding, it is necessary to make explicit to the mothers the basis of their concern over children's eating so that they understand it; and, moreover, since in the subcultural groups prizing large children the mother's self-esteem with respect to being a good mother is bound up with achieving this end, it is necessary to deal with the cultural values and to alter them before such a mother would be receptive to the practice of permissive feeding.

It is very important to stress the lack of awareness which the parent will have of his own values. Indeed, one must ask whether it is not true that much of what is alleged to be "unconscious" (in the strict psychoanalytic sense) only appears to be so in the average parent, and consists instead of internalized aspects of the culture; the latter being not actively repressed but simply "pre-conscious," so to speak. Where these implicit cultural values play a determining role in the parent's behavior, the educational program must first make one conscious of these values which he has earlier acquired by calling them forth and opening them to conscious examination by the parent. In this regard a parallel might be drawn between parents exposed to educational programs, and, say, college sophomores when exposed to their first course in cultural anthropology in which they discover that many of their heretofore unexamined values, such as their religion, their orientation toward achievement, their modes of disciplining the deviant, the manner in which they express friendship, and the form of their marriage are but single instances of the wide range of human possibilities of choice in such matters.

It is in this context that one better understands the observation that parent education has produced a tendency in parents to become dependent on professional experts in child care and family matters. One may recognize the parallel between this process and the college sophomore who, having challenged with the aid of his teacher the beliefs which he has held up to now, strives to find an intellectual and ethical security in the adoption of some new set of values. Odd though they may appear to the adult, he clings to them fervently and the function which they serve in stabilizing his personality should not go unnoticed. Indeed, one sees a parallel also to the traditional sequence in the therapeutic process where the patient is deeply challenged as to his attitudes toward life and where, if the challenge is successful, the transitional phase occurs, involving transference to the therapist who plays a stabilizing role in the patient's personality; the transference then must be worked through until the patient becomes independent. In like manner, then, the parent challenged as to his basic beliefs about the values inherent in child rearing turns to the expert educator to provide him with a new set of ends and means to be used in rearing his children and relies upon these values to structure his relation with his child. Where the parent educator seeks his own ends rather than those of the parent, he now has a willing and compliant follower. In contrast, where the aims of the parent educator are to render the patient more competent to seek his own values, he must help the parent stand on his own feet, for having challenged the parent's traditional values, he must now work with him until he has consciously and independently selected that new set of values which he wishes to pursue.

Parent education in this country probably has not needed to be especially concerned with the influence of such internalized cultural values upon parent role performance. The reason is that our society includes a variety of subcultural groups possessing different values which, through our marked social class and spatial mobility, are brought into close contact with each other. This serves to challenge the respective values of each subcultural group, making each conscious of its traditional beliefs, and leading each to examine the values of his own group and to compare them with those of others. Indeed, as we pointed out in the first chapter, this loosening of tradition in child care has moved parents toward rationalizing the parental role and has contributed to the demand for parent education. Were a parent education program to operate in an isolated sixth-generation Vermont culture, in contrast, it would be much more important first to face the fact that much of the parent's behavior in such a group would be traditional, habitual, and unanalyzed, and that the educator's first job would be to render the parents self-conscious about their behavior before further steps in the educational program would be effective.

INTERPERSONAL AND SOCIAL CONTROLS

Parent education is viewed as an attempt to influence and change the social role of the parent in our society. This role, like all roles in social interaction systems, is a set of regulated ways of behaving and of prescribed ends to be achieved, which are consonant with the more general function ascribed to the social system of which the role is a part. Thus, the parent role, being part of the parent-child system, is regulated by rules about the aims to be sought and the appropriate behavior to reach these which are established by the members of society and in turn enforced by them. Members of groups who share this common culture share also a mutual sense of obligation, rightness, and moral necessity regarding the performance of the customary behavior which constitutes the culture of the group. The individual, in his role as the parent, seeks to discharge his responsibilities in a way which elicits approval from the groups to which he belongs or, in any case, seeks to avoid their punishment. He knows the behavior prescribed for his role and knows as well the censure which is forthcoming from his group for failure to conform.

As a social scientist, one is struck by the fact that parent education seems to operate as if the parent existed in a social vacuum, as it were, whereas actually each parent's behavior is embedded in social situations involving the other parent, relatives, the community, and others. The parent is not isolated. Other members of the society have the legitimate authority to exercise control over parents' role performance, to make certain that the values prescribed for the role are sought and the appropriate means are utilized. The omnipresent other spouse in the family system, the close relative such as the parent's parent, not to speak of other relatives such as sisters or brothers, or one's neighbors, are authorized to seek informally to influence the parent so as to conform to the values of the society.

Very little seems to be known about the reception accorded to parent education materials by other members of the parent's groups when a parent seeks to put them to use. Yet one can hardly doubt that the effects of parent education do not occur in the social vacuum which seems to be implicitly assumed in many programs. Indeed, the one study of which we know that deals with this problem (5) clearly exhibits the influence of other family members upon the outcomes of education. In this study, referred to above, the effectiveness of parent education counseling of mothers in increasing permissive feeding of infants depended in large part upon the approval of the idea by the husband.

Probably one of the most obvious controlling influences within the family upon the parent has been most neglected in parent education. This is the influence of the child upon the parent, arising from the fact that the child himself has rights and legitimized modes of control regarding his relations with his parents. Each parent-child relation is different, and in the course of interaction over time certain norms arise which determine what is legitimate behavior on the part of *both* parent and child. Marked departures from this normatively regulated course of parent-child interaction are viewed as deviant, and are reacted to with efforts to control, to bring the deviant member back into line. It is true that where the child is still an infant, not yet a social being in the true sense of the word, it is only the parent whose behavior has to be reckoned with. But beyond a given age, probably age two, the parent is influenced by the child's receptivity to changes which the parent attempts to introduce into his child-rearing practice. The emphasis in parent education has been upon the inabilities of the parent as an individual to put something into practice, so that when the parent says "I can't do that," the interpretation has been that the practice does not fit in the parent's personality. Equally cogent is the interpretation that the parent cannot engage in a certain new practice because the child resists the parent's change, and responds to this perceived deviance with all of the controls over the parent which he has at his disposal, including appeals to the other parent, to his sibs and to the neighbors, threatened withdrawal of affection, reactive deviance ("being bad"), and many others.

A closely related problem involves the issue of who in the family has the responsibility for making decisions about appropriate child-care practices in specific areas of child rearing. This is seen most clearly with respect to the allocation of the decision-making power between a mother and father in a family, where responsibility for certain kinds of decisions is prescribed and is customarily given to one spouse at the expense of the other. It thus follows that a parent education program may seek to influence one parent, usually the mother, with regard to aims or means in some child-care area, whereas in fact it is the socially given responsibility of the other parent to determine the practice in this area. For example, observation would suggest even to the most casual observer that a parent of the same sex as the child has the responsibility for certain decisions regarding child rearing, while the parent of the opposite sex has the decision authority with respect to other matters. Any attempt by one parent, whether under the influence of a parent education program or not, to usurp the decision-making power which custom gives to the other will be viewed as an intrusion of authority and will be dealt with by resistance.

It would seem to follow that some parents, for example, fathers, may be the more appropriate clientele for educational matters involving discipline or perhaps the handling of money, whereas mothers are the appropriate clientele in other areas. Moreover, the allocation of decision authority within a family almost certainly varies with social class and cultural background, so that even further specification of the program's clientele would seem desirable.

The failure of almost all parent education programs to assess the social setting into which they introduce their educational materials, the failure to recognize that the mothers who are primarily involved in such programs have husbands, parents, and neighbors with whom they must deal, is lamentable, since it is recognized that in many instances the net result of introducing change on the part of one member into the family system is to produce interpersonal friction, resentment, and hostility between husband and wife, which in turn is probably detrimental to the child. It is to be hoped that the conceptual model of parent behavior underlying educational programs will be expanded so as to recognize that, while the parent may consciously seek new values, there are other human beings whose approval he must obtain before he can successfully pursue them; and that parent education programs in their planning and operation will give due attention to the possible consequences of the parent's education for his or her relations with other members of the family.

GROUP STRUCTURAL DETERMINANTS

A fifth determinant of parent behavior can be viewed as one which arises from the structural characteristics of the family group. In recent years in sociology there has been a very rapid growth of research on small groups (9) which has dealt with the effects upon behavior of group members, of the size of the group, of heterogeneity, of type of leadership, of patterns of communication, and of other group characteristics. Clearly the family is a small social group, and there seems good reason to believe that many of the research results for small groups other than the family may be found to be true also of the family and, in this sense, to be pertinent to the question of causes of parent behavior.

While at the present time we know little of the way in which such structural characteristics may in fact determine parent behavior, we have selected for discussion the property of group size to exemplify why we believe they are pertinent to parent education planning and why further research involving a direct study of such structural determinants of family interaction seems of fundamental importance. With respect to group size, while a direct transfer of findings from the experimental research on small groups to the family itself is not suggested for reasons given later on, the argument may be put as follows: Group size influences characteristics of interaction between group members. Thus, the parent role performance may be in part determined by the family size.

Research has demonstrated two correlates of group size which appear to have implications for parent behavior. First, five years ago Mills reported a study (16) of three-person *ad hoc* problem-solving groups, showing that the groups split up into units of two and one, with the isolated member being spoken to less and contributing less to the conversation, whereas the two members in the coalition interact much more heavily. Research in progress on groups of other sizes shows that in four-person groups, a unit pattern of two and two usually develops, with the result that a member is not isolated.

These same patterns may not emerge, it is true, in the only-child and two-child families, respectively. Indeed, in research (23) on three-person family groups composed of mother, father, and son about twelve years old, the development of coalitions of two against one occurred but was unstable through time; that is, positions in and out of the coalition tended to rotate among the family members. This implies that the cultural norms governing interaction in the family prohibit the continuing isolation of any member in the family, and that parents and child, actively though not necessarily consciously, try to avoid any permanent teaming up of one set of members against another.

The point now for parent education and for parent role prescriptions generally is that recommendations to parents of how to rear their children, either from parent educators or from the role prescriptions indigenous to their culture, may suggest or demand that the parent treat his child in a way which conflicts with the natural pressures of the group structure. The success of the parent may be limited, struggling as he is against powerful behavioral determinants deriving from group structure. The effectiveness of parent education is to the same extent limited when it makes recommendations about parent behavior where the behavior is not fully under the parent's control. Indeed, one can go farther and ask if it is even good policy to try to set people in opposition to the forces of group structure.

As a second example, we refer to research (22) on the rates of participation in discussion of members of college classes of sizes varying up to 12. In the analysis of the data, one plots the relation between the rank order of group members' participation (for example, who participates most, the next to most, and so on) and the actual frequency of participation in terms of total number of actions. The relation between these two variables is that of an exponential curve in which the highest participating member talks about twice as much as the next ranking member, who in turn talks a third more than the next in rank, and so on. As group size increases the tail of the curve extends farther, so that in groups of six, seven, and up, those members low in rank-order participation talk very little indeed. The ranks are stable across group meetings, as is the exponential relationship.

One would suppose that the rank positions of participation are the expression of personality characteristics of the group members, such as extroversion, need for affiliation, and the like. If this is the case, then one could not argue that the participation pattern is determined by structural properties of the group, but rather by personalities of the members. In a subsequent critical test of this hypothesis (3) after duplicating the earlier results with *ad hoc* groups, the groups were reconstituted so that new groups were composed of the highest participating members from the previous groups, on the one hand, and the lowest participating members, on the other. In these reconstituted groups the distribution of participation showed the same exponential pattern as in the first groups. This result argues most effectively for the determining influence of group structure in contrast to personalities of the members.

One would hypothesize that the same pattern of participation occurs in the family, around the dinner table or during an evening in the living room. Thus, different members of the family would have different rank orders of participation, and hence both parent and child are exposed by virtue of this group structure determinant to continuing and systematic differences in their interaction in the family. As family size increases, those members who participate least assume a position in which their participation must be very small.

The normative regulation of family interaction has its counterpart with respect to participation patterns also. Probably parents seek to equalize the participation of children in family matters and thus struggle to prevent the development of the exponential pattern described previously, in which one child participates greatly and the least participating child becomes withdrawn. The difficulty of achieving this clearly must increase as family size increases, and it may be that in four- or five-child families it is impossible.

Other findings of probable pertinence include those showing that members in groups of an even-numbered size are more antagonistic than those of an odd-numbered size; and that both tolerance of deviation and lower levels of tension in interaction accompany increasing group size.

In sum, parent education programs may be asking parents to behave in ways which are extremely difficult, perhaps impossible, because they operate at cross purposes with the determinants of parent behavior inherent in the group structure.

ECOLOGICAL AND PHYSICAL FACTORS

The sixth influence on parent behavior considered here consists of the ecological and physical aspects of the environment which impinge on the parent. Parent educators vary considerably in their understanding of such realistic aspects of the parents' role. On the one hand, the written materials of the U.S. Children's Bureau are prepared most cautiously to avoid making recommendations with which physical or ecological factors would interfere. On the other hand, one finds famous works with little sensitivity to the trials of the average parent, as in the Gesell and Ilg (6) descriptions of the typical behavior day of a given age child, which may point out that at five o'clock such a child likes to have his supper in his own room.

We can do no more in this section than speculate on some of the ways in which these factors are important, because apparently there is no body of research relating the physical environment of the parent to the child-rearing practices which he employs. A few examples of the way in which such factors may influence the parent serve to call attention to our need for greater understanding here.

Consider the effects of comparative poverty upon the home environment where the absence of labor-saving devices, the absence of assistance in child care in the form of baby sitters or other persons, the absence of adequate medical care, generally depressing surroundings, and the like, may well make it hard to be cheerful, to be resourceful and creative in child rearing, to give deliberate attention to one's parental role when one is oppressed by matters of higher saliency, such as getting the day's work done under difficult conditions.

Consider also the fact that at the present time almost two million mothers with children six or under are active in the labor force, and the fact that the mother is working has consequences of several kinds for her family role. In such families the older children are frequently pressed into service to act as parent substitutes. The working mother who sees her children for only a short time during the day may feel the need to compress into this short period of interaction with her child all of those elements of love and discipline which a nonworking mother is able to distribute throughout the whole day with the child, and, indeed, may be called upon to do this in her own mind even when the child is not concerned about it.

Consider, too, the various possible effects of physical crowding resulting from restricted housing space, involving such factors as increased frequency of physical exposure between brother and sister on the one hand, between parents and children on the other; or overstimulation between family members, resulting in many instances in a gradual attrition in the emotional equanimity of the mother so that it is much more difficult, if not impossible, for her to maintain the equivalent level of acceptance and supportiveness for her children as is reached and held by the mother who is able to withdraw and regenerate her emotional resources.

These examples simply suggest the need for some research on this problem which would further help to differentiate the clientele and methods of parent education in terms of the child-care practices which their environment permits them to undertake.

CONCLUSIONS

The purpose of this chapter has not been to demonstrate the falsity of the assumption parent education makes about parents, but to stress that it has limited applicability and that there are other well-validated assumptions about the causes of parent behavior.

The applicability of the basic assumption of education, that the parent is autonomous and deliberately and consciously selects his ends and means in child rearing probably varies with the area of child rearing. As we have said, it may apply in the area of child-rearing practice devoted to training youngsters to use money and not in the area of training children to control sexual motivation or to control aggression. Moreover, the applicability of this model of man probably varies with the individual; this is to say that individuals differ in the degree to which their behavior may

have these conscious volitional and rational aspects. In some individuals this type of behavior may play a much larger role than
in others where the latter are hemmed in by a variety of restrictions, internal and external, so that there are few conscious and
volitional characteristics to their behavior. Certainly a large
amount of research is desirable here to further clarify the
validity of parent education assumptions.

Recognition of the many contributing causes of parent behavior leads to closer examination of the limitations of parent
education. This is valuable not only in helping one avoid educational efforts which hold no promise of success. It is of value also
because it can spare both the educator and the parent the frustration and unhappiness that can result from educational programs
being supported that are in opposition to the influence of other
determinants of parent behavior. As we have pointed out, the
major recognition of parent education of this point has been with
regard to unconscious determinants. Here the argument has been
that the attempt to educate where the motivating factors are
unconscious produces anxiety and guilt in the parent. But clearly
the same argument applies to efforts to change child-rearing
practices where it is impossible to do so because of the authoritative position of someone else in the family or because of the
limitations arising from inadequate housing, to name but two
examples.

Recognition of the various causes of parent behavior leads also
to an appreciation of the value of the programs which stem from
these rather different conceptions of man. Thus, one can recognize that where some aspect of parent behavior arises from unconscious and repressed motives, the means of change involve
therapeutic procedures. One understands that when change is
asked of a mother in an area where the husband has authority the
change also will involve efforts to change the beliefs of the husband. Where the working mother is concerned, the emphasis of a
program may be upon providing supervised after-school activities for the child in order to afford the mother a brief time at
home alone for her housework or just for the privacy and quiet
which she may desperately need to reestablish her emotional
equilibrium. As Grams has pointed out (7), the issues in parent

education parallel those of education in general. Our public schools do not assume total responsibility for educating the pupil nor should they, recognizing that pupil behavior springs from a variety of sources which hinder or aid the learner's academic achievement, and that the home, the church, and others all share responsibility for education. Parent education could with profit develop the same viewpoint.

One sees now also that it is wrong to raise the question of which kind of program, for example, educational, therapeutic, eugenic, environmental manipulation, or the like, is the "right" program. Rather, all programs may proceed from valid assumptions. The adequacy of such assumptions, however, and hence the program, vary with the individual client, with the area of role performance involved and with other characteristics. It follows that one cannot discuss the question of whether one program is better than another, for example, therapy in contrast to education, without studying its application to a specific situation in which the facts are available about the causes of the client's behavior. One surmises also that certain kinds of parent behavior which may produce troubles for the child are not to be dealt with by one of these measures but require instead a full-scale attack. This is to say that certain aspects of parent behavior involved in the production, of, say, mental illness in a child, may stem from many causes at once and hence may require not simply therapeutic procedures for the parent, or simply education, or raising the family's economic level, but all of these and still others to change the situation.

REFERENCES

1. Adorno, T. W., Else Frenkel-Brunswick, Daniel J. Levinson, and R. Nevitt Sanford, *The Authoritarian Personality*. Harper and Bros., New York, 1950.
2. Biber, Barbara, "Basic Assumptions and Goals of Parent Education" in *Taking Stock in Parent Education:* Proceedings of the 1953 Conference for Workers in Parent Education. Child Study Association of America, New York, 1953, pp. 12–17.
3. Borgatta, Edgar F., and Robert F. Bales, "Interaction of Individuals in Reconstituted Groups," *Sociometry*, vol. 16, 1953, pp. 302–320.
4. Brim, Orville G., Jr., *Individual Selection in Cultural Change*. Unpublished doctoral dissertation, Yale University, New Haven, 1951.

5. Brim, Orville G., Jr., "The Acceptance of New Behavior in Child-Rearing," *Human Relations*, vol. 7, 1954, pp. 473–491.

6. Gesell, Arnold, and Frances L. Ilg, in collaboration with Janet Learned and Louise B. Ames, *Infant and Child in the Culture of Today:* The Guidance of Development in Home and Nursery School. Harper and Bros., New York, 1943.

7. Grams, Armin, "Some Suggestions," *Children*, vol. 6, 1959, pp. 78–79.

8. Gruenberg, Ernest M., "The Prevention of Mental Diseases," *Annals of the American Academy of Political and Social Science*, vol. 286, 1953, pp. 158–166.

9. Hare, Paul, Edgar F. Borgatta, and Robert F. Bales, *Small Groups:* Studies in Social Interaction. Alfred A. Knopf, New York, 1955.

10. Hart, Irvin, "Maternal Child-Rearing Practices and Authoritarian Ideology," *Journal of Abnormal and Social Psychology*, vol. 55, 1957, pp. 232–237.

11. Herskovits, Melville J., *Man and His Works:* The Science of Cultural Anthropology. Alfred A. Knopf, New York, 1949.

12. Kelly, E. Lowell, "Consistency of the Adult Personality," *American Psychologist*, vol. 10, 1955, pp. 659–681.

13. Korsch, Barbara Maria, "Practical Techniques of Observing, Interviewing and Advising Parents in Pediatric Practice as Demonstrated in an Attitude Study Project," *Pediatrics*, vol. 18, 1956, pp. 467–490.

14. Kubie, Lawrence S., "Psychoanalysis and Marriage: Practical and Theoretical Issues" in *Neurotic Interaction in Marriage*, edited by Victor W. Eisenstein. Basic Books, New York, 1956, chap. 2.

15. Linton, Ralph, *The Study of Man*. Appleton-Century Co., New York, 1936.

16. Mills, Theodore M., "The Coalition Pattern in Three Person Groups," *American Sociological Review*, vol. 19, 1954, pp. 657–667.

17. *Psychoanalytic Study of the Child*. International Universities Press, New York, 1946–1957, vols. 1–12.

18. Sanford, Nevitt (issue editor), "Personality Development During the College Years," *Journal of Social Issues*, vol. 12, 1956, pp. 1–70.

19. Sears, Robert R., Eleanor E. Maccoby, and Harry Levin, *Patterns of Child Rearing*. Row, Peterson and Co., Evanston, Ill., 1957.

20. Spock, Benjamin, "Values and Limits of Parent Education" in *Communication in Parent Education:* Proceedings of the Ninth Annual Institute for Workers in Parent Education. Child Study Association of America, New York, 1955, pp. 7–13.

21. Stanton, Howard R., "Mother Love in Foster Homes," *Marriage and Family Living*, vol. 18, 1956, pp. 301–307.

22. Stephan, Frederick F., and Elliot G. Mishler, "The Distribution of Participation in Small Groups: An Exponential Approximation," *American Sociological Review*, vol. 17, 1952, pp. 598–608.

23. Strodtbeck, Fred L., "The Family as a Three-Person Group," *American Sociological Review*, vol. 19, 1954, pp. 23–29.

CHAPTER FOUR:

Aims of Parent Education

THE AIMS OF PARENT EDUCATION require analysis from two points of view, the ethical and the scientific. First, one must consider the aims of educational efforts in terms of the ultimate values being sought. The concern here must be with ethical issues, namely, whose values are to be realized, those of the parent or the parent educator. And since we conclude that in some degree it is always the values of the parent educator that are sought, the ethical problems arise of how his values are to be introduced into the program and which are to be given priority.

Second, whatever values are sought, their achievement requires certain changes in parents. Such changes, of course, are desired by the parent educator on the basis of his theories regarding the effects of parents on children, and may range from more lenient toilet-training practices to greater knowledge of child development by the parents. But the possibilities of producing such changes by education are affected by practical considerations, such as the intelligence and social background of the parent, his personality, and his family structure. Thus, from the scientific viewpoint our analysis must deal with the ways in which theories of parent-child relations and of the educability of parents combine to set the specific practical working goals of parent education, embodied in types of "good parents" which the different programs seek to produce.

ETHICAL ISSUES IN THE CHOICE OF OBJECTIVES

The parent-child relation is a stable social interaction system, charged by society with the function of producing children com-

petent in their role as children, and competent later in their
adult role. Like all such social systems, it is regulated by normative beliefs or sanctions about how the participants are to behave
so as to achieve such an end. Child rearing in the parent-child
system has as part of its function the inculcation, through training, of certain personal characteristics: behavior patterns, belief
systems, and values which are held to be desirable by adult
members of society. The selection of characteristics to be produced in the child through training is in the last analysis an
ethical choice, dependent on what one believes to be the good
person. Research has amply demonstrated that there are broad
differences between cultures in their conception of what constitutes the good person, that there are differences between subcultural groups in our society, and that even within these there are
idiosyncratic differences arising from the special personality
characteristics of the individuals. It follows that in selecting aims
to be reached in child rearing, the parent educator will differ
from some of the groups and some of the individual parents with
whom he works. Moreover, research is now showing that even
within the sets of values held by individual members of our
society, including parent educators, there often is conflict. Not all
of the personal characteristics we prize may be obtainable in the
same person: the selection of one may require the rejection of
another.

Avoidance of the Ethical Issues by Parent Educators

The problem of conflict of values between parents and parent
educators, and between the values of parent educators themselves, to our knowledge has not been systematically considered
in the literature on parent education. There are several well-
regarded works (e.g., 9, 40, 63) which attack parent education
on the grounds that it has made the modern American parent
anxious about his child's development and dependent upon parent educators for advice. These works, however, are not concerned with basic ethical issues, but rather with the fact that
some parent education programs produce ill effects, so that un-
desired results occur; changes in parent education procedures

might produce different results, it is argued. While we return to this problem in detail in a subsequent chapter, it suffices simply at this time to note that such ethical issues as whether or not it is legitimate to carry out parent education at all, and if so, on what moral grounds, are omitted from critical works of this kind.

The probable value conflicts of the kind under discussion here have been obscured by at least three familiar procedures: taking refuge in generalities, making statements of things to be "against," and making fatuous assertions that everyone knows what a good child is, anyway. While one cannot argue that resort to such procedures is deliberate, it is clear that stating aims in such a way that everyone can agree with them avoids the very difficult task of stating specifically at a workable level just what ends are to be sought.

Considering the first, Helen Witmer pointed out in her survey of parent education a generation ago (70) that the avowed aims of her sample of programs at that time were broadly stated and consisted of desires to "promote effective family life." The aims of the parent education program of the Works Progress Administration during the decade of 1930 were stated in terms of helping "parents in the care and guidance of their children," and of helping "to improve conditions of home and family life." (67) The aims of the National Congress of Parents and Teachers include those of "raising the standards of home life" and "securing for every child the highest advantages in physical, emotional, spiritual and social education." (33) The general aim of the Parent Education Project of the University of Chicago (41) is that of developing "mature, responsible citizens in a free society."

We do not believe these examples of general statements of parent education aims are unfair to the field. Indeed, the statements which we have given are some of the few available; other parent education programs are impressive in the degree to which they avoid formally stating, even at this general level, the ends they seek to achieve. Given only such global statements, not to speak of no statements at all, one can avoid the challenging task of wrestling with ethical issues.

The second way in which critical ethical problems are obscured is for parent educators to state their aims in negative terms, referring only to bad things which are to be avoided. Hence, one is against mental illness rather than for mental health; security is not necessarily sought, but insecurity is to be eliminated; gentleness may not be a virtue, but brutality clearly is an evil. In this matter, the parent educators do not, to be sure, stand alone. Various authorities (12, 38, 44) reporting on conferences, programs, and available literature describe the considerable reluctance of professional persons in the field of mental health to state just what mental health would be. With respect to family service organizations generally, Foote and Cottrell (31) have shown that the aims of such agencies historically have been negatively stated, and that some such organizations are now moving from remedial and therapeutic work, through a phase of preventive services, to programs seeking to promote positive values, and that concomitant with the last stage of development is the task of stating just what such positive values should be.

While it may be generally true of human endeavors that the objectives sought are negatively stated, the fact remains that in parent education, as with its companions among activities directed to human betterment, the statement of evils to be avoided hides the problems of what goods are to be sought.

With respect to the third procedure which masks the potential value conflict and the need for choice, namely, the assumption that all agree on good adult character, or the nature of mental health, the research literature in cultural anthropology is rich in documentation of the differences between cultures in their conceptions of the valued adult personality. Benedict's classic comparison (11) of the Pueblo and the Navaho, Mead's equally famous contrast (50) of the Dobu with the Arapesh, the theoretical work of Linton (45), the well-known shorter analyses of various cultures (e.g., 43, 48), all show the great variety of conceptions of the good person which exist among cultures. The research literature describing contemporary cultures continues the documentation of the cultural relativity of values: Kluckhohn's comparison of Mexican with American culture (42); Farber's comparison of the socialization values of English and American parents (29); the impressive analysis of differences in "paths of life" recently presented by Morris (52) in which several major world cultures are compared, all these attest to the fact that different people pursue different values. Within the United States, ethnic and social class differences in conceptions of the desirable character have been heavily documented by research: the work of McClelland (49) and of Strodtbeck (65), centering on Italian, Irish, and Jewish differences; and of Davis and Havighurst (21), and of Sears, Maccoby, and Levin (61), describing race and class differences, all are pertinent to showing differences in values.

Given the manifold differences between and within cultures— orderliness versus spontaneity, vengeance and aggression versus gentleness and timidity, a future time orientation versus an emphasis on present gratifications, a sense of potency over nature versus being one with nature, an emphasis on self-discipline and responsibility versus social skills and feelings of acceptance, a high achievement drive versus personal inner security, submission to authority versus encouragement of independence—given differences such as these, one may well ask how the parent educator can assume that everyone knows what a good adult character consists of, or that the traits of adult mental health are known and agreed upon. The facts are, to take the latter point first, that when concepts of mental health are phrased as meaningfully specific traits, there is little agreement as to whether such characteristics are pertinent to mental health or not; nor do we know yet whether or not there are many "mental healths" rather than a single universal conception, depending on the stage of an individual's life cycle and on the interrelation of an individual's personality and the specific cultural setting in which he lives (19). With respect to the assumed agreement on the good adult character, it has been too well documented (e.g., 22, 35, 55, 60) that many professions, and specifically educators and therapists, emphasize middle-class values and continually run afoul of disagreements on fundamental conceptions of the good life with the lower-class members of their clientele. There seems no reason to believe that this would not be true also of parent educators.

In sum, vague general statements, negatively stated goals, and the assumption of universal agreement about good character have permitted the parent educator to avoid important ethical issues.

Whose Values Are to Be Sought?

Twenty years ago Jean Carter (17) pointed out that there were substantial differences among parent educators in their perceptions of their moral rights. The same differences seem to exist today. Some believe that "we know what children need" (1, p. 9), believe that they are justified in influencing parents to pursue these ends, and seek to provide parents with information on how to achieve them; others accept and clarify the parents' ends, say they are value-free themselves insofar as they can be, and seek also to help parents achieve their ends. We see that the first would treat the parent as an instrument through which the aims of parent educators are achieved. The second would treat the parent as a professional client who is to be assisted, through professional advice, in attaining his own ends.

The question of whose values are to be sought in parent education is usually stated as a dichotomous choice; namely, should the parents' or the parent educators' values be dominant? This seems to confront the parent educator with the need to choose one or the other of these two positions. He might say that his proper role is to assist parents in clarifying their own values for their children, and also, since he is in possession of certain special knowledge pertaining to child development, of assisting parents in the achieving of such values. On the other hand, he himself possesses values with respect to children in our society, and he might take the position that his role is to promulgate such values to parents, and to provide them with information about how to reach these, his own, ends.

We believe that the formulation of the ethical problem as a choice between parent and parent educator values has been unfortunate; has established a false dichotomy, and has obscured the true problem. The parent educator cannot be value-free, as some claim; he cannot avoid the intrusion of his values into the educational program. The ethical problem thus becomes one of the *way* in which the values are introduced into the program, whether autocratically or democratically. Most programs can be ordered along this continuum, with the so-called "value-free" programs actually falling at the democratic pole of the continuum.

Consider first the programs in which the values of the parent educator are openly emphasized and actively pursued, with no claim of being value-free. Most parent education programs have as their aim the furthering of a set of values which the parent educators themselves hold and believe desirable for parents to pursue. Such programs include the vast parent education activities of the Protestant and Catholic Churches. For example, one publication regarding parents' groups in connection with the church states that the aim of some groups is a better understanding of children. "Some groups are established almost wholly for this purpose. Leading teachers, child psychologists, doctors, and other experts are brought to the group for lecture and discussion of child care and growth. This is the major purpose of your group. Be certain not to neglect the religious growth of the child. One of the functions of parents' groups is to help them overcome their frustration because they cannot answer their children's questions about God, Christ, the Holy Spirit, death, immortality, and aspects of religious belief." (23)

Much parent counseling under public health and clinical auspices, and many mass media enterprises and discussion group programs stress special values. One finds statements that "the discussion leader represents an ego ideal to the group and should embody accepted standards" (54, p. 203) and lists of principles (values) to guide the parent group leader; for example, "Race experience shows marriage best when all emotional power [is] directed into marriage, not outside it. Necessary for deep loving, protection of children, etc." (34, p. 72) One need not argue the merits of this point of view, but simply note that there would be certain families in this country that would not consider such a marriage to be the best. In programs of this type, the purpose is to instill in parents the belief in desirability of the goals of child rearing set by parent educators, and to instruct parents in the most efficient child-rearing practices (based on current scientific theory) as means of reaching these goals. To these, parent education must appear as a method of making over the personality of the members of society closer to the educators' ideal image, of bringing about a massive reconstruction of the basic personality structure of the society. As one program has put it (36), "To great souls all men are children, easy of approach and craving sympathy. Parent education teachers are missionaries of no mean order, spreading the gospel of truth, security and happiness."

In the democratic programs, where the parent educator believes (although mistakenly) that he takes a value-free position, it is proposed that the parents' values are to be implemented through education. Almost thirty years ago it was argued that parents should not be treated "merely as instruments for rearing children in accordance with the standards and methods presented by experts or authorities." (37) Recently it has been suggested that "in the coming years, in order to keep our experts from imposing their own ideas and values on the not-so-expert we may need to weave into all codes of professional conduct the principle of *habeas mentem*." (59, p. 832). The often-stated aims are to provide the parent with information helpful in reaching his ends, and to help him explore and systematize his own values. An acceptable statement of the aim of many such programs is to increase parent competence and rationality in role performance, by making him better able both to select his own values for the child, and to achieve these through child-rearing practices.

The parent group program of the Child Study Association of America is an example. As Auerbach (3, p. 4) has described the program, "by means of shared thinking around common problems, parents are consciously exposed to varied experiences from which they can make choices suitable to their own needs and situations." Dybwad and Goller, in describing the aims of the program (25), point out that while many parent educators have seen their role as the "transmitter and interpreter of positive cultural ideals and values," that is, as attempting to set values for the parents, actually the group leader should help parents to an appreciation of cultural differences and variations in the aims of child rearing, hence providing them with an opportunity to select from this range of variation in values. In part, this position suggests that parent education should support and encourage as much variability in the aims of parents as parent educators urge parents to give their children.

However, we emphasize that it is a serious mistake to think of this second position as "value-free"; and to do so is misleading and unrealistic. Since the claim of being value-free is widely accepted as the solution to the ethical problem, something more needs to be said to indicate why it is not possible.

There are several reasons why this is the case. First, as others (e.g., 71) have pointed out, scientific findings are incomplete and their implications for practice ambiguous. It is *not* enough to claim that one is "just presenting facts," for such facts must first be chosen and then stated intelligibly, that is, with some meaning and in relation to other facts. The parent educator in the middle-man role of transmitting and interpreting factual findings to parents, and having values of his own pertaining to children, may unknowingly color his choice and interpretation of scientific data in terms of his own value system. Indeed, the vast research on the distorting effects of one's own wishes when interpreting ambiguous situations suggests that the parent educator, however much he tries to remain value-free in his discussions, may find it impossible to keep his own values from influencing the discussion of materials.

Second, a closely related point is that values enter into the selection of the content of the program, in deciding what should be stressed, what omitted because it is unimportant. Neubauer writes that the parent group leader "guides the discussion by selecting points from the material produced by the group . . . [and] . . . has a responsibility of underlining those contributions of group members which evidence strength and healthy attitudes." (53) But by whose standards are such contributions to be judged if not the parent educators'? And if this problem still exists in group discussion, where at least the topics are raised by the parents, how much more of a problem it must be in the preparation of mass media materials where the audience is anonymous and their values unknown.

Third, consider the common instance in which parents insist that parent educators supply the values, that is, tell them what is right. In Chapter I it was noted that in the United States people have been led to reexamine their own traditional cultures, and that this is manifested in reconsideration of the question of what a child should be. Sottong (62) has pointed out that parents may be confused as to exactly what their culture is, and, indeed, whether it is the culture that should be transmitted. Along with this goes serious self-doubt on the part of the parent as to whether he is the proper person for the child to emulate. Coleman (20) points out that in this moral vacuum science becomes a major source of standards for direction even though one should know that science itself does not supply standards, but rather information in order to achieve such standards. This misconception of the role of science may lead the parent to demand that the parent educator tell him, on the basis of scientific research or the parent educator's superior knowledge, what values he now should seek for his child. Indeed, educators must watch carefully because parents very rapidly adopt and follow rigidly the suggestions of parent educators, and really need to be induced to explore them, rather than taking them on faith. It follows that programs should challenge the parents' values, even when the parent educator himself agrees with them, so that parents better understand the basis of their own choice.

Fourth, and probably most important of all, the parent educator is often confronted with a parent who wishes to rear a child in terms of values with which the parent educator strongly disagrees. Certainly such occasions raise doubts in the mind of the parent educator about the morality of his own value-free position. Should he at this time introduce his own point of view as a contradiction? Should he take no position at all? Should he mildly object, indicating simply that "others disagree" with this particular parent? Consider the parent who wishes to rear a selfish, aggressive child who will have a strong achievement drive, and who will use honesty or dishonesty, depending on the situation, to further his own ends, rather than having internalized the former; all in order, as the parent states, that the child can "get along in our competitive business society." To what extent, and in what ways, should the parent educator assist the parent to achieve these ends when his own personal beliefs are that these are evil? Can he honestly maintain that his own values do not enter into his exchanges with this parent?

This latter question confronts all individuals with superior knowledge and authority when dealing with those not so endowed. Thus, to draw an analogy with the parent-child relation, the parent may take the position that his own values are to be unquestioned, that his child is but an instrument for the embodiment or achievement of his own ends, and that the child's desires and conceptions of the good are unimportant. Or the parent may endeavor to take the position that he has neither the right nor duty to rear the child according to his own values, but rather that it is the child's ends alone which should be served. But the first is undemocratic, and the second a delusion. The parent is responsible both for helping the child to clarify, make realistic, and achieve his own values in some instances; and for stating to the child and insisting upon adherence to his own parental values in other instances. Consider the example wherein the child with fragile bone structure and a history of broken bones wishes to go out for the school football team. Here the parent must know what he himself wants, for example, health or athletic success for the child. He must be honest in stating this to the child and then work with the child so that *he* is clear himself as to his wishes, and their consequences if followed. The decision is then the child's to make, except in those instances, of which this is probably one, where the child is too little or too ignorant to understand the consequences, or where the parent feels so strongly about some value that he simply cannot live satisfactorily with the child unless he adheres to it. Here the parent must speak with authority if the child selects the wrong value, and actively prohibit its pursuit.

In summary, if the parent educator is to work in the best traditions of democracy he does not autocratically enforce his own values, nor does he take refuge in the false claim of being value-free. Rather, he must continually attend to the role of his values in his work. Sometimes he can, and must, speak with conviction and authority rather than assist in the achievement of ends he believes are wrong. Sometimes, as in the field of health, science speaks with authority and one had best listen. Sometimes maturity thus must speak to youth. The decision to defer the parents' values, or to stress one's own, recurs continually throughout parent education activities, and requires the persistent application of intelligence, self-knowledge, and honesty. The objective is to achieve an educational program which speaks with moral conviction on some matters and assists the parent toward his own ends in others. The educator must know and state his own values, work with parents to do the same with theirs, assist in the achievement of those which are agreed upon, seek democratically to win the parent to his point of view, where they disagree, by rational persuasion, and, finally, withdraw and refuse to help where the parent insists on the pursuit of goals which the educator believes to be evil.

What Values Are Sought?

If the parent educator cannot avoid being influenced by his own values, it is pertinent to ask what values he holds. We have called attention to the great variations in values, in conceptions of the good person, which exist among cultural groups. The values of parent educators are undoubtedly determined by their own cultural background, mixed with their knowledge of child development and clinical research, and certain idiosyncratic ideals.

One cannot present a systematic appraisal of parent educators' aims, since most programs do not state their aims, or else state them in obscure general terms. Past efforts to make such appraisals are not of much help. One can, however, give some examples. The Parent Education Project of the University of Chicago, whose general purpose we have noted as developing mature, responsible citizens, further specifies six characteristics. These are: feelings of security and adequacy, understanding of self and others, democratic values and goals, problem-solving attitudes and methods, self-discipline, responsibility, and freedom, and constructive attitudes toward change (41). Programs stress the development of trust in others by the child (14), the ability to accept leadership (7), and similar discrete traits. Values guiding some programs may be understood by inference from statements of "what children need," such as the feeling of being wanted or of inner security, of being recognized and treated as an individual, and so on (e.g., 27). Aims are embedded in a variety of statements to parents of what parents should do in child rearing, such as providing tasks which the child can solve so that he develops a sense of competence; making toilet training contingent on maturational level, so that the child does not develop anxiety and feelings of inadequacy; handling infant-feeding schedules in such a way that the infant develops a basic sense of trust of others, rather than mistrust; providing teaching and example in the area of sexual behavior so that the value of continence prior to marriage is instilled (e.g., 34).

The one solid kind of information on parent educator objectives is historical. The record shows clear shifts in aims from concern over moral characteristics, to physical health characteristics, to a recent emphasis, as pointed out in the Appendix, upon emotional or mental health characteristics of the child (57, 66, 68, 69). For example, Vincent, in his exhaustive coverage of the infant care literature since 1890 (68), describes the shift in emphasis from a concern with infant mortality and health to a concern with psychological factors. In 1890 to 1894, 64 per cent of the articles were concerned with mortality and 4 per cent with psychological loss to the child; in the period 1945 to 1949, the respective percentages were 11 per cent and 32 per cent.

The ambiguous and ineffectual statements of aims of parent education programs have masked, as we have pointed out previously, the critical issue of the choice of values to pursue. Such vague statements also hide possible conflicts within the values actually held, so that a given parent education program may be striving for incompatible objectives. As our knowledge of personality development grows, it increasingly suggests that many facets of the personality held to be desirable are incompatible.

For example, it seems to us fair to state that many parent educators would hold as desirable the values of a sense of inner security, of a desire for achievement, of independence of judgment, and of getting along well with others. We might cite, then, to exemplify the kind of conflict which may be hidden in parent education aims, several research studies.

A study by Ausubel and others (4) shows that youngsters who are valued for themselves rather than for what they do, possess stronger feelings of security and self-adequacy, but score low in achievement motivation; in contrast, youngsters extrinsically valued by their parents, that is, valued for what they do, while high in achievement drive, are to a greater degree insecure. A study by Dynes and others (26) concerning the relation between level of aspiration and experience in the family, demonstrates that unsatisfactory interpersonal relations in the family were, for college students, significantly related to high aspiration levels, whereas satisfactory relations were related to lower levels. As the authors point out, "Since increasing attention is being given to the development of happy and socially well-adjusted persons by some of our institutions and social agencies, the question arises whether modifications will occur in the future to the success orientation of American society." (26, p. 214) This research may thus pose a choice for parent educators as to which of two possible values should be sought for the child, since the evidence suggests it is not possible to achieve both in the same person.

Another example of possible value conflict is delineated in the work of Riesman (56), among others, and can be phrased as the degree to which it is desirable for a child to be sensitive to group demands, to conform to socially accepted customs, in contrast to being independent of group demands; or, in Riesman's terms, the degree to which it is desirable to be other-directed rather than inner-directed. Current research on the origins of conformity motivation suggest that in the near future we may be in the position to describe those child-rearing practices which produce relatively greater desire for conformity on the one hand, as opposed to independence on the other. Given such knowledge, the ethical choice is posed.

In the past several years, efforts have been made to prepare statements of aims suitable for the service professions such as parent education. The statement by Foote and Cottrell (31) of the components of interpersonal competence is one of these. The authors present six such components: health, intelligence, empathy, judgment, autonomy, and creativity. Another well-known work is the report on conceptions of mental health, prepared by Jahoda (39) for the Joint Commission on Mental Illness and Health. These efforts may reflect the stirring and unrest among parent educators and others about their current ambiguities in the area of values, and may point to the decade ahead as one in which this cardinal problem will receive more of the serious attention it deserves.

SCIENTIFIC ISSUES IN THE CHOICE OF OBJECTIVES

The Selection of Practical Working Goals

The ethical choices of the parent educator, reviewed in the previous section, determine in part the objectives of the educational program. In addition to the ethical considerations, there are a number of scientific or practical matters, namely, those pertaining to the effects of parents on children and to the various determinants of the educability of parents, which also exert a powerful influence over the objectives selected for the educational program. Together with the ethical issues, these matters dictate the kinds of changes in parents which are believed to be desirable and possible, and which child-training practices are seen as both valuable and teachable. The ethical choices and the conclusions one draws with respect to the scientific and practical matters combine to give several kinds of instrumental or working goals of parent education programs. Customarily these are expressed in conceptions of the "good parent" held in different educational programs. Recognize that these are not ideals so much as they are blends of the desirable and the practical, which constitute realistic objectives in the minds of various parent educators. It is these types of "good parent" as working goals that are discussed in this second part of Chapter IV.

The establishment of working goals requires a conception of the ethically most desirable parent, as well as certain assumptions about the way in which parents are educated and the effect they have on their children. We have pointed out in preceding chapters and in the first part of this chapter, that these matters are far from clear in parent education theory. Many ethical issues are unresolved; and in spite of the vast research on child development, our knowledge of the effects of parents on children's personality is still in a rudimentary stage; and in a like way, our understanding of the limitations imposed by personal and social characteristics of parents upon their ability to learn and change in child rearing is still in a primitive state.

The fruits of this ambiguity and ignorance, as must be the case, are a number of vague conceptions of actual working objectives. In the paragraphs that follow we present seven conceptions of the "good parent" which seem to be used as working goals of one or another program. In isolating and naming these types of working goals we have erred on the side of drawing with a heavy hand, putting body where perhaps there is none, in order to provide points of reference for a discussion of working goals in terms of types. Some may feel that these are caricatures of the aims of certain programs. We admit that in some cases they are overdrawn, but we emphasize again that their purpose is to provide points of reference in terms of which our discussion of working aims can proceed. The types discussed in the subsections below include: the rule-following parent, the loving and accepting parent, the parent with an understanding of child development, the parent who understands his influence upon his children, the problem-solving parent, the home manager, and the comfortable, relaxed, natural parent.

There are some general points to be made about this typology before moving on to a more detailed examination of each type. First, this classification serves heuristic purposes and is not meant to be a basic theoretical classification. Other individuals, looking at the procedures and implicit objectives of parent education programs might well arrive at a different classification of working goals. It is to be noted in particular that this typology, which seems to describe the aims of parent education programs, bears no resemblance to typologies of personality found in the social science literature. To take some familiar examples, the introversion-extroversion distinction, or the dimension of dominance-submission, are not represented in this typology.

Second, it should be stressed that an educational program may pursue more than one objective concurrently, so that it is not the case that some one and only one of the types of "good parent" described below is associated with a given educational program. The objectives are not mutually exclusive. Indeed, at the end of this chapter we argue that parent education should develop a conception of multiple objectives, should have several different working goals, depending on the personal and social characteristics of the various parents who participate in the program. This is a necessary conclusion from earlier considerations, that types of good parents are determined in part by beliefs about the effects of parents on children and about the educability of parents. Since these two vary for different groups of parents, it follows that the objectives should also differ.

For each of the seven types mentioned below we endeavor to show how it reflects certain combinations of ethical goals and of practical and scientific considerations regarding the kinds of persons that parents are. The criticisms presented in parent education literature of each of these types are briefly reviewed. The discussion of criticisms must be speculative, since there are little or no data on the consequences of a parent behaving in one or another of these ways; for example, it is still much a matter of conjecture whether or not a relaxed and comfortable parent has better results in achieving a certain personality characteristic in a child than does a somewhat anxious, self-conscious, involved, and knowledgeable parent. Hence, our discussion of the merits and criticisms of each type must be based largely on theoretical materials.

Types of "Good Parent" as the Working Goals

1. **The Rule-Follower.** Many people believe that the chief goal of the parent educator is that each parent be acquainted with expert

advice and opinion on child rearing, and to be trained to follow such expert judgments. The emphasis upon advice giving and adherence to expert judgment has had two phases during the course of parent education. The earlier emphasized parents' *behavioral* practices, often of a quite specific kind such as training the child in the use of a spoon. More recently, the substance of advice has to an increasing degree dealt with the affection of the parent for the child, recommending certain attitudinal responses to be made by parents. As we have pointed out in an earlier chapter, this new emphasis came in the largest part out of the influence of Freudian psychology. However, in both aspects, behavioral and emotional, the orientation is toward the parent who is a follower of advice.

In this section we deal with the first of these, namely, the "rule-follower"; whereas in the subsequent section we deal with the "loving and accepting parent." Regarding the first, it is true that such a goal dominated many parent education programs during the 1920's and also some during the first part of 1930. This first objective arose logically from the conception of parent education associated with the establishment of the child research stations during the 1920's. The conception was one in which research on children would discover new facts about desirable child rearing, and parent education would then transmit such information directly to the parents in the form of expert advice on how to rear children.

One must stress, on the other hand, that there were outstanding programs during these decades which did not have the "rule-following parent" as a working goal. There were countertrends and, as Brown (15, p. 5) points out, by 1930 there was evidence that leaders in parent education were well aware of the limitations of this approach. By the 1940's the importance of this objective, compared to the others cited, had undergone a significant decline. At the present time there are few programs in which this instrumental goal is still pursued. These often occur in situations where the program is dominated by medical personnel (pediatricians, general practitioners). Studies of parent education programs in certain medical settings (e.g., 2, p. 28) show "that many doctors expect mothers to be passive, compliant, submissive; to listen attentively and receive the doctor's findings; to give information when he asks for it and to follow recommendations to the letter." This is an outcome of the more general medical approach to clients which partakes of a formality and reliance upon expert status characterizing the medical practice as a whole. In addition, the thinking of medical personnel about the educability of parents has been insulated from the challenge of clinical materials stemming from psychoanalytic theory.

Several events combined to bring about the decline of the "rule-following parent" as an important working aim of educational programs. One was the growing belief that dependency of parents upon experts causes parental anxiety over their own role performance, a tension and rigidity in the interpersonal situation, a lack of creativity in unanticipated child-rearing situations, and other such consequences, all of which are judged to be undesirable for the child. During the 1940's there were at least two attacks upon parent education for pursuing the objective of a "rule-following parent." One by Kanner (40) and another by Bauer (9) state a number of the alleged undesirable effects produced as a result of pursuing this objective, reflecting opinion current at that time.

In addition, Sottong (62) and Baruch (8) have pointed out that as child development knowledge accumulated during this period there was no convergence toward a common set of principles by the experts, but rather that the contrary occurred. There was a shift toward a conception of multiple causation of such complexity that each expert was left to emphasize his own particular whim or interest in the area of personality development. The parent, still trying to rely upon experts, clinging to the conception of single causation and looking for simple answers, could not (and cannot) understand the multiplicity of answers that were given to him, and the fact that all of them were to some extent correct.

Third, competing conceptions of the desirable parent arose during the two or three decades involved and, since no research had accumulated to support the belief that the parent following expert advice reared children superior to other parents, the competition among goals of necessity proceeded in terms of appeal to professional backgrounds and personal idiosyncrasies of the parent educator, rather than to scientific appraisals of relevant evidence of which there was none.

2. The Loving and Accepting Parent. This second working goal shares with the first the conception of the parent following expert advice, but differs in its greater emphasis upon love and acceptance. Very few programs would state this as their actual working aim. However, as pointed out above, this objective from the mid-1930's became of increasing importance and in some programs became the sole objective.

The criticisms here are similar to those directed against conceptions of the good parent as an expert rule-follower. They appear in more recent articles or books (e.g., 10, 16) generally critical of parent education, which parallel the earlier works of the 1940's. The more recent criticisms, however, seem much less temperate, more polemic and less thoughtful, than the similar works appearing in the 1940's.

The outstanding criticism (discussed in Chapter III) has been that love and acceptance are not characteristics which are changeable through education, because they lie deep in the personality. Hence, those pursuing this good can produce much damage in the parent in the way of guilt over his own inadequacies.

A second criticism has been that the parent should not strive to express love and affection, for unless it is spontaneous it is of no value. Baldwin (6, p. 25) calls attention to the fact that if a social role *requires* characteristics such as friendliness or love, it is almost self-defeating. He points out that certain acts might be required in a role and certain consequences may be required or prohibited but that love and similar expressions of feeling cannot be deliberate or contrived.

A third criticism has been the standard one applied to all of these working conceptions, namely, that we lack the data to demonstrate that the loving and accepting parent does in fact have children whose characteristics are more desirable than those of children of other types of parents. We have commented on this in earlier chapters and simply stress again that much of what is taken as evidence of the importance of these parental characteristics is derived from clinical cases and is not evidence from scientific studies.

This second aspect of reliance upon experts, in which the "good parent" is viewed as a loving and accepting person, has rapidly declined in importance under the criticisms of the kind sketched above. The belief that education can do little to change parents' feelings, as well as the absence of documentation that this is an important factor in child development, has turned parent education programs toward some new and different working objectives.

3. The Parent Who Has an Understanding of Child Development. This type and the following are both aspects of a more general goal of producing an informed parent. In this section we consider the parent with an understanding of the way in which children develop; in the next, the parent who understands the effects of his behavior upon the child's personality.

There are many parent education programs which try to increase the parent's knowledge of child development. Principles of child care need not be added, for it is assumed that knowledge alone results in improved parent behavior. How might this work? One hypothesis has been that understanding of child development powerfully influences the parent's interpretation of the child's behavior. The underlying argument is that knowledge of child development equips the parents with a new set of concepts or labels to describe or classify the child's behavior.

Surely the most influential of these new labels is the one of "normality"; it provides an example for analysis. Assume that a parent has learned that more than 50 per cent of six-year-olds tell lies occasionally, or that several studies (13, 47, 51) show the frequency of nail-biting in a number of samples of public school children to be 50 per cent or more; or that two-and-a-half-year-old males tend to be aggressive toward family members. The new knowledge means that these behaviors are taken out of the realm of the odd and disturbing into the comfortable realm of "normal development" where the parent knows that time and maturation are on his side.

The reinterpretation of a child's behavior through new concepts goes beyond simply the abnormal-normal distinction. New labels for motives, abilities, and other characteristics may be learned. For example, the parent may recognize that when the older sibling hits the younger it is not because of hatred or evilness or inherited criminal tendencies but rather because he currently is jealous of his younger sibling. It is argued that the value of new and more accurate labels is that the parent is made less anxious and more accepting of the child. We would not deny that this is often the case. On the other hand, the outcomes of gaining knowledge may be other than this and the parent educator should consider these alternatives. For example, the knowledge that more than 50 per cent of six-year-olds lie may lead the parent to accept the behavior as normal for that age, which indeed it may be, statistically. But the fact may be that it is only because of parental intervention with this normality that the rate of lying declines from the age of six; that the child's maturation does not bring about a natural decline in lying, but that the decline occurs because his parents prohibit him to lie even when he is six.

The second major hypothesis regarding the value of understanding child development is that the parent knows of the child's needs at the time and thus can minister to them. Now it is possible to separate knowledge of the kinds of things that concern children, the interests they have, the worries they struggle with at different ages, from suggestions or discussion of what parents might do about it. However, the implicit assumption is that knowledge of needs at various ages leads the parent naturally to respond to them intelligently. This assumption must often be wrong. For example, the parent may learn to identify a child's questions about sex at a certain age as being the expression of a natural interest but this is only partly helpful to the parent if he does not have available the child-rearing skill of responding to this natural interest. Therefore, the criticism has followed that information also is needed by the parent about methods of sex education, in addition to his appreciation of the child's interest in the subject.

We have been unable to find any study reporting correlations between a parent's factual knowledge of child development and his confidence in his role, or the overall happiness or good adjustment of his children. A simple research project here on the relation of parental knowledge to characteristics of their children would be of real value. In spite of the absence of satisfactory evidence on results the transmission of child development information has been part of education from the very beginning. At present it is an important end of almost all parent education programs. Informal evidence about the kind of programs which parents themselves desire suggests that they do prize factual information of this kind. This indicates that teaching child development facts to parents probably will continue as a major focus for parent education for some time.

4. The Parent Who Understands the Effects of His Behavior on Children. The other type of knowledgeable parent, closely related to the foregoing, is the parent who understands the effects of his own behavior upon his child. This type of parent, as a working goal of educational programs, does not occur so frequently as does the type just discussed. This particular working goal has been most clearly manifest in the parent education program of the St. Louis Mental Health Association, and in the accompanying evaluation study of the St. Louis County Health Department (58).

This broad objective of various programs seems usually to become a much simpler one of teaching the parent that he has a powerful influence upon his child, and of getting him to accept his causal involvement in his child's development, instead of believing that "all children are born bad," or "he gets it from Uncle Willie," or other irresponsible views. This may reflect a more general change in society by educated people toward perceiving themselves as causal agents of others' behavior, which is demonstrated in the treatment of delinquency and crime, divorce, educational failure, and the like.

Still, a more powerful influence probably is the lack of adequate information on the specific effects of parents on children, which forces parent education to seek this more limited objective, for current facts support only the *general* conclusion that parents are an important influence.

Critics (e.g., 5) of programs with this objective have pointed out that a sense of causal involvement can shake the faith of parents in their own abilities to rear children; that a parent should not believe that his every act has a permanent effect upon the child, or that the process of child development is easily deflected and distorted by parent behavior. It is implied that programs with the working goal of parents who understand their effects upon their children cannot stop with "involving" the parent, but must complete their education (as in the St. Louis program mentioned earlier) by teaching the concept of multiple causation. The understanding can be given that parental effects upon the child are part of a pattern of multiple causation, so that the parent sees that the child's personality is determined not alone by the parent's behavior.

5. The Parent as Problem-Solver. This fifth instrumental goal is one of establishing through education a parent who is competent to deal effectively with the day-to-day child-rearing situations which confront him; to utilize as a basis for his decisions the best information available, as well as to integrate and apply this information creatively. Here the parent is neither a rule-follower nor an information learner, although both are involved in his problem-solving skills.

The arguments for this objective of parent education have been that one does not wish to develop parents who conform to expert advice, because the parent becomes anxious and dependent and the advice may not be correct for specific situations. Nor does one wish only to educate the parent in the factual information described above, important though that information is, since the information always needs application to specific situations. Hence, advocates of improving parent problem-solving say that the educational program should include consideration of varying situations and even of the problem-solving process itself; that is, how one should proceed in making a child-rearing decision.

This objective is not new in parent education. For example, Groves said thirty years ago that education of parents will prove of little value if a system of recipes or plain information is all that is taught. Rather, "it is [the] adaptability to meet rapidly changing conditions that both husbands and wives and parents require to pass successfully the tests of every day experience." (32, p. 55)

In a current Kansas City program the view is that "parents must solve their own problems—parents can gain knowledge, insight, and vision which will be of real value to them in solving their own problems." (28) Others (e.g., 24) suggest as a criterion of success of parent education the development in parents of a problem-solving approach. And in the workshop reports from the 1954 annual nationally attended institute for parent educators of the Child Study Association (18) the most frequent statement of goals for parent education was that of helping parents achieve the ability to accept themselves, to discover their own strength, and to develop the ability to find their own answers in handling their children.

If there has been increased interest in this kind of objective for parent education, perhaps it is part of a broader movement in the service professions generally. Sanford (59) has described four phases in the history of man's dealing with his own health, and suggests that we are moving into the fourth phase, that of creativity. He states that we are seeing a secularization of the health and welfare professions and the growth of an anti-expert attitude among people who want to learn to solve their problems in their own way. Foote and Cottrell (31, pp. 27–28) make a related point in their general discussion of the current convergence between professionals and laymen. They say that it is not too early to speak of the "professionalization of parenthood," in which each parent is concerned with improvement of his own performance, under his own creative initiative. While this professionalization initially may limit the joys and ease with which one conducts family living, the authors suggest that this is a decade of transition to one in which the emphasis will be upon the joys of competent performance as parents, rather than on the difficulties and the threats of failure.

Probably there are no parent educators who would disagree with the desirability of the working goal of a competent "problem-solving parent." The criticisms instead have been that this is a realistic objective for a limited group only; that the average parent, by virtue of moderate intelligence and considerable emotionality, cannot acquire the problem-solving attitudes and skills referred to here. The discussion of ability factors as determinants of parent behavior presented in Chapter III is pertinent here. It is pointed out that there are individuals who cannot live without simple traditions, who are unable to create their own synthesis or philosophy; and that although the more intelligent, or better educated individuals might acquire such problem-solving skills, most individuals will always need to rely on others to do much of their thinking for them.

6. The Parent as Home Manager. This conception of the good parent, and also the seventh type (the "comfortable, relaxed, natural parent") discussed next, can be viewed as reactions to the five types described above. The emphasis on home management is in part a reaction against giving rules or information on how to rear children in the attempt to change interpersonal relations. It is argued that parent education should avoid demanding of parents any acts which they cannot practice voluntarily, so as to not make them guilty over failures. It is argued that parental acts toward the child are in large part involuntary, arising from habit or unconscious motives. Parent education, therefore, should focus on the relatively impersonal aspects of the parent role which are consciously controlled. The parent should be taught how to manipulate the environment so that its effects on both parent and child are beneficial.

This is a theoretical approach in which both personality traits and the external situation are seen as causes of parent and child behavior; in this instance the emphasis is not on the personality component, but on teaching the parent how to change the situational component of the causes of behavior.

The emphasis on teaching home management stems also from the availability of content to be taught and the fact that present-day mothers have had less opportunity to learn the folk wisdom, the many simple administrative procedures, which make a home run smoothly. Faris (30) in particular has stressed how this capital, this heritage, may be lost because the new modern family is isolated from the older, more experienced generation. The materials to be taught are much more those of home economics than of child development. Children need to be fed, playtimes planned, toys purchased, "five o'clock hours" managed, supper prepared, routines established, friends visited, baths given, and homework completed.

It is proposed that parent education should educate parents in simple techniques and skills of handling children comparable with those of nursery schoolteachers, and in home economics materials; for example, to phrase requests to a child in such a way that he will more readily comply. Or in a case where the mother finds herself irritable, give her information on how to arrange rooms and playthings so that the child does not create a situation in which he irritates her. If some aspects of child care irritate the mother, but not the father, or one of the children irritates one parent but not the other, apportion the parental responsibility so that each parent avoids those situations which irritate him. Or if it is known that when the child is age three the mother may need to spend more time with him, the appropriate educational course is to teach her how to run her home during that period so that she actually has more time.

This kind of working goal clearly is very different from the working goals mentioned previously. It is not by itself a commonly accepted working goal in educational programs. However, it is an important objective for many of the programs under the auspices of home economics groups in university extension programs or in small communities. It also is a working goal of some cooperative nursery school programs, and is emphasized in some excellent mass media for parents, such as *Baby Talk* magazine.

The objections to this conception of the good parent are varied. One is that it is irrelevant to the improvement of interpersonal relations and mental health; that education in the significant aspects of the parental role has been avoided, and the easier, but rather aimless path taken. The fact is that we know nothing about the effects upon the family of the parent being skilled in home management. It may be true that the level of health of members of a family "managed" in this way is actually less than where the "management" is somewhat inefficient, but where the parent understands stages of child development and is sensitive to the child's inner needs.

A second objection is that this conception is incomplete. It has been said that managerial techniques must be integrated with knowledge of child development and other areas, or else such techniques are ineffective, or even employed in undesirable ways. In the example given earlier of the mother of the three-year-old, the salient point is *what* she does with the extra time gained by her improved management. Does she spend it with the child? Does she understand why, or do it sullenly? Perhaps she spends too much time. The concern of many is that the parent who takes a managerial attitude toward her children, untempered by understanding of the children and her influence on them, may soon become an unsympathetic authoritarian.

7. The Comfortable, Relaxed, Natural Parent. The last type of major working goal of parent education programs is that of comforting the parent, of making him feel secure. As one person has put it, "Helping parents gain a greater measure of security is the primary end and aim of parent education. It is far more important than helping them acquire facts concerning the bringing up of their children"; and later: "any method used should be used so as to contribute to this end." (8, p. 33)

One advocate of this aim is Benjamin Spock, probably the most notable of current parent educators. In an important address to parent educators in 1955 (63) he stated that "the only question you have to ask yourself is 'Will this make them [parents] more comfortable or will it make them more guilty?' My impression is that you rarely help them by making them guilty and that you *always* get a reflection of better management of the child by making them more comfortable." He states that parents should not be warned about unfortunate outcomes of minor common behavior problems, should not be made dependent on experts, should not be made to feel guilty and regretful for what they have already done; and that one should recognize that "we cannot (and should not attempt to) change them too much by our teaching."

In his nonprofessional writing, especially his recent revision of his famous work for parents (64) Spock takes the position that the parents should trust themselves, that instinctive or natural behavior prompts most parents to give children what they need, and that parents should go ahead according to the code of child rearing they feel most comfortable with, without any qualms of conscience.

This newer goal is properly understood as a reaction to the emphasis on parents becoming aware of themselves, their motives, their effects on their children, which appears in various educational programs. Lowy, for example, says that parents should understand their children's needs, but in order to do so they must be able to understand their own needs. "It would be desirable, therefore, that every potential parent have an opportunity to examine his own personality." (46, p. 27) It also is a reaction to the anxiety and guilt produced in some parents by the pursuit of other objectives noted above.

Some parent educators respond to this new goal by pointing out that it is yet to be demonstrated that a comfortable, relaxed, natural parent is better for children than the more anxious or self-conscious parent, for example, the "causally involved" parent discussed above. A second and more powerful criticism is that comforting the parent is hardly compatible with increasing his information or of changing his child-rearing practices. There will be occasions when it is necessary that the parent be discomforted in order for these other goals to be reached. Spock states that he does not mean that one gives approval to the parent for something he is doing which one considers unwise (63). But, unless the parent already is behaving in ways agreeable to the parent educator, in which case no education is necessary, one can hardly both comfort the parent and at the same time not give approval to him for something considered unwise. It is true that one can discuss with the parent in a nonhostile way whatever the parent is doing wrong, but the fact remains that before learning takes place the parent must be brought face to face with facts which will discomfort him, namely, his own behavioral inadequacies at the present time.

Granted the soundness of this criticism, then, this working goal must be viewed as unrealistic, and simply as the product of an emotional reaction to certain parent education consequences. The sentiment it expresses has already been included in more carefully thought out programs, which continue to give advice, information, problem-solving skills, and management hints, but in as comforting and nonpunitive a way as is compatible with effective education.

The Development of Programs with Multiple Working Goals

It will be apparent by now that several of the working goals are incompatible, and that it is desirable for each parent education program to clarify the instrumental aims of the program so as to avoid conflict. We have pointed out, for example, that the objective of making parents more comfortable and relaxed may well be incompatible, at least initially, with that of informing parents about their effects on children. Also, the competent and creative problem-solver will be a person quite different from the individual highly dependent upon, and conforming to, expert advice about child rearing.

This plea for clarification of goals does not mean parent education programs should have but one concept of the good parent, should have but a single working goal. The demands are quite otherwise; namely, for multiple conceptions of the good parent, there being a different goal for different kinds of personal and social situations. Each parent's behavior is influenced by his defenses, his intelligence, the normative attitudes of the family members, the degree to which they are bound to the traditions of their culture, the limitations placed upon them by their socioeconomic circumstances, and others discussed in Chapter III. Thus, realistically the objectives of parent education programs should be consonant with maximizing the change which can be produced in a desirable direction, but embody as working goals those changes which are consonant with the characteristics of the parent. It can hardly be doubted that there are some persons who can be better parents if they are ignorant of child-rearing information, but instead are made comfortable along the lines that Spock recommends. There are some who find it difficult to develop a feeling of love and affection for their child, but can be good managers, so that the home life is pleasantly organized and there is little occasion for friction. In sum, parents and their families are varied, and parent education can work with multiple conceptions of the good which apply to different personalities and situations.

The basic difficulty in tailoring the objectives to the individuals he attempts to reach is that the parent educator (unlike the elementary schoolteacher, by way of contrast) knows almost nothing about his students. Lacking this information, most parent educators take the path of setting a single goal for all parents, instead of facing the problem squarely and demanding that research supply the necessary information. Even rudimentary efforts to classify parents according to intelligence, ethnic origin, family size, degree of education, and the like would permit some improvement in relating working goals to different kinds of parents. In the years ahead, much more information will be needed. The study of types of parents, how the types are to be recognized, and how realistic aims can be set for them, is a matter of great importance.

REFERENCES

1. Allen, Winifred Y., and Doris Campbell, *The Creative Nursery Center:* A Unified Service to Children and Parents. Family Service Association of America, New York, 1948.

2. American Public Health Association, *Health Supervision of Young Children.* The Association, New York, 1955.

3. Auerbach, Aline B., "Parent Discussion Groups: Their Role in Parent Education," *Parent Group Education and Leadership Training.* Child Study Association of America, New York, 1953, pp. 1–8.

4. Ausubel, David P., Earl E. Balthazar, Irene Rosenthal, Leonard S. Blackman, Seymour H. Schpoont, and Joan Welkowitz, "Perceived Parent Attitudes as Determinants of Children's Ego Structure," *Child Development,* vol. 25, 1954, pp. 173–183.

5. Bakwin, Harry, "The Aims of Child Rearing," *New England Journal of Medicine*, vol. 248, 1953, pp. 227–231.

6. Baldwin, Alfred L., "The Psychological Processes Underlying Behavioral Uniformity" in *Conference on Cross-Cultural Research on Personality Development*, by David F. Aberle, Alfred L. Baldwin, John W. Whiting, Robert R. Sears, Daniel Miller, and William E. Henry. Kansas City, 1955, mimeographed.

7. Barnes, Marion J., "The Educational and Therapeutic Implications in Working with Parent Study Groups Around the Problem of the Normal Preschool Child," *American Journal of Orthopsychiatry*, vol. 22, 1952, pp. 268–276.

8. Baruch, Dorothy W., *Parents and Children Go to School:* Adventuring in Nursery School and Kindergarten. Scott, Foresman and Co., Chicago, 1939.

9. Bauer, William W., *Stop Annoying Your Children*. Bobbs-Merrill Co., Indianapolis, Ind., 1947.

10. Beecher, Willard, and Marguerite Beecher, *Parents on the Run*. Julian Press, New York, 1955.

11. Benedict, Ruth, *Patterns of Culture*. Penguin Books, New York, 1946.

12. Bernhardt, Karl S., "Report of the Research Symposium on Mental Health and Child Development," *Bulletin of the Institute of Child Study*, University of Toronto, Canada, 1955.

13. Birch, L. B., "The Incidence of Nail Biting Among School Children, Part II," *British Journal of Educational Psychology*, vol. 25, 1955, pp. 123–128.

14. Blatz, William E., "Insight into Parenthood," *Bulletin of the Institute of Child Study*, University of Toronto, Canada, vol. 19, 1957, pp. 12–16.

15. Brown, Muriel W., *With Focus on Family Living*. Vocational Division Bulletin 249, Office of Education, Government Printing Office, Washington, 1953.

16. Bruch, Hilde, "Parent Education or the Illusion of Omnipotence," *American Journal of Orthopsychiatry*, vol. 24, 1954, pp. 723–732.

17. Carter, Jean, *Parents in Perplexity*. American Association for Adult Education, New York, 1938.

18. Child Study Association of America, "Parent Education: Its Ends and Goals," *Workshop Reports:* Proceedings of the 1954 Conference for Workers in Parent Education. The Association, New York, 1954, pp. 17–32.

19. Clausen, John A., *Sociology and the Field of Mental Health*. Russell Sage Foundation, New York, 1956.

20. Coleman, Jules V., "Mental Health Education and Community Psychiatry," *American Journal of Orthopsychiatry*, vol. 23, 1953, pp. 265–270.

21. Davis, Allison, and Robert J. Havighurst, "Social Class and Color Differences in Child Rearing," *American Sociological Review*, vol. 11, 1946, pp. 698–710.

22. Davis, Kingsley, "Mental Hygiene and the Class Structure" in *A Study of Interpersonal Relations* edited by Patrick Mullahy. Hermitage Press, New York, 1949, pp. 364–385.

23. Department of the Christian Family, *Program Suggestions for Parents' Groups.* The Department, Nashville, Tenn., undated.

24. Duvall, Evelyn, and Sylvanus Milne Duvall, *Leading Parents' Groups.* Abingdon-Cokesbury Press, Nashville, Tenn., 1946.

25. Dybwad, Gunnar, and Gertrude Goller, "Goals and Techniques for Parent Education," *Casework Papers.* Family Service Association of America, New York, 1955.

26. Dynes, Russell R., Alfred C. Clarke, and Simon Dinitz, "Levels of Occupational Aspiration: Some Aspects of Family Experience as a Variable," *American Sociological Review*, vol. 21, 1956, pp. 212–215.

27. Eckert, Ralph, *Handbook on Parent Education.* Bulletin of the California State Department of Education, Sacramento, 1950.

28. Family Life Education Department of Kansas City, Missouri, Public Schools, *Parent Education Handbook.* Curriculum Bulletin No. 96, June, 1955.

29. Farber, Maurice L., "English and Americans: Values in the Socialization Process," *Journal of Psychology*, vol. 36, 1953, pp. 243–250.

30. Faris, Robert E. L., "Interaction of Generations and Family Stability," *American Sociological Review*, vol. 12, April, 1947, pp. 159–164.

31. Foote, Nelson, and Leonard S. Cottrell, Jr., *Identity and Interpersonal Competence: A New Direction in Family Research.* University of Chicago Press, Chicago, 1955.

32. Groves, Ernest R., "Education for Family Life" in *Family Life Today*, edited by Margaret Rich. Houghton Mifflin Co., Boston, 1928, pp. 49–57.

33. Hayes, Anna H., "Guides and Goals for P.T.A.'s," *The Parent-Teacher Organization.* National Congress of Parents and Teachers, Chicago, 1944.

34. Health Publications Institute, *Education for Responsible Parenthood.* The Institute, Raleigh, N. C., 1950.

35. Hollingshead, August B., *Elmtown's Youth.* John Wiley and Sons, New York, 1949.

36. Indiana Works Progress Administration, *Second Annual Parent Education In-Service Training Institute.* 2d ed. Indiana WPA, 1936, mimeographed.

37. Iowa White House Conference on Child Health and Protection, *Proceedings.* Copyright, 1932, by Planning Commission, Iowa White House Conference, April, 1932.

38. Jahoda, Marie, "Toward a Social Psychology of Mental Health," *Problems of Infancy and Childhood:* Transactions of the Fourth Conference, Supplement II. Josiah Macy, Jr. Foundation, New York, 1950.

39. Jahoda, Marie, *Current Concepts of Mental Health.* Basic Books, New York, 1958.

40. Kanner, Leo, *In Defense of Mothers:* How to Bring Up Children in Spite of the More Zealous Psychologists. Charles C. Thomas, Springfield, Ill., 1941.

41. Kawin, Ethel, *Parenthood in a Free Nation.* Parent Education Project, University of Chicago Press, Chicago, 1954.

42. Kluckhohn, Florence, "Dominant and Substitute Profiles of Cultural Orientations: Their Significance for the Analysis of Social Stratification," *Social Forces*, vol. 28, 1950, pp. 376–393.

43. Kluckhohn, Clyde, and Henry A. Murray, editors, *Personality in Nature, Society, and Culture.* 2d rev. ed. Alfred A. Knopf, New York, 1953.

44. Lemkau, Paul V., "Local Mental Health Services," *Annals of the American Academy of Political and Social Sciences*, vol. 286, 1953, pp. 116–125.

45. Linton, Ralph, *The Cultural Background of Personality.* Appleton-Century-Crofts, Inc., New York, 1945.

46. Lowy, Louis, *Adult Education and Group Work.* William Morrow and Co., New York, 1955.

47. Malone, Anthony J., and Maury Massler, "Index of Nail Biting in Children," *Journal of Abnormal and Social Psychology*, vol. 47, 1952, pp. 193–202.

48. Martin, William E., and Celia B. Stendler, editors, *Readings in Child Development.* Harcourt, Brace and Co., New York, 1954.

49. McClelland, David C., A. Rindlisbacher, and Richard de Charms, "Religious and Other Sources of Parental Attitudes Toward Independence Training" in *Studies in Motivation*, edited by David C. McClelland. Appleton-Century-Crofts, Inc., New York, 1955, pp. 389–397.

50. Mead, Margaret, *From the South Seas:* Studies of Adolescence and Sex in Primitive Societies. William Morrow and Co., New York, 1939.

51. Michaels, Joseph J., and Sylvia E. Goodman, "Incidence and Intercorrelations of Enuresis and Other Neuropathic Traits in So-Called Normal Children," *American Journal of Orthopsychiatry*, vol. 4, 1934, pp. 79–106.

52. Morris, Charles, *Varieties of Human Value.* University of Chicago Press, Chicago, 1956.

53. Neubauer, Peter B., "The Technique of Parent Group Education: Some Basic Concepts," *Parent Group Education and Leadership Training.* Child Study Association of America, New York, 1953, pp. 9–15.

54. Pollak, Gertrude K., "Family Life Education: Its Focus and Techniques," *Social Casework*, vol. 34, 1953, pp. 198–204.

55. Pollak, Otto, *Social Science and Psychotherapy for Children.* Russell Sage Foundation, New York, 1952.

56. Riesman, David, *The Lonely Crowd:* A Study of the Changing American Character. Yale University Press, New Haven, 1951.

57. Rockwood, Lemo, *Origins and Development of the Movement for Education for Marriage, Family Life and Parenthood in the U.S., 1900–1948*, with Major

Emphasis on Developments During the Past Twenty-Five Years. Unpublished manuscript, 1948.

58. St. Louis County Health Department, Mental Health Research Program, *An Evaluation of a Preventive Community Mental Health Program.* Clayton, Mo., 1956, mimeographed.

59. Sanford, Fillmore H., "Creative Health and the Principle of *Habeas Mentem*," *American Psychologist*, vol. 10, 1955, pp. 829–835.

60. Schaffer, Leslie, and Jerome K. Myers, "Psychotherapy and Social Stratification," *Psychiatry*, vol. 17, 1954, pp. 83–93.

61. Sears, Robert R., Eleanor E. Maccoby, and Harry Levin, *Patterns of Child Rearing.* Row, Peterson and Co., Evanston, Ill., 1957.

62. Sottong, Philipp C., "The Dilemma of the Parent as Culture Bearer," *Social Casework*, vol. 36, 1955, pp. 302–306.

63. Spock, Benjamin, "Values and Limits of Parent Education" in *Communication in Parent Education:* Proceedings of the Ninth Annual Institute of Workers in Parent Education. Child Study Association of America, New York, 1955, pp. 7–13.

64. Spock, Benjamin, *Dr. Benjamin Spock's Baby and Child Care.* Pocket Books, Inc., New York, 1957. (This book is a new version of *The Pocket Book of Baby and Child Care*, originally published under the title *The Common Sense Book of Baby and Child Care* by Duell, Sloan and Pearce.)

65. Strodtbeck, Fred L., "Family Interaction, Values, and Achievement" in *Talent and Society*, by David C. McClelland and others. D. Van Nostrand Co., New York, 1958.

66. Sunley, Robert, "Early Nineteenth Century American Literature on Child Rearing" in *Childhood in Contemporary Cultures*, edited by Margaret Mead and Martha Wolfenstein. University of Chicago Press, Chicago, 1955, pp. 150–167.

67. United States Works Progress Administration, *Proposed Scope of the Emergency Education Program in the Works Progress Administration.* Bulletin No. 19, WPA, Washington, 1935.

68. Vincent, Clark E., "Trends in Infant Care Ideas," *Child Development*, vol. 22, 1951, pp. 199–209.

69. White House Conference on Child Health and Protection, *Education for Home and Family Life:* Part I, Elementary and Secondary Schools. Century Co., New York, 1932.

70. Witmer, Helen L., *The Field of Parent Education:* A Survey from the Viewpoint of Research. National Council of Parent Education, New York, 1934.

71. Wolfenstein, Martha, "Introduction to Part III, Child Rearing Literature" in *Childhood in Contemporary Cultures*, edited by Margaret Mead and Martha Wolfenstein. University of Chicago Press, Chicago, 1955, pp. 145–149.

CHAPTER FIVE:

Clientele of Parent Education

WITH OUR CONSIDERATION of the assumptions and aims of parent education now completed, it is possible to analyze the problem of who are, and who should be, the parents who participate in educational programs. In our analysis of this topic of clientele we discuss first the data which describe who in fact are reached by parent education. We then consider the question of which parents logically should be involved in such programs.

NUMBER AND CHARACTERISTICS OF PARENTS REACHED

How Many Are Reached?

As Helen Witmer pointed out in 1934 (43, pp. 34–39), it is probably impossible in terms of absolute numbers of this country's population to answer the question: How many are reached by parent education programs? The central difficulties are the varieties of programs, which number in the thousands and which may be unknown outside their respective communities, and the difficulties of obtaining comparable reporting from such varying programs as are known.

One might surmise, however, that there is hardly a literate young mother in the United States who is not reached by one or another mass media attempt to influence her maternal behavior. The distribution of the Children's Bureau pamphlets numbers in the tens of millions, and the sales of current paper-covered books on child care number in the many millions; *Parents' Magazine* has a circulation of nearly two million; *Baby Talk* about half a million; the total circulation of four leading women's magazines, each carrying parent education materials, is more than 15 million; the Gerber Products Company alone has distributed some 20 million copies of its pamphlet for mothers. Also, a great distribution of pamphlets, many of which include parent education materials, occurs through the reading-rack programs of major industrial and business concerns, for example, General Motors.

A somewhat different approach to the question of who are reached would be to determine the percentage of parents never reached, and subtract it from the total population of parents. However, the two basic studies of this kind (4, 25) while reporting separately the percentages of their samples never reached by specific techniques, for example, newspaper columns, do not report totals for those never reached by any technique. Therefore, we are unable at the present time even to estimate from the few careful sampling studies available the probable number of parents not reached by any educational technique.

Characteristics of the Parents Reached

Even though one is unable to state absolute numbers, existing studies do indicate the characteristics of those parents who are reached by parent education programs.

1. Socioeconomic Status. Most of the major studies pertaining to the socioeconomic characteristics of parents reached use data from the decade 1920 to 1930 and a few years thereafter. The other studies were made in recent years, so that there is about a twenty-year gap in our information. However, these studies, though made many years apart, all clearly demonstrate that the percentage of parents reached by parent education varies directly with the person's socioeconomic status. This generalization should probably not be extended to include extreme upper-class groups, for whom few data are available.

Witmer's review of the literature up to 1934 (43, pp. 34–39) summarizes several unpublished studies of characteristics of persons attending parent discussion groups. These studies show a regular increase in absolute numbers of participants paralleling an increase in their educational and occupational status.

Anderson (3) and Davis and McGinnis (13) have made studies of characteristics of parents attending study groups in Minnesota. Anderson's data are for the period prior to 1926, the Davis and McGinnis data for the period 1926 to 1932. Anderson's analysis of 540 participants shows that they come from upper- and middle-class backgrounds. The Davis and McGinnis study, based on records of over 90 per cent of all groups conducted during the above-mentioned period and including more than 10,000 parents, shows in a five-class breakdown that 64 per cent were from the upper three classes, 31.5 per cent were from the bottom two classes, with 4 per cent being rural. The comparable figures for the occupational distribution in the state of Minnesota as a whole for 1929 were some 22 per cent in the upper three classes, 54 per cent in the bottom two classes, and 24 per cent rural. Moreover, the number of different groups and number of sessions of each group attended by parents varies directly and significantly with social class.

Both studies also reported on characteristics of parents enrolled for reading (correspondence) courses at the University of Minnesota. Anderson finds the 750 enrollees in his sample to be primarily upper- and middle-class, and Davis and McGinnis report that of the approximately 4,000 parents in their sample, two-thirds were from the three upper classes.

Anderson's study of 1936 (4), based on data from the White House Conference national survey of about 3,000 families, is an extensive source of information. Comparisons are presented of the percentages of each social class exposed to various educational techniques, including books, pamphlets and magazines read, radio talks listened to, articles on child care read in newspapers and magazines, and attendance at child study or discussion groups. In all comparisons, using a seven-fold class differentiation, the exposure to these educational techniques varies directly with socioeconomic class. For example, some 80 per cent of Class 1 had read books on child care within the past year, compared to 27 per cent of Class 7; some 66 per cent of Class 1 had been members of child study groups, compared to 24 per cent for Class 7.

A recent survey by Boek and others (7) of New York State mothers found that a wide range of literature was seen (nearly 80 different items) and that the distribution of exposure by social class shows the usual positive relation. This relation between social class and parent education literature seen was largest for books such as Spock's *Common Sense Book of Baby and Child Care* and Eastman's *Expectant Motherhood*, and somewhat less for two New York State books for mothers. White, in a recent study (40) of 74 mothers, found no class differences in reading parent education materials in newspapers and magazines, but a significant difference favoring middle-class (as contrasted with lower-class) mothers in the mention of specific books.

Also, Stendler's data from a smaller recent study (30) suggest that lower-class parents may more frequently refuse to go to school for parent-teacher conferences. Another report (19) states that among fathers eligible to attend a course for expectant fathers at the Chicago Lying-In Hospital, a random sample of 100 each of those who did attend and those who did not shows that the fathers who attended were proportionately more often from the middle and upper socioeconomic classes.

These results seem to parallel those of recent studies of who are reached by therapeutic programs (10, 26, 35). While we definitely do not mean to imply that data from therapeutic programs may be generalized to parent education, it is worth noting that these studies show that exposure to and willingness to seek therapeutic help for problems varies directly with social class.

In summary, data spanning a twenty-five year period clearly demonstrate a direct relation between socioeconomic status and amount of exposure to parent education activities.

2. Sex. Several of the studies cited above present their data in such a way that one may compare the relative numbers of mothers and fathers reached by parent education. Witmer's review (43) shows that some 90 per cent of study group members are women. Anderson (3) reports that, of 1,290 members in either study groups or correspondence courses, only one was a man. In another report Anderson (4) indicates that all parent education techniques reach proportionately more mothers than fathers;

for example, for the total sample some 50 per cent of mothers had attended study groups compared to 10 per cent of the fathers. More recently Rowland (28), reporting on two samples of parents in New Orleans, finds that the readership of educational pamphlets mailed to parents of all first-born children in Louisiana is greater for mothers than fathers.

Thus, the data support the conclusion that while fathers are not untouched by parent education programs, proportionately more mothers are reached.

3. Age of the Children. Assumptions that parental behavior during the period of early childhood is more influential on the child's physical and mental health than is the parental behavior during later years have resulted in parent education programs being more frequently directed to parents of younger children. This is especially clear in the area of mass media. Thus, the Children's Bureau's earliest publication was *Infant Care,* which was followed by publications pertaining to later age groups. This is true also of the work of Gesell and his colleagues, of the widely distributed *Pierre the Pelican* pamphlet series of the Louisiana Society for Mental Health, as well as of many other series of publications. Unpublished data from the Child Study Association of America indicate a decided preponderance of books for parents over the past fifty years pertaining to care of the infant and preschool child.

Parents seem more frequently to expose themselves to parent education activities concerned with care of the younger child. With regard to discussion groups, Witmer's review (43, pp. 34–39) of analyses of membership shows substantially greater enrollment in groups concerned with pre-adolescence. However, and in contradiction, the Davis and McGinnis survey of Minnesota study groups (13) shows enrollment about equally divided among study groups centering on preschool, school-age, and adolescent children.

With respect to mass media, the Davis and McGinnis survey shows that for correspondence courses one-half of the mothers were studying the age group under one to five years and one-third the age group six to eleven years. Various publication figures attest to the greater distribution of materials pertaining to younger children. For example, approximately 35,000,000 copies of the Children's Bureau's *Infant Care* have been distributed, compared to 11 million and 10 million copies of publications for prenatal and age one to six groups, respectively, the two closest competitors.

In the United States there are almost three-fourths as many ten-to-fourteen-year-old children as there are children under five. On this basis, the evidence supports the conclusion that parent education programs are proportionately more often directed to, and in fact reach, the parents of younger children.

Type of Educational Technique

Another aspect of the problem of who are reached concerns not the characteristics of the parents but rather the relative power of different techniques to reach parents. In this sense the question becomes: Which technique reaches the greater number of parents? Note that we are not concerned here with relative effectiveness of techniques in producing change, but only their outreach. Data are available from two extensive studies on this point. One of these is Anderson's report (4). Based on replics of 483 mothers reporting on their sources of information regarding infant care, the data show that some 54 per cent use pamphlets, 44.5 per cent books, 41 per cent the nurse, and some 30.5 per cent the pediatrician. The second study was carried out by the Michigan State Department of Mental Health (25). Subjects were selected by quota sampling from experimental and control counties, with a total of 1,000 each in the experimental and control groups. This study gives a rank order of percentages of the sample relying on different techniques, and the ranks, from highest to lowest percentage of use, are: reading materials, doctors, lectures, and study groups. Results of the two studies, carried out some twenty years apart, are comparable if "pamphlets and books" in the first are equated with "reading materials" in the second, and nurse and pediatrician equated with "doctor." The Michigan study gives further data on the absolute number (totals of both experimental and control groups) of persons reached by three techniques. Thus, some 784 had read child-care books, while 195 had not; 182 had attended lectures, while 788 had not; and 32 had attended study groups, while 930 had not.

These two studies both point to the same tentative conclusion: reading materials have the greatest outreach; nurses, pediatricians, and unspecified doctors the next greatest; lectures next; and study groups least.

Unanswered Questions

The results of these studies indicate that proportionately more middle- and upper-class mothers of young children are reached by parent education. Results also indicate that reading materials reach more parents than do other educational techniques.

Several types of research on the question of who are reached by parent education seems desirable. First, a major study remains to be made of the number of parents unreached by any educational technique. We suggest that this could be answered most easily by modern national sample survey studies, rather than by attempts to enumerate all who are reached by some given program.

Second, it would be desirable to have more research data for the modern period describing who are reached in terms of such social characteristics as socioeconomic status, sex, and age of child, as well as others, for example, ethnicity.

Third, new ground could be broken by studies comparing parents reached by parent education with those not reached, within a given socioeconomic group, with respect to several personality characteristics. It is surprising that we have been unable to find any study of this kind. Since exposure to those programs requires participation, that is, motivated action on the part of parents, one might raise such questions as whether parents reached by educational programs are more anxious, more submissive, or possess greater feelings of competence in child rearing than those who are not reached.

Fourth, our information on the power of different educational techniques is inadequate and research profitably could be directed to investigations of the relative outreach of the techniques of mass media, individual counseling, and study groups.

These briefly indicated research areas have been mentioned as if they were discrete lines of investigation. On the contrary, it must be emphasized that the most profitable research course in the future is to analyze the interaction effects of several factors. Thus, our research question would not be: Are more people reached by lectures than study groups? but rather: What kinds of people are reached more often by what kinds of techniques?

Some of the existing data show these interaction effects clearly. For example, Anderson's report (4), while showing that mothers proportionately more often than fathers are reached by all techniques, indicates a strong interaction effect between sex of the parent and social class level. The mother-father difference in exposure is much *less* at the lower- than at the middle-class level. While it is true that the percentage of fathers reached increases regularly by social class, the increments are small. The data on the mothers also show a regular increase in exposure by social class, but for the mothers the increase is very great. The size of the mother-father difference in exposure to parent education, therefore, increases directly with the class of the parents.

Another example of interaction effects concerns the interaction between social class and educational technique. In both the Michigan study (25) and the Anderson report (4) the number of persons reached by reading materials increases regularly and substantially with social class. The Michigan study shows that this is also true for lecture and study group techniques. However, in the Michigan study the use of the physician as a source of information *decreases* proportionately as socioeconomic status increases. In sum, while in terms of absolute numbers reached, the rank order of effectiveness is reading materials, medical sources, and lectures or study groups, the interaction effects are such that the middle- and upper-middle class groups are reached relatively more often by reading, lecture and study groups, whereas the lower classes are reached relatively more often by medical sources of information.

These two examples demonstrate that further research will be much more powerful if it includes in its design a consideration of the possible effects of interaction of factors.

WHO ARE THE APPROPRIATE CLIENTELE?

The rational basis for selecting a clientele for parent education is that of assuring maximum program effectiveness. There are two characteristics to be considered in estimating program effectiveness, namely, "educability" of the parents, and "need" on the part of the parents. With respect to the first, we have pointed out in Chapter III that there are important variations in the degree to which parents can be changed as a result of an educational experience and that consideration of the educability of parents is of basic importance in parent education planning. With respect to the second, it was pointed out a generation ago (41, pp. 4–5) that advocates of education for family life are well aware that a project of education must meet the challenge of why human beings need to be educated for so natural or everyday an undertaking as parenthood. This is to say that a parent becomes a logical candidate for education only on the premise that his role performance is less competent than it could be and, hence, that there is room for improvement through education.

These two characteristics of parents, namely, educability and need, are independent of each other in the sense that one cannot predict one from knowledge of the other. The appropriate course of action to follow in order to find those parents most suitable as clientele for a program is, therefore, to discover those persons characterized by relatively great need and educability. The possession of either one of these characteristics, without the other, would limit the effectiveness of the program.

Participation of Parents as a Criterion of Need and Educability

The usual procedure of parent education is to avoid systematic appraisals of either parent need or educability, and instead to take as clients those parents who voluntarily participate in educational programs. It is our belief that the issue of selecting a clientele is not solved by "taking those who participate" because this provides inadequate criteria of both need and educability.

The arguments which traditionally have been advanced in support of using "self-selected" parents as clients must now be considered carefully.

It is true that participation in educational programs must be a motivated act. The assumption is then made that the motive involved is a need on the part of parents for further information, discussion, or other types of help; that is, it represents an admission of less than optimal competence on their part. The one study we know of describing motivation for participation was made by May Shirley some twenty years ago (29) and pertains to attendance at study groups. In 125 home interviews of study-group members the responses to the question of "What they wanted from study groups" were rather mixed, and as Shirley writes (p. 89), "These members were vague as to what they wanted from study groups. More than 40% merely said 'help in guiding children' and over 20% said specifically that they 'did not know what they wanted.' Some implied again that curiosity was their motive, by saying 'I wanted to find out what it was all about.' A few wanted 'whatever I could get,' and others didn't want, need, or even expect to get anything."

One can hardly challenge seriously the assumption that parents sufficiently motivated to seek parent education have thereby indicated a feeling that they might become more competent by participating in an educational program. Even though some motives other than concern over one's role performance as a parent may be involved in participation in programs (for example, the desire for social life), nevertheless, when such other motives are subtracted, as it were, from the desire leading to participation, one can safely assume that there remains the major component of parents' concern over their role performance.

The concern of parents over their adequacy may in turn have several causes. As Rockwood points out (27), it is normal and understandable for young married couples to be anxious concerning their role as parents, until they know they will be able to master it. Most young people today have not had the opportunity, prior to becoming parents, to prove to themselves that they can carry it out successfully, since they have had little prior par-

ticipation in child care in their own families. A second source of
parents' concern may be not so much the feeling of ignorance,
but a desire to be reassured in their belief that they are really
doing a good job. This source of concern is important because of
the comparative isolation of the modern parent from others with
whom he can compare his behavior, and from whom he can
determine whether or not he is being a "good parent." A third
point suggested by Wolfenstein (44), and Foote and Cottrell (15)
is that interest in parent education represents a feeling of incompetence only in the sense that the parent believes that there is
something better than tradition, that the growth of scientific
knowledge of child development leads to principles of child rearing superior to those possessed already and which are desirable
to know. That some of the feelings of parents about their own
possibilities for improvement may have been produced by parent
education itself does not obviate the fact that the parents *now*
perceive themselves as being able to improve in various ways.

Granted that the attention of parents to educational programs
indicates that they are concerned to improve or strengthen their
role, this does not mean that they are in greater need or are more
incompetent than parents who do not attend. Even the few
existing facts challenge such a deduction. For example, participation is significantly greater among upper-middle-class than
among upper-lower-class parents, but this hardly warrants the
inference that the former therefore are less competent and more
in need by any standard. As another example, the fact that the
vast bulk of participation is by parents of younger children and
that there is a gradual decrease in participation as youngsters
proceed through the adolescent period, does not permit one to
conclude that parents of adolescents are more competent than the
parents of younger children.

Ignorance of the true distribution of parent competence and
the use of attendance as the criterion of need tends to inhibit the
effectiveness of parent education. For democratically oriented
programs, it robs them of their maximum efficiency by directing
their efforts to parents who may be less desirous of education than
others who do not attend, for whatever reason. For the more

authoritarian programs, it may involve them with a clientele who are already competent in the areas of special concern to the parent educators and whose feelings of incompetence, which motivate them to attend, pertain to matters of little interest to the educators.

There is one further argument offered by parent educators which favors as clientele those parents who attend programs or who participate in other ways; namely, since they already have indicated their interest in parent education, they are most likely to learn from participation. This argument, however, has no merit at all, since we do not know the relevant characteristics of the persons who do or do not participate. We have discussed this point before, so a single example here will suffice. One could maintain that those who are sufficiently motivated to participate in programs are in fact much too anxious about their role as parents really to profit from education and that the most suitable clientele of programs in terms of beneficial effects are those parents who are not so anxious that they participate voluntarily. This is to say that in the absence of available data one might argue that the same motives that lead parents to participate also render them relatively uneducable because of the underlying conflict and anxiety which cause the participation. Therefore, parent education might be more effective with those that it does now not reach at all.

Educability of Parents

The educability of parents has already been discussed in previous chapters. In Chapter III we considered several influential determinants of parent behavior, such as unconscious motivation, cultural traditions, and immediate social controls within the family and neighborhood. For example, where an appeal through education is made respecting a certain kind of change, the parent is unable to be educated in this area if the behavior involved is under unconscious control. In like manner, matters of family size or of beliefs of one's spouse place limitations on the effectiveness of the educational programs. Chapter III also described the ways in which the actual working goals of parent educators are adapted to the realistic limitations placed upon parental change by these various determinants of their behavior. We pointed out that ideally one should appraise beforehand the relative influence of the different determinants of parent behavior in different areas of child rearing so that programs can be tailored accordingly, but that this demands an appraisal of parents with respect to social and personal factors which lies considerably beyond the present resources of parent education. Now we look at this same matter from a slightly different vantage point, namely, its implications for selecting the clientele of an ongoing program.

Different programs vary in aims, content, and method, and it follows that the best clientele for one type of program will not be the same as that for another. Ideally the clientele of a given program should be those parents most educable with respect to the content being presented and by means of the method employed. It may be that for some programs where the emphasis is on developing in the parent a conception of personal involvement in, and multiple causation of, the child's behavior, as well as problem-solving skills of a general type, the appropriate clientele must be those of more than moderate levels of intellectual ability, and perhaps with some college training. In other instances where the program is oriented toward creating or educating a parent to perform child-rearing practices in accord with expert judgment, the clientele might consist of parents somewhat liberated from their cultural traditions, somewhat high on dependency needs, and so on. In programs where a discussion group is employed, it may be possible to tolerate to a greater degree parents whose child-rearing practices are protected from change by personal defenses since some of these, even within the confines of the educational method, can be dissipated through group discussion. In contrast, mass media programs or other programs directed to an anonymous audience where the dissipation of defenses cannot occur, may be wisely restricted to clientele whose child-rearing practices are open and subject to comparatively more conscious manipulation.

The efforts made by parent education programs to deal with this question have been of only a rudimentary kind. For example, the Child Study Association of America makes a preliminary and informal screening of parents prior to accepting them as members of a parent discussion group, seeking to eliminate (and refer to appropriate counselors) those parents whose concern about their child-rearing practices indicates considerable anxiety and unconscious conflict. The Louisiana Society for Mental Health seeks as clientele of its program parents at a specific age level, but goes one step beyond the efforts of most programs in this respect. It selects as clientele for certain types of information pertinent to stages in child development, the parents whose children are several months younger than the age to which the material pertains. Parents thus are educated prior to the establishment of habits and of mutual expectations of parent and child, rather than after, when these must be changed. This could be done in pediatric and public health nursing contexts also, but has received only occasional attention.

In part, the inadequacies of selection of clientele stem from inadequate knowledge of the effects of interaction of parent characteristics with types of programs. In large part also they arise because of the practical inability to appraise parent characteristics relevant to their educability, even if we knew what these were. As stated in the previous chapter, there seems little one can do about the latter, barring the development of more adequate methods of appraisal and of financial and personnel resources which make it possible to put such client selectivity programs into effect. Concerning the former, Chapter IX stresses the need for research on the value of educational programs which takes into account various interaction effects of content, method, and clientele. Hopefully, research would find that the characteristics of parents which importantly influence their educability are distributed among easily identifiable social groups, so that the selection of a clientele can be made in terms of variables like education, occupation, ethnicity, and others easy for the parent educator to identify. At the very least, the parent educator should continually ask himself what characteristics of parents are pertinent to their ability to profit from his educational program and in what ways he might most easily identify parents having those characteristics.

Needs of Parents

The second important criterion in selecting clientele for programs is the need of parents for the information transmitted by the program. This raises the basic question of how competent parents are in child rearing, and the question of whose standards are to be invoked in the appraisal of parent competence.

In a not inconsiderable number of programs the issue of parent competence is ignored and the assumption is made that everybody is in need. Thus, some parent educators argue (e.g., 22, 34) that all categories of parents should be covered and that all families need instruction and counsel in parent education. Indeed, some suggest that parent education should be compulsory (23). Extreme *a priori* assumptions about the lack of parent competence are often made by such groups and are illustrated by the following statement: "Often [the teacher] is hopelessly handicapped by the ignorance, indifference or inefficiency of the home teacher [i.e., the parent] who from four to six years has, all untrained, been giving daily, even hourly, instruction and demonstration in physical and mental hygiene, motor skills, habit formation, family and community relations, honesty, obedience, and personal property rights. In fact, the parents have been training the child in all the fundamentals of education except the academic and technical subjects for which training is demanded by law." (42, p. 18) The hazards of assuming that all parents are incompetent are impressively shown in one study (37). This study in progress at one of our major universities used a panel of psychiatrists and child development psychologists to judge the accuracy of the beliefs and knowledge of a sample of parents with respect to child development and child rearing. This same panel also judged the accuracy of ideas expressed in articles containing advice to parents in leading commercial mass media. The findings are that the parents score higher in knowledge and beliefs than do the articles in the mass media. This sample of a group of midwest parents is already more knowledgeable and more competent than the authors (or the material) to which they are exposed in the mass media.

The attempts to develop criteria of need so that parents could be differentiated on this basis have been naive, makeshift solutions which must reduce the effectiveness of any program. Some have suggested certain social categories of parents as in greater need than others; for example, it is the high school graduate parent who is in most need of information, or the parent most difficult to reach and communicate with who needs the most help. Others have suggested accepting the parents' judgments as to their needs, but this is not a convincing answer to Witmer's question (43) of what one should do about those parents who believe that they are getting on so well that they should be left alone. What is one to do, for example, when faced with a situation reported in a study (20) of 150 Ohio farm couples made in 1954, which finds that only some 20 per cent of the women in the study indicated that their lack of knowledge and certain home management practices, including child development and family relations, affected the happiness and unity of their homes? This is to say, four out of five women felt their competence was such as not to handicap the happiness of their homes. Is it valid, therefore, to assume that these women are not in need of parent education?

It is our intention to analyze the kinds of information about parents that are logically relevant to making judgments of their competence. Then we will review the actual information which has been provided by research. There is so little of this that the two steps together serve to delineate areas of critically needed research about parent behavior which would assist parent education in its judgments as to the type and degree of parent need for assistance from educational programs.

The standards for appraising parent competence vary according to the instrumental aims of the parent education program, as described in the previous chapter. It would be unprofitable to attempt an analysis of parent competence in relation to each of the working goals. Instead, we have gone back to the more basic ethical distinction between programs which definitely try to advance the values of the parent educator, and programs where these values are introduced democratically (the so-called value-free programs). For purposes of quick reference, we will call the former "autocratic" programs and the latter "democratic" programs. This is not to say, of course, that any one program has all the ingredients of either type, but that programs do tend to fall in one or another of these patterns. The distinction will be sharpened somewhat beyond what is the case in reality; however, it is necessary to give us reference points for the analysis.

In general, in the first type the standards against which parent competence is judged are autocratic, for it is the parent educators' values for the child that are at issue, and parent behavior is judged competent to the degree that it corresponds to the behavior believed suitable for attaining them. In the second type of program the criteria of competence are more democratic, for it is primarily the parents' ends for the child that are accepted and sought in parent education, and judgment of competence is made in terms of whether the parents are capable of achieving their ends.

1. Types of Data Pertinent to Judging Parent Competence. In this section we present a brief logical analysis of the kinds of data which are pertinent to judging parent competence. Considering first the democratic programs, pertinent data with respect to parent competence fall into two classes: those pertaining to the parents' ends and those pertaining to the means they use to reach them. With reference to the first, relevant data would be those which showed parents to be confused as to what ends are desirable, for it suggests that they could gain from education new ideas which would deepen and enrich their own planning for their children. Also important information about ends is that showing the ends sought by parents for their children to be unrealistic. The ends actually may conflict, so that not all are actually achievable; or they may simply be physically impossible in themselves.

Information pertaining to *means* is of interest where it indicates that parents actually need more or better information about ways to achieve the goals which they hold for the child. There would seem to be two important subclasses which describe parents' competence in terms of means. First, there would be data showing that the ends parents seek are not in fact reached by the means they use. This requires one to know what their ends are so that one can determine whether or not they are reached; or, and more commonly, one may use statements of parents that they are not reaching the ends they desire as indication that they need to improve in their choice of child-rearing practices.

Second, one may have knowledge of the current child-rearing practices (means) of parents and judge them to be inadequate for the achievement of the ends being sought. But this obviously requires that one know also the ends which they seek, and herein is a danger. Since the latter data are difficult to obtain, the democratically oriented parent educator may simply assume what parents want—for example, a child who feels secure—and judge their behavior as adequate or not with respect to this assumed aim. The danger, of course, is that parents might want something quite different. However, where the parents state what they want for their child *and* where observation shows that their behavior on the basis of scientific knowledge will not achieve this aim, the judgment of lack of competence in means is legitimate.

Turning now to the authoritarian program in which the goals of parent educators are actively sought, the pertinent data fall into the same two classes pertaining to ends and means, although within these classes they differ from the above in substance. Thus, the data pertaining to the competence of parents with reference to selection of ends do not bear on questions of realism, confusion, and conflict of ends. Rather, they would simply describe the ends. The parent educator himself then judges whether or not these are "right" ends in terms of his own standards. For example, an indication that the parents seek to make their children completely obedient, to "break their will" in the phrase of a century ago, constitutes grounds for the parent educator's judging such parents incompetent, where he disagrees.

With reference to the adequacy or competence of the *means* used by parents, there are two subclasses of relevant data, as was true in the discussion concerning democratic programs. The difference is that here judgment of means is made in terms of their adequacy in reaching the goals of parent educators, not the parents. First, there are data showing that the ends of parent educators are not being reached; for example, high rates of mental illness are used as direct evidence that child-rearing practices of parents are inadequate. Second, there are data describing what parents actually do in child rearing; one could then draw the conclusion on the basis of scientific knowledge that such practices are inadequate to reach parent educators' ends.

In summary, considering the two types of programs together, there are several logical types of information which pertain to the competence of parents: first, that pertaining to ends, whether confusion, conflict, or "correctness" is involved; second, that pertaining to means, either inferred from the degree of successful goal attainment, or comprising direct descriptions of the parental practice. These types of data can define those parents who are less competent than they might be, by their own or parent educator standards, and perhaps who would profit most from parent education.

2. Available Data on Parent Competence in the Selection of Ends. In our discussion of the logical classes of data relevant to parent competence we mention two types of data about ends. One type pertains to parents' confusion about the ends; the other pertains to the realism, achievability, and for some programs with an authoritarian emphasis, the desirability of the ends which parents actually seek.

With respect to the first, we have been unable to find any data of a systematic kind which report the concern of parents over what the ends of child rearing should be. Most information obtained from "parents' questions" concerns means to achieve ends, for example, "how to make the child eat better" rather than "how fat he should be," or "is this something that a parent should stress?" This information has been mistakenly interpreted as if it pertained to aims of child rearing. Instead it suggests that parents may be unconfused about what they want but considerably confused about the means of achieving their ends.

This difference is not surprising, since the aims of child rearing are derived from basic values of the culture; whereas the actual child-rearing practices tend to be technical matters, and hence are more changeable by the impact of scientific knowledge. Also, the relative isolation of new parents in America may keep them ignorant of child-care practices. This would not be true with respect to the aims of child rearing, since the latter are acquired during their own childhood along with other basic cultural values. The parent therefore enters his role with a set of aims which he should seek, but through lack of prior experience, or access to parent models, he does not have the technical competence to achieve these ends.

This is not to say that some parents are not puzzled about what the aims of child rearing should be. One would anticipate that this would be true more frequently of groups in the process of assimilation to American culture where their culture of origin is undergoing a change. We might find this also in segments of a socially mobile society such as our own, where there are social class differences in the aims of child rearing and where persons moving upward (or downward) from one class to another may be puzzled over what new aims they should adopt. It is probable also that there are some areas of child rearing in which the aims are less clear than in others. In areas where the culture is changing, perhaps with respect to the degree of submissiveness or independence that is desirable, one would anticipate confusion in parents' minds about appropriate goals; in others, perhaps with respect to the desirable attitude toward achievement, where the change has been less, one might well expect less confusion. However, all this is speculation. The conclusion we stress here is that data describing the need of parents for help in selecting ends to be sought are apparently nonexistent.

A second type of data pertinent to the parents' ends would be information on the ends which they do in fact seek. This information then needs to be analyzed, for the democratically oriented program, as to the realism and conflict of the ends, and for the authoritarian program, in terms of the desirability of the ends according to the standards of parent educators. As was the case with the first question, pertaining to parents' confusion over ends, we find here also that there is little information. It is remarkable that there is almost no research describing what parents seek to achieve through child rearing. A few isolated studies, for example, one comparing fathers' aims for sons and daughters (1), another comparing English and American descriptions of the desirable child (14), a third (40) comparing middle- and working-class mothers in their choice of very general ends; for example, "happy" versus "good" are about all that we have of a systematic nature.

Lacking these primary facts, the tendency has been to infer the ends which parents seek from data describing their actual child-rearing behavior. This is a hazardous practice. Child-rearing behavior is based on beliefs, whether explicit or not, held by parents about how to achieve in their children the characteristics deemed desirable by society. It is not only possible, but highly probable, that different groups have different beliefs of how to reach the same ends, so that inferring from differences in behavior that different ends are sought would be erroneous. To give an example, one description of Polish immigrant families (18) indicates that there is no important aspect of the parent role which might be termed "giving love" to the child. This contrasts markedly with the stress in certain middle-class ethnic groups on "giving the child affection" in order that he may feel wanted, secure, and lovable. To infer that Polish parents are not concerned with their children feeling wanted and secure and lovable is unwarranted. They may simply believe that the way to achieve this does not involve overt demonstrations of affection to the child, but instead springs from regular feeding, or some other culturally prescribed means.

If we had research describing the ends of parents, it might show several ways in which parents could profit from educational programs. First, it might show that there are ends sought which are not in fact realizable. This may be because the characteristics sought are, to a major extent, genetically determined; hence, are not achievable through parent influence. One might argue that this would not be the case, since both cultural values and the prescribed means of obtaining them are generally adjusted on the basis of centuries of experience to what is in fact possible for man. But it is not yet clear either to groups of parents or to groups of social scientists what is truly possible or impossible. Parents may also hold ends which are unrealizable for other than a genetic reason; namely, they seek two or more characteristics which are incompatible and which are impossible to achieve in one child. Here, too, we know little about what these might be, but we have cited before at least one recent study (5), which suggests that a feeling of security and a high desire for achievement are characteristics of this type.

Research may show still another way in which parents could profit through educational programs. It may be that parents, whether idiosyncratically or by virtue of their common cultural background, hold aims for the child which are inconsistent. The inconsistency may be such that one or the other is impossible of achievement, in which case they fall into the category above. But they may be inconsistent in a lesser sense in that they are possible of achievement but at some emotional cost to the child. Inconsistent aims may be sought in the same stage of a child's development or the aims may be inconsistent from one stage of development to another. The aim of producing a girl who is chaste at whatever cost during adolescence, and who with her husband is sexually uninhibited and cooperative after the wedding ceremony, is a classic instance in social science literature.

To know that parents generally or in subcultural groups hold ends which are difficult or impossible to achieve, provides justification for educational programs designed to help parents clarify their desires and reestablish their aims for the child on a more realistic basis. What we need, therefore, for this broad problem of parent competence is an investigation of the kinds of ends which parents hold, especially those they are most concerned about and feel most confused about; and the way these vary by subcultural groups, by the age and the sex of the child, by family size, sex of parent, and the like. Given our current lack of knowledge, even the most rudimentary survey would be of value to parent educators in the planning of their programs.

3. Available Data on Parent Competence in the Selection of Means.
The other basic type of information which would provide help
in selecting a clientele concerns the means (child-rearing practices) which parents use to reach their ends. The value of such
information differs, depending upon whether the educational
program has a democratic or an authoritarian emphasis. We will
consider the democratically oriented programs first.

In discussing the logical classes of data on means pertinent to
parent competence where the program has a democratic emphasis, we said that if one knew the aims of parents and also
knew their child-rearing practices, one could then on the basis of
scientific knowledge draw the conclusion that parents were rearing children in ways not conducive to the achievement of their
ends; and, therefore, that their selection of means was less competent than it could be. However, in light of the preceding section
discussing the lack of information about ends which parents in
fact seek, the data describing actual child-rearing practices are of
little current value to democratically oriented programs.

A second type of data pertaining to means and to democratic
programs is the information given by the parents themselves
about their areas of ignorance and about the areas in which they
perceive themselves to need help in selecting child-rearing practices. This includes the category of "parents' questions" about
how to achieve certain ends in their child rearing; and if there
is a large amount of such questioning, it clearly suggests that
parents portray themselves as able to profit from educational
programs.

What is remarkable, however, as was true in the case of parents' ends, is that there seems to be no systematic investigation on
a large scale of the areas of concern to parents. A few studies of
small and unrepresentative groups (6, 39) suggest that aggression,
discipline, and sibling relations stand out as areas of parental
concern in which the child-rearing advice is considered to be
helpful. Probably better research (and certainly larger-scale research) was done during the early 1930's. The Child Study Association's pamphlet, *Parents' Questions*, was based on informal
tabulations of parents' questions in discussion groups over a

period of many years. The studies cited in Helen Witmer's survey of parent education research (43) include several studies of mothers' rank ordering of various "problems." These earlier surveys are of little value to us now because we do not know whether their findings would be true of mothers today.

Where the democratic parent education program makes use of individual counseling or discussion group methods, the absence of information is not so much a problem, since the content of the education is based on the concerns which emerge in the discussion. Still, it would follow that if such concerns were not expressed by parents in these counseling or group situations one would not know logically how to proceed, since the program is oriented to their needs and there is no prior information as to what these are. In the field of mass media where this *ad hoc* information is not available, since one must select the content in advance, the absence of prior knowledge of parent concerns has even greater consequence. Insofar as the mass media program remains democratic, it must simply guess at the things which concern parents.

All of this suggests that a very simple, inexpensive, and most instructive research project would be one in which a sample of parents would respond to a list of items on child rearing, indicating those for which they thought education would be of service to them. It further suggests that a continuing assessment of parental interest in one or another type of information would provide a strong foundation for parent education programs.

We turn now to a consideration of data pertaining to the means parents employ which are of special relevance to programs with an authoritarian emphasis, that is, which stress the ends of the parent educator. In such programs at least four different kinds of information become relevant.

First, there is information on the degree to which ends of parent educators are being achieved, which permits inferences as to the competence exercised by parents in rearing children. Second, there is information on the actual overt behavioral practices of parents, leading to judgments as to their competence or incompetence with respect to achieving the aims of the parent educators. Third, there is information on parent beliefs and attitudes regarding child rearing. This third class of data has two subdivisions: (1) data on parent beliefs about appropriate practices which can be compared with the beliefs held by experts of how to achieve the ends they hold desirable, thus permitting judgments as to the "correctness" of parent beliefs; (2) data on parents' perceptions of "problems" in children which, in comparison to expert opinion as to what constitutes a true problem, permit judgments of parents' competence in this area. Let us consider these in order.

In contrast to the democratic programs where one needs to know the ends of parents in order to assess their competence in achieving them, the situation for the more authoritarian programs is much simpler. One need only to assess the degree of achievement of the ends held by parent educators; then armed with the assumption that parents are the effective agents in achieving such ends, the inference follows that if the ends are not achieved parents must be using unsuitable means. This point of view has been present for a generation or more in parent education literature.

An illuminating comparison can be made on this point with the use of statistics on physical health and safety. Such statistics describe the degree to which the aims of, say, health departments are being achieved and provide the support for preventive programs. For example, statistics on preventable home accidents lead readily to educational campaigns for families about home safety. It is true that in the area of physical health these statistics permitting inference as to parent competence are more readily available and more accurate, and also that the relationship of parental action to the effect is to a greater degree understood. Nevertheless, in several areas the parent educator concerned with other than physical health aims finds justification for his program in the statistics available. Thus, statistics on rates of hospital admission for mental illness spurred many educators to further efforts, with the aim of reducing the incidence of mental illness. Recently, Clausen (10) has described several studies of the mental health of noninstitutionalized populations which provide some impressive statistics, namely, that as many as one-third of both urban and rural populations may suffer from impairment of function by virtue of psychiatric symptomatology, and that only about one-seventh were entirely free of signs of emotional disturbance.

The rapid rise in rates of juvenile delinquency since World War II, together with the advance of the point of view that delinquency is caused by parents, has led many organizations to develop educational programs to combat delinquency. In several cities the courts now require parents of delinquents to establish contact with family service agencies for counseling and education. In New York support has been recently provided in the city budget for parent education programs in areas having high delinquency rates. These types of educational efforts are understandable, given the assumption that parents are effective agents in retarding the achievement of these ends; and, second, given the belief that such ends are desirable whether the parents believe them to be desirable or not. This is not to say, of course, that parents do not desire mental health and nondelinquent behavior for the child, but only that this is not logically necessary in order that the authoritarian parent education program find its justification in such statistics.

The second type of relevant information about means comes from the large body of research data which describe actual parent practices in child rearing. The most important part of this information for the parent educator is that describing child-rearing practices in terms of social class differences and, to a lesser extent, by race. There is a great amount of such information dating from the pioneer study reported by Anderson (4) and continuing up to the numerous studies currently under way. Bronfenbrenner (9) in an excellent recent review has summarized the results of some 15 major studies of this type covering the past twenty-five years. He summarizes the descriptive data on a variety of child-rearing practices, such as age of weaning, age of toilet training, nursing versus bottle feeding, type of independence training, authoritarian relations, and others. In addition to giving descriptive data, he demonstrates the existence of consistent differences between classes across the various studies during the past years, and also systematic changes through time in social class child-rearing practices, including several middle- and lower-class reversals of practice with respect to items such as severity of discipline. The substantive findings of Bronfenbrenner's review are too extensive to summarize here, but they are of utmost value to every parent educator, constituting the best available summary of descriptive data on parent behavior.

Additional information of this kind is scattered through a variety of other studies. It does not deal directly with class differences and so does not appear in the Bronfenbrenner review. A comprehensive bibliography of such additional studies has recently been prepared, with the type of study and the data it presents classified in a brief review (8). There is much rich material, and one can do little more than ask for more of these studies, with greater differentiation among parent practices with respect to the area of child rearing and to the characteristics of the parent, such as ethnic origin, age, and sex.

The descriptive information just referred to on parent behavior provides a basis for the autocratic parent educator to make judgments as to parent competence or lack of it in child-rearing practices, in terms of the aims which he as an educator seeks and in terms of his theory as to which behavior is most suitable for achievement of such aims. Given these data, the current theories of child rearing then could lead to the conclusion that there are some areas in which parents would be judged less competent than in others; this in turn leads to planning parent education programs so as to emphasize areas of greater need as determined by the parent educator.

The third type of information which is valuable to the authoritarian-oriented program concerns parent beliefs and attitudes regarding child rearing. These data are important, both because such attitudes and ideas are thought to underlie child-rearing practices which may not be conducive to achieving the aims of the parent educators, and because they may directly influence the child in an undesirable way. It is necessary, of course, just as was true with respect to the descriptive material on parent behavior itself, for the parent educator to have some theory relating parent beliefs and attitudes to the achievement of his ends, so that he can judge whether or not they indicate that the parent is competent; that is, holds the correct beliefs and attitudes. The assessment of parent competence in this respect customarily takes the form of comparing parent beliefs and attitudes on various aspects of child rearing with the beliefs and attitudes held by experts on the same matters.

Several of the important studies of this kind date from almost a generation ago. A study in 1934 asked two samples of parents for their agreement or disagreement with a lengthy set of statements about child rearing (2). Their responses were then compared with the approved responses made by a number of experts in child development. The average percentages of agreement between the parents' responses and the approved responses for the two separate samples were 50 and 61 per cent, respectively. In a similar study in 1939, using more than 150 parents as subjects, the percentages of correct responses ranged from 19 to 100 per cent, with the average being 75 per cent (11).

A recent study (38) employing an attitude instrument found that over 200 undergraduate males enrolled in social science classes had attitudes superior, in the judgment of experts, to the attitudes of mothers of problem children; were similar in attitudes to mothers of nonproblem children, but were inferior with respect to clinical psychologists, that is to say, persons with expert competence in this area. In another study the subjects comprised both young parent couples and undergraduate women engaged in professional courses of study (33). The findings were that the feelings and attitudes of these young professional and pre-professional parents and students did not differ significantly from those held and approved by specialists.

A somewhat different type of study used as subjects the parents of children with difficulties who were referred to the children's psychiatric service at Johns Hopkins (24). An analysis of some 1,500 consecutive case histories showed more than a third in which parental misconceptions (mistaken beliefs) played an important part in the development and management of the difficulty. Thus, in 392 cases of enuresis, there were 100 "errors" in explanation by parents, for example, weak kidneys; for tics, 55 out of 68 cases had misconceptions as to the cause; for temper, constipation, speech difficulties, the proportions were 22/97ths, 87/420ths, and 46/167ths. In 56 cases heredity was used as an explanation of specific things such as just mentioned; although perhaps this is less, rather than more, than one would expect.

With the exception of the last-mentioned, all of these research studies have used as subjects persons of comparatively high education. This raises the question of whether the findings could be generalized to persons of lower education; and, indeed, raises the more general question of the degree of agreement between parents and experts which is found in terms of education, ethnicity, race, or whatever. There is some information on the differences between groups of parents in this respect, but the research does not point to a uniform conclusion. In a study carried out in Michigan which evaluated the effectiveness of the *Pierre the Pelican* pamphlet series (25), the results show that parents answering attitude and belief questions in ways judged superior by experts came more frequently from higher levels of education and from higher occupational positions. Moreover, these superior answers were positively correlated with the mother being older when the baby was born. The latter finding may simply reflect the fact that older mothers tend to come from a higher educational level. One of the earlier studies cited above (2) reports the same finding for differences in educational level and, in addition, reports no differences of importance between mothers and fathers.

A study by Cole and others (12) illustrates how complicated this problem may be. This careful research, done in the Salt Lake City area, reports on 200 personal interviews with a stratified sample of parents. The younger groups showed somewhat more assimilation of psychiatric concepts in the child-rearing field, but in terms of knowledge of cause and treatment of emotional disturbances, no correlation was found with age. It is of great interest to note that apart from this single age difference, no other socioeconomic variables were related to superior beliefs or attitudes. This means specifically that the education of the parents was not related to the superiority of answers. The interpretation of the superiority of the younger groups which was found could be that these groups are now actually in the process of acquiring information pertinent to child rearing and, hence, are more receptive to the new information generally available to parents.

These different studies demonstrate that parents know less than the experts when they are rated on the expert's scales; and it shows also that the competence of parents as assessed in this manner does sometimes vary by socioeconomic and other characteristics of the parent, although these variations are as yet hardly explored. Much more work could be done in this area which would be of help to parent education. While it is true that there are probably many small unpublished research studies on this problem which have been made by different parent education organizations, and have been used in planning particular programs, such efforts do not obviate the need for a major research undertaking in this aspect of parent competence. Parent education needs to know more about the distribution of ignorance and misinformation by specific areas of child rearing. It needs to know how much variation in beliefs and attitudes occurs with respect to mothers and fathers, or between different communities, or between parents of children of different ages. Even the picture with respect to the education of the parent is unclear. While one might wish to argue *a priori* that education must be positively related with superior knowledge about child rearing, the value of the study by Cole and others lies in the fact that it finds no such variation.

The fourth and last type of information relevant to assessing, by autocratic standards, parent competence in choice of means, is closely related to the material discussed just above. It consists of data on the opinions of parents concerning the severity of emotional disturbance indicated by different kinds of child behavior. These data consist of survey results, and such things as their reasons for referrals of children to professional organizations for treatment. These data are customarily compared to the standards provided by expert judgment, and the competence of parents then duly assessed. The information gains its importance from the belief that if parents adequately understand symptomatology in their children, it follows that they are knowledgeable about child rearing and are sensitive to the important characteristics of child development.

There seems to be no single outstanding study directly concerned with the assessment of parents' competence of this nature. In an older study by Stogdill (32) designed after some earlier studies of teachers' competence in the perception of children's behavior, it was found that parents and mental hygienists differed in their opinions as to the seriousness of different kinds of children's behavior. Parents, more often than mental hygienists, considered serious (that is, an important problem) such things as disobedience, disrupting the quiet routine of the house, and breaches of etiquette. The reverse was true for such items as introversion, withdrawal, suspiciousness, sensitiveness, and the like. These findings parallel the earlier findings with regard to the study of teachers versus mental hygienists, in that the former overemphasize "acting out" symptoms and underemphasize the "withdrawing" symptoms in comparison to mental hygienists.

Clausen (10, pp. 13–14) has reported that a major study as yet unpublished of attitudes toward mental illness, carried on by the National Opinion Research Center, "indicates that the concept is for most people ill-defined and not clearly understood." Clausen goes on to say that it shows there is a tendency to think of the acutely disturbed psychotic whenever mental illness is mentioned rather than the neurotic, and to employ mechanistic and naively empirical cause-effect explanations. Along with this is the tendency to normalize deviant behavior in ways that make it rational and acceptable, thus indicating perhaps an effort to distort and normalize the situation for the purpose of avoiding social stigma.

On the other hand, studies have been made which indicate that the picture presented above is incomplete and that parents may be more competent than the parent educator realizes in their appraisal and understanding of the child's behavior.

Gardner (16) points out that the great bulk of cases referred to child guidance clinics at the present time come not from social agencies and hospitals, as was true two decades ago, but rather are brought to the clinic by parents themselves who seem to have become more alert to symptoms. Reports (17) from the major study of parent education of the St. Louis County Health Department provide information on the relation between clinical diagnoses of children and the number of symptoms of disturbance in the children as reported by their mothers. As the frequency of symptoms reported by mothers increased, the degree of severity of the child's disturbance as judged by clinicians also increased. This indicates that mothers are not insensitive to symptomatology and that a mother's report of four or more symptoms or perceived problem areas is a very good indicator that the child is somewhat seriously disturbed.

It is highly desirable that we obtain more information on the variations in parent competence along socioeconomic and other lines in judging the disturbances of children. The basic work on social class and mental illness of Hollingshead and Redlich (21) shows clearly that attitudes toward mental illness vary with social class. Data reported for two clinics (31, 36) indicate for both that about one-fifth of the parentally referred children are referred by fathers. These data raise the question of whose responsibility it is in the family to decide when a child is ill and whether mothers and fathers differ in their ability to make this judgment. It is perhaps clear that the major surveys suggested here which bear on this aspect of parent competence would aid the planning of a parent education program, in that the program would focus on demonstrated areas of incompetence as they exist in different subcultures, and with respect to different aspects of child behavior.

In closing this section, the general conclusion is that if the different kinds of data described above relating to parent competence, with respect both to ends and means, were available, a direct result could be educational programs focused on specific areas of need. In the absence of such information, parent education must continue to make various secondhand solutions to the problems it faces; that is, it must continue to take attendance as an indication of need of some undifferentiated kind, must continue to utilize informally gathered parents' questions based on inadequate samples as a guide to program planning, or must make inferences from failures to achieve fairly obvious ends, such as mental health for all, that programs which seek to educate parents toward better child rearing are justified.

REFERENCES

1. Aberle, David F., and Kasper D. Naegele, "Middle-Class Fathers' Occupational Role and Attitudes Toward Children," *American Journal of Orthopsychiatry*, vol. 22, 1952, pp. 366–378.

2. Ackerley, Lois A., "The Information and Attitudes Regarding Child Development Possessed by Parents of Elementary School Children," *University of Iowa Studies in Child Welfare*, vol. 10, 1934, pp. 113–167.

3. Anderson, John E., "The Clientele of a Parent Education Program," *School and Society*, vol. 126, 1927, p. 179.

4. Anderson, John E., *The Young Child in the Home:* A Survey of Three Thousand American Families. Report of the Committee on the Infant and Preschool Child, White House Conference on Child Health and Protection. D. Appleton-Century Co., New York, 1936.

5. Ausubel, David P., Earl E. Balthazar, Irene Rosenthal, Leonard S. Blackman, Seymour H. Schpoont, and Joan Welkowitz, "Perceived Parent Attitudes as Determinants of Children's Ego Structure," *Child Development*, vol. 25, 1954, pp. 173–183.

6. Barnes, Marion J., "The Educational and Therapeutic Implications in Working with Parent Study Groups Around the Problems of the Normal Preschool Child," *American Journal of Orthopsychiatry*, vol. 22, 1952, pp. 268–276.

7. Boek, Walter E., Edwin D. Lawson, Marvin B. Sussman, and Alfred Yankauer, *Social Class Maternal Health and Child Care*. New York State Department of Health, Albany, May, 1957.

8. Brim, Orville G., Jr., "The Parent-Child Relation as a Social System: I. Parent and Child Roles," *Child Development*, vol 28, 1957, pp. 343–364.

9. Bronfenbrenner, Urie, "Socialization and Social Class Through Time and Space" in *Readings in Social Psychology*, edited by Theodore M. Newcomb, Eugene L. Hartley, and Eleanor E. Maccoby. 3d ed. Henry Holt and Co., New York, 1958, pp. 400–425.

10. Clausen, John A., *Sociology and the Field of Mental Health*. Russell Sage Foundation, New York, 1956.

11. Coast, Louise C., "A Study of the Knowledge and Attitudes of Parents of Preschool Children," *University of Iowa Studies in Child Welfare*, vol. 17, 1939, pp. 157–181.

12. Cole, Nyla J., Orla M. Shaw, Jack Steneck, and Leonard H. Taboroff, "A Survey Assessment of Current Parental Attitudes and Practices in Child-Rearing," *American Journal of Orthopsychiatry*, vol. 27, 1957, pp. 815–822.

13. Davis, Edith A., and Esther McGinnis, *Parent Education:* A Survey of the Minnesota Program. University of Minnesota Press, Minneapolis, 1939.

14. Farber, Maurice L., "English and Americans: Values in the Socialization Process," *Journal of Psychology*, vol. 36, 1953, pp. 243–250.

15. Foote, Nelson N., and Leonard S. Cottrell, Jr., *Identity and Interpersonal Competence:* A New Direction in Family Research. University of Chicago Press, Chicago, 1955.

16. Gardner, George E., "American Child Psychiatric Clinics," *Annals of the American Academy of Political and Social Science*, vol. 286, 1953, pp. 126–135.

17. Glidewell, John C., Ivan N. Mensh, and Margaret C.-L. Gildea, *Behavior Symptoms in Children and Degree of Sickness*. Paper read at the 112th Annual Meeting of the American Psychiatric Association, Chicago, Illinois, May 4, 1956. Washington University School of Medicine and St. Louis County Health Department, mimeographed.

18. Green, Arnold, "The Middle Class Male Child and Neurosis," *American Sociological Review*, vol. 11, 1946, pp. 31–41.

19. Hare, A. Paul, and Rachel T. Hare, "Classes for Prospective Fathers," *Marriage and Family Living*, vol. 14, 1952, pp. 206–207.

20. Hillman, Christine H., "Areas of Need of Young Rural Homemakers," *Journal of Home Economics*, vol. 46, 1954, pp. 377–379.

21. Hollingshead, August B., and Frederick C. Redlich, *Social Class and Mental Illness:* A Community Study. John Wiley and Sons, New York, 1958.

22. Indiana Works Progress Administration, *Second Annual Parent Education In-Service Training Institute*. 2d ed. Indiana WPA, 1936, mimeographed.

23. International Union for Child Welfare, *Child Welfare in Relation to the Family:* Proceedings of World Congress, 1954. Geneva, Switzerland, 1954.

24. Jacques, Elliott, "Miscomprehensions of Parents Concerning Child Health and Behavior," *American Journal of Orthopsychiatry*, vol. 12, 1942, pp. 202–213.

25. Michigan State Department of Mental Health, *A Report of Some Aspects of the Effectiveness of the Pierre the Pelican Mental Health Pamphlets*. Lansing, Mich., 1952, mimeographed.

26. Redlich, Frederick C., August B. Hollingshead, and Elizabeth Bellis, "Social Class Differences in Attitudes Toward Psychiatry," *American Journal of Orthopsychiatry*, vol. 25, 1955, pp. 60–70.

27. Rockwood, Lemo D., *Origins and Development of the Movement for Education for Marriage, Family Life and Parenthood in the U.S., 1900–1948*, with Major

Emphasis on Developments During the Past Twenty-Five Years. Unpublished manuscript, 1948.

28. Rowland, Loyd W., *A First Evaluation of the Pierre the Pelican Health Pamphlets*. Louisiana Mental Health Studies, No. 1, Louisiana Society for Mental Health, New Orleans, 1948.

29. Shirley, May, *Can Parents Educate One Another?* National Council of Parent Education, New York, 1938.

30. Stendler, Celia B., "Social Class Differences in Parental Attitudes Toward School at Grade I Level," *Child Development*, vol. 22, 1951, pp. 36–46.

31. Sternberg, Harriet, "Fathers Who Apply for Child Guidance," *Smith College Studies in Social Work*, vol. 22, 1951, pp. 53–68.

32. Stogdill, Ralph M., "Parental Attitudes and Mental-Hygiene Standards," *Mental Hygiene*, vol. 15, 1931, pp. 813–827.

33. Stott, Leland H., and Dorothy V. Mummery, "Adult Attitudes Toward Ascendant Behavior in Young Children," *Merrill-Palmer Quarterly*, vol. 2, Spring, 1956, pp. 110–120.

34. "UNESCO Expert Meeting on Parent Education," *International Child Welfare Review*, vol. 9, 1955, pp. 166–168.

35. United States Department of Health, Education, and Welfare, *Evaluation in Mental Health*. Public Health Service Publication No. 413, Government Printing Office, Washington, 1956.

36. United States Department of Health, Education, and Welfare, *Health Services and Juvenile Delinquency*. Children's Bureau, Washington, 1955.

37. University of Illinois, Institute of Communications Research, *The Development and Change of Popular Conceptions About Mental Health:* Summary Report. Urbana, Ill., 1958, mimeographed.

38. Walters, James, and Barbara Bridges, "Attitudes of Single Men Towards Child Guidance," *Journal of Home Economics*, vol. 48, 1956, pp. 109–113.

39. Weinstein, Morris, "A Controlled Role-Playing Approach as an Education Technique in Mental Hygiene Concepts," *Dissertation Abstracts*, vol. 14, 1954, p. 867.

40. White, Martha Sturm, "Social Class, Child Rearing Practices, and Child Behavior," *American Sociological Review*, vol. 22, 1957, pp. 704–712.

41. White House Conference on Child Health and Protection, *Education for Home and Family Life:* Part I, Elementary and Secondary Schools. Century Co., New York, 1932.

42. White House Conference on Child Health and Protection, *Home and School Cooperation*. Century Co., New York, 1932.

43. Witmer, Helen L., *The Field of Parent Education:* A Survey from the Viewpoint of Research. National Council of Parent Education, New York, 1934.

44. Wolfenstein, Martha, "Introduction to Part III, Child Rearing Literature" in *Childhood in Contemporary Cultures*, edited by Margaret Mead and Martha Wolfenstein. University of Chicago Press, Chicago, 1955.

PART TWO. PROCEDURES AND RESULTS

CHAPTER SIX

Content of the Educational Program

THE SELECTION of content for educational programs for parents is a specific instance of the more general process in an educational effort of selecting a curriculum. There is a parallel between the choice of content in parent education and the choice of curriculum for the training of engineers, preparing a course of study for third-grade students in the public schools, determining the sequences of courses in college as one moves from freshman to senior year, and other similar cases. The materials presented to parents are one part of the means of achieving the working goals of the program. The other part is the actual method of instruction ("educational methods") which is considered in the following chapter.

The choice of content should be governed by theoretical considerations which relate means to ends; that is, considerations which relate presentation of certain kinds of content to the achievement of the specified ends of the parent education program. However, it has been pointed out in prior chapters that there has been little thought about, or clarification of, the ends of parent education, and it must follow that the choice of parent education content can hardly have proceeded on a rational basis since there were no guiding principles to regulate the choice.

The effectiveness of a certain class of content will depend on the relative influence of various determinants of parent behavior such as intelligence, reviewed in Chapter III, and on the specific needs of the parent as considered in Chapter V. There has been little formal attention given to the problem of relating the content of a program to the characteristics of parents. One study a generation ago by Ojemann (24) had judges rate the importance of different types of parents (for example, mothers versus fathers, parents of young versus older children) being taught child development principles of different types (pertaining to physical growth, emotional needs, and so on). In contrast to this study, attempts of others to relate content to parent characteristics consist of presenting materials on children of the same age as the child of the parents participating in the program; or of questioning parents about materials which would interest them the most, and then presenting these materials. This latter is especially true of commercial organizations in which the content of the program is determined in most part by systematic consumer surveys, using standard market research techniques, of samples of parents.

There is a wide range of information of varying types that could be used as the substance of a parent education program. A program could present information on child development stages (physical, emotional, social, or intellectual), as well as advice to parents on ways of handling such developmental periods. Information could be presented on parent behavior itself, consisting of data on child-training practices in different cultures and descriptions of American parents' behavior, feelings, and attitudes. A program could emphasize case studies of parents' modes of handling a given child-rearing situation, with related discussion by parents of how they themselves deal with the situation. The content of the discussion could be derived from observation and analysis of a specific child, for example, as in nursery schools. An educational program could emphasize discussion of selected basic research studies of child development and parent-child relations, or more generally, of human personality as a whole. Another type of content comprises principles of home management in all of its aspects, and not just that of child rearing. All of these types of content are presented in parent education programs, either singly or in combination.

The selection of content in parent education has lacked a sound theoretical basis. Historically it has ranged from the discussions of parental techniques in "breaking the child's will," through the discussions of the early parent groups of the Child Study Association of America, who together read Rousseau's *Emile* and discussed applications to their own behavior as parents (7), to the more recent major considerations of developmental stages of the child's growth, and their significance in his personality development. The availability of information of certain kinds has led to its emphasis in programs, with little self-criticism as to the desirability of employing this content in contrast to some other. It is commonly recognized (e.g., 16, 37) that the overwhelming bulk of content in parent education programs consists of two major types. These are content referring to child development (norms, stages, phases, and the like) and content consisting of advice to parents (whether this pertains to handling specific developmental stages or to general child-rearing patterns, for example, showing affection). The other kinds of subject matter mentioned above also occur in one or another program, but infrequently as compared to developmental materials or advice.

In the sections which follow we consider for each of these two major types of parent education content their historical development, the probable validity of the data, and their probable effects upon parents in the light of our preceding discussions of theoretical principles of parent behavior. At the end of this chapter we consider briefly the other possibilities in parent education content, and analyze their probable usefulness in achieving the aims of parent education.

CHILD DEVELOPMENT NORMS AS CONTENT

The data on child development norms comes from two major sources: the research centers concerned with experimental studies of child development and the clinical specialties represented today by psychoanalysis, psychiatry, and clinical psychology. From the beginning, both emphasized developmental sequences. The work in the clinical tradition was from the earliest oriented toward "stages," since much of Freud's analysis of personality development was cast in terms of stages through which the child passed; for example, the Oedipal period and the latency period. The descriptive work on children done in the child research stations from their beginning around 1920 emphasizes the physical, mental, and social development of children. This contrasts with the emphasis on emotional development in the clinical tradition. These developmental data (of one or the other type) were quickly adopted as standard content in parent education programs. It is important to recognize that in a great many parent education programs the developmental information was transmitted relatively free of advice to the parent as to how such stages should be handled. One thinks of Gesell and Ilg's *Infant and Child in the Culture of Today* (11), a best seller (nearly one million copies) with predominantly developmental information and very little advice.

At the present time the parent educator has a wide array of formulations of child development stages from which he can choose. These include a number of theories concerned with emotional development such as those of Freud (12), Sullivan (22), and Erikson (8); works on the development of the child's self-conception and other social behavior such as those of Mead (19) and Gesell and Ilg (11); theories of mental growth such as Piaget's (25); and many others.

The important point is that these formulations of child development show wide disparity in the stages set forth in their descriptions. For example, while it is true that Sullivan, Mead, Freud, and Piaget all seem in agreement that the first stage of the child's development can be loosely referred to as autism or unreality, they diverge rapidly in their conceptions of subsequent stages. However, such diversity should *not* be taken as an indication of spuriousness or lack of validity of any particular theory. A delineation of developmental stages of the child is always directed to the specific predictive problem which the theorist faces. They are classificatory concepts which describe the child's development in terms of phases which are supposed to relate to something else; for example, either to later events, or to the readiness of the child for certain experiences. It follows that for varying fields of endeavor, different classification systems would be appropriate. For different problems one may want to use legally defined stages, motor skill or muscular stages, emotional stages, stages recognized by the society itself in its customs, stages of self-awareness, or any of the others.

It is not that the more recently formulated stages are more valid or better than the earlier, but rather that they are concerned with aspects of child development not described by previous systems. On the whole, they do not compete, but rather supplement each other. These various formulations of child development command the attention of the parent educator, and he is charged with the decision as to which are suitable content for the educational program. One basis of choice is the aspect of child development concerned. This choice of developmental norms for presentation is determined in part by the professional orientation of the parent educator. In Chapter II we pointed out that most programs have either a child research center orientation or a clinical orientation. The material on developmental stages resulting from these two interests indicates the former to be substantially more concerned with physical and social development, while the latter heavily emphasizes the emotional aspects of child growth. Since the concern of parent educators, and subsequently parents, historically has shown a change from outward to inward characteristics of the child, that is, in the direction of a greater concern with emotional well-being, one would guess there has been a shift toward greater use of developmental norms pertaining to emotional growth. This is only a supposition and requires a content analysis of program materials for documentation. The one existing study of this matter, however, does support our observation. Ojemann and his associates (23) made a study of articles appearing in five popular monthly magazines at three time intervals during the period 1900 to 1945. The results show that the physical aspects of development did in fact receive more attention in the sampling of 1924 to 1925, which was the middle one of the three sampling periods.

One point *is* clear: it is the virtual absence in any parent education program of normative material pertaining to the child's

intellectual development. This is the more surprising, since some
of the very best normative data available are on cognitive development in children (27). In Yu's survey (42) of 50 recent books
on child development and child care he reports that almost none
includes any material on intellectual development, although
physical, social, aesthetic, and emotional development are
stressed. One current exception is the curriculum of the Parent
Education Project, University of Chicago (14) in which the materials on middle childhood include developmental characteristics of children in the intellectual sphere. In this case the program materials are based on Piaget (25).

There are other issues in choosing developmental norms for
content than the area of personality with which they deal. One
of these is individual variability in development. A generation
and more ago the presentation of stages affixed the onset and
termination of stages to quite specific ages of the child. Such rigid
affirmation of child development stages was supplanted in time by
an emphasis upon the variability, around a given age norm, of
the onset and termination of stages. Whether this change arose
because of observations of the effects upon parents of presenting
such age-specific normative data, namely, that parents became
concerned when their child lagged behind age norms, or because
of the greater empirical demonstration of the actual variability by
further study of children, the fact is that the emphasis grew
tremendously.

This in turn has been supplanted, in the past decade, by still a
third conception of stages. It might be viewed as an extension of
the concept of norm variability but it really deserves separate
consideration. This is the conception (e.g., 8, 31) of child development as a sequence of stages through which the child passes, but
at his own rate, and with such inter-individual variability as to
invalidate the idea of age norms. The earliest age norms suggested that children exhibit behavior x at about a certain age,
and that this is normal for this age in our culture. Phases, sequences, epochs, and the like suggest that children pass through
a normal phase (at whatever age) in which they exhibit behavior
x, and there is predictability of sorts because this phase follows in

sequence some other phase regardless of the age in which it occurs. The shift away from age-specific norms to the conception of a developmental but age-free sequence increases the validity of the statements on development, since it takes account of the very wide age variability in children. Yet it leaves unanswered whether or not such sequences, even apart from the ages, are valid; that is, whether there actually are certain phases which inevitably occur in child development.

This leads to the issue of validity of the norm formulations, a third matter to be considered by the parent educator. Regrettably, most of the information on the social and emotional aspects of child behavior is based on samples of inadequate size and/or on clinically disturbed populations. For example, some years ago Malinowski's analysis (18) of the child-rearing practices of the Trobrianders showed that the Freudian formulation of the Ocdipal phase did not apply, and perhaps was descriptive of certain upper-middle class or upper-class Viennese children at the end of the last century, and only for the clinically disturbed among these; at the very least, the universality of the Oedipal phasc was no longer a tenable belief. The limited generality of several more Freudian or other psychoanalytic stage concepts was indicated by Sears (28) in the early 1940's, and more recent appraisals (e.g., 12), while giving a slightly altered picture, continue to stress the lack of solid evidence for some of the formulations.

The inadequacies of sample size and representativeness in some of the work of Gesell and his colleagues (e.g., 11) have recently been made clear in Senn's description (31) of the sample. For the basic survey made in 1925 the sample consists of 107 white middle-class New Haven children, all second generation and northern European in background. The sample was supplemented by "random" children visiting the clinic. In the follow-up study the sample was even smaller: there were semi-annual examinations of 16 boys and 20 girls at age three, and of 11 girls and 7 boys at age six. The data for the ages from five to ten come from 50 children, examined at half-year intervals, supplemented by data on 14 children from a private school.

What is one to say in summation? How can the parent educator estimate the comparative validity of existing stage or sequence formulations? The answer seems to be that he cannot, because with rare exceptions there are not relevant research data. Only in the area of physical growth are the facts available (36) which would permit the parent educator to talk of developmental sequences with the certitude of science. In other spheres he must recognize that the formulation of stages is mostly impressionistic theory, without adequate empirical foundation. If he does choose to treat child development as a matter of stages and sequences, it would seem to be his responsibility at this time to stress their hypothetical nature to his clients.

We leave behind the unresolved problem of validity and move on to consider the probable effects on parents of learning child development norms (even assuming they are valid). The discussion of effects of information of this kind must involve us in speculation, since the evaluation research on the effects of educational programs reviewed in Chapter IX is not concerned with the distinctive effects of using child development or other aspects of content. The evaluation studies actually have never differentiated between types of content. The arguments favoring the selection of child development norms as content in the educational program must be based on theoretical grounds. It is our plan to consider the merit of such theories.

It will be necessary to have an example at hand when some points which follow are analyzed. A good example is the data on lying from the recent report of Jean W. Macfarlane and others, *A Developmental Study of the Behavior Problems of Normal Children Between Twenty-One Months and Fourteen Years* (17, pp. 102–104). The data refer to the following types of behavior: *Category 1:* frequent, habitual first reaction to deny or distort facts; compulsive lying; lying to gain ends even when truth is effective; *Category 2:* lies habitually in almost any emergency; *Category 3:* lies occasionally to avoid scolding, punishment, or when under pressure to make a good impression. These three category descriptions together constitute "problem lying" in the Macfarlane study, and the total of parental reports of this type of behavior in their children gives the percentage of liars among their children. The percentage distribution is as follows:

Age in Years	Percentage
1¾	0
3	15
4	35
5	50
6	55
7	30
8	40
9	30
10	15
11	10
12	10
13	10
14	5

When data such as these on child development are included in parent education what might be the effects on parents? In Chapter IV we pointed out that child development information provides a parent with new concepts or labels to explain his child's behavior, and especially with the label "normality." For example, the 25 per cent of the parents in a large sample survey (20) who answered yes to the question "Does it upset you to think your child may lie?" could now view their children's behavior as normal, as part of a stage or sequence in ordinary development. They acquire, as some have put it, a "developmental perspective on behavior." (2) The outcome assumed to occur by most parent educators and which probably does occur for many parents, is that the parent becomes less concerned over specific characteristics of his child's actions, more relaxed, less punitive and restrictive, with the resultant good effect on the child.

But there are two other results, originally unanticipated, which also follow when parents learn child development norms. Both are viewed by most as undesirable. The first occurs in the case where the child's behavior is considered desirable, for example, control over urination, but he is slow (below the norm) in achieving such control. The second occurs in the case where the child's behavior is normal, in the sense of being average for his age, but the behavior itself (for example, lying) is considered undesirable.

The first of these unanticipated effects is familiar: it is the increase in worry and concern about the child, in excessive demands upon the child, as the parent acquires more and more developmental information about children. Indeed, so closely has this been associated in popular as well as professional literature, with the response of some parents to the information presented in the work of Gesell and Ilg (11) that one might refer to this consequence as the "Gesellian dilemma."

The fact is that normative standards are for parents a mixed blessing, either comforting them or dismaying them as the case may be, depending on the position of their child with respect to such standards. The efforts to free developmental stages from being age-specific has not, and probably cannot, solve this dilemma, since the parent faced with the notion of epochs or sequences or stages is as much concerned with the normality of the sequence as he is with the age normality of the child. Insofar as the child development information, age specific or not, presents a concept of normality of development, then if the child is behaving favorably with respect to the norm, the parent is comforted. But to the extent that the child is not, the parent ordinarily increases in apprehension and makes more demands upon the child.

Why should this occur? It arises from the tremendous motivation of ordinary parents to assure themselves that their children are normal. This motivation in turn has its roots deep in the value system of the society as a whole. Recognize that in every social system there is some function which is performed for the society at large. In some of these relations, including the parent-child, the teacher-pupil, and the master-apprentice, the primary function is training society's members. In the former the broad function is the physical care and training of the child so that he becomes a suitable member of society, both as a child in the child's role and later on as an adult performing an adult role.

Parents ordinarily have acquired the desire to carry out the demands of their role. Their life experience prior to parenthood usually results in motives to be a good parent which become internalized and strong; that is, become personal values of a very powerful kind. In addition, there are both social and legal controls over parents to ensure their correct role performance.

It is against this background that one can clearly see the sources of the parent's powerful motives to view his child as normal. For the educated parent, who sees himself as an important cause of his child's behavior (and in societies where he is viewed as such), a normal child is taken as proof that he has performed adequately in his role as parent and that he deserves the rewards contingent upon this. For the parent who believes in genetic determination, the normal child proves the purity and value of his family stock. For the religious parent who may believe (as men have from time immemorial) that God punishes children for the misdeeds of the adults, the normal child is proof of their morality, substantiating their claims to being good.

One interesting expression of this demand by parents to be reassured that they are adequate has been pointed out by Strang (34). The author states that it has been very difficult in the public school systems to get parents to accept a grading system based on a child's performance in relation to his ability, in place of the traditional grading system based on universal standards; that is, where the child's performance is compared with that of others of his age group. To grade the child's efforts according to the child's own capacity fails to answer the parent's deep concern of how his child compares to others.

The "Gesellian dilemma" thus follows from normative data on children because of the ego involvement of parents in the child's role performance. Where the child is shown to be normal or better than normal with respect to some desirable characteristic the consequence should be a happy and unanxious parent. But where the child is shown (by normative data) to be engaging in age-inappropriate behavior, or in a sequence of development somewhat different from that alleged to characterize the normal child (for example, he has not learned to control his urination, or has failed to move on to less frequent lying after age six) then what is the parent's reaction? The parent sees this as a sign of deviance in the child, which reflects upon his own personal worthiness, with an understandable increase in parental anxiety and demands upon the child to alter his behavior.

Nor is this latter group small in number. Given the fact that developmental norms indicate the average, it follows that at least as many parents must have children below the norms as otherwise. Hence, at least as many could experience an increase in anxiety and worry and resultant pressures upon the child as would experience a decrease of such anxiety and a relaxation of pressure upon the child. Where statistical data giving averages are absent, as in conceptions of developmental "sequences," one could not assign proportions of more or less anxious parents in this way. But it is probable that most current sequence formulations have low validity, so that most parents find their youngsters developing in a way other than that described as normal in sequence, with consequences similar to the foregoing.

The second unanticipated consequence of using child development norms as content is closely related to the aforementioned. It was stated earlier that this consequence often occurs where a child's behavior is "normal," but is viewed by the parent as undesirable. The actual consequence referred to is the onset of "permissiveness" or lenient child care in parents to a degree which is punishing to them, frightening to the child, and astonishing to the parent educator, who asserts that this result was not his intention. The parent, grimly holding himself in check while his child runs rampant, to the detriment of the home, the family, and the community, is a familiar picture. Many will say that this is unfair, that it is but a caricature of a parent who has been taught child development norms. But few would deny that a great many parents have come to tolerate behavior in their children which they disapprove of, on the grounds that it is only normal behavior for that age and that the child will grow out of it naturally. How does this permissive attitude arise and what might be *its* consequences for the parent-child relation?

The responsibility for this outcome, even though unintended, belongs to the parent educator. Child development norms have been presented in a manner which strongly implies that child development stages are intrinsic and occur independently of parent elicitations, with the parent's proper role being to provide a nurturant environment so that the inherent characteristics of the child can unfold in their natural sequence. However much the parent educator may think this is a parody of permissive child training, the fact is that parents have so interpreted the data he presents.

The reason for so erroneous an inference on the part of the parents is not hard to find. Most of the data on child development, and especially its mode of presentation to parents in this country, fail to make clear the fact that the child development norms apply to individuals brought up in specific social environments, where there are specific parent demands on the children. The influence of parents in actively eliciting maturation from the child, in moving him on from one stage to another by demanding new actions, is not considered in the presentation of child development norms. Discussion of such norms usually does not include the possibility that the norms occur because parents, sharing a common culture, demand this behavior from the children; the implication instead is that these norms are the expression of intrinsic characteristics of the natural child.

Unfortunately, the actual studies of child development never have included enough data on the ways in which parents of different backgrounds demand different kinds of behavior from their children. The data we do have, mainly anthropological, strongly suggest that so-called developmental norms, while showing in part the universally inherent characteristics of children's growth, are also specific to given cultures or subcultures, and depend in significant part upon what is demanded by parents. Benedict (4) has indicated the way in which cultures differ in the age and nature of changes made in parents' demands upon children. Aberle (1) has described certain shifts which may occur in the responsibility for child care between parents as the child matures. Baldwin (3) reports significant differences in parental behavior and demands toward youngsters at the three- and nine-year-old levels.

To return for the moment to the data presented on children's lying, which showed lying to decrease after age six, one cannot conclude that this decrease occurs naturally as an expression of a child's inherent nature. The lying may instead decrease as a result of greater parental and other social demands upon the child to tell the truth after the age of six.

This common misconception of child development norms may have further consequences of its own. One has been remarked on many times by others; that the parent who is permissive to the child even when he thinks the behavior wrong, because the behavior is described as normal, will become frustrated, aggressive, and hostile toward the child in other child-care areas; or even worse, will simply withdraw from the child, with a sometimes serious impairment of the relationship. A second consequence is not so obvious, and also is more speculative. It may be that the parent who misunderstands developmental materials and is very permissive will find that his child does *not* progress, but stays at this current stage of development. For example, where the parent is exposed to the developmental material on lying and concludes that he should be permissive regarding his child's lying at age six, he may find that the child continues to lie since there is no demand from the environment to change his ways.

Granted that parental intervention is an important force in the child's development, the relation of development of a child through intrinsic maturation and the elicitation of behavior by parental demands upon the child can be shown schematically in the chart at top of the next page.

In cell A the child's maturing behavior unfolds in congruence with the changing parental expectations; in cell D the child is not changing, nor does the parent expect new things of him. Cell B describes the case where the parent demands behavior from the child which he "is not ready to perform," and cell C instances the child wishing to perform certain behavior, but which the parent inhibits by contrary demands.

Child's maturational tendencies

Parents' prescription for child	Able and/or willing	Unable and/or unwilling
Should do it	A	B
Should not do it	C	D

SCHEMATIC RELATIONSHIP OF PARENTAL DEMANDS TO
CHILD'S READINESS

The relationship in cell A is often advocated by parent educators and often becomes changed into extreme permissiveness. The point to be made here is that the child's development may not be a natural flowering of inherent tendencies, but rather that a relationship such as that in cell B may be necessary to elicit it. To illustrate, the argument has been that parents should not expect a child to walk and climb prior to the "necessary" physiological maturation and development of the child's ability to understand what is being expected of him. The same argument has been applied with respect to other physiological, or more specifically neurological, developments such as the ability to pick up and handle spoons or other eating utensils. One would not want to deny that with respect to these heavily physiologically determined acts the relationship A may be valid, although even these may depend on children being encouraged by the environment in some degree. But especially suspect is the conception of development in cell A when nonphysiological characteristics, such as lying, sibling rivalry, or concern over opinions of one's peer group are at issue. Nevertheless, viewpoint A is given to parents without any indication of why these social characteristics of children should appear at all, apart from the demands of parents that such behavior or attitudes be developed on the part of the child.

If the selection of content for parent education programs includes developmental information based on samples of children in this country, the parent educator must face squarely the question of what the implications may be for the parent. Where there seems to be a clear physiological basis, as in walking, probably much is to be gained if the parent adjusts his demands to such maturational characteristics of the child. Where emotional and other characteristics are concerned, and the physiological base is not clear, the question remains as to how developmental norms should be interpreted by the parent. Are they something which the parent should seek to obtain by virtue of his demands upon the child (as in cell B), or are they something which he should view as natural in the course of the child's development (as in cell A) if he simply permits the child to mature in his own way?

ADVICE TO PARENTS AS CONTENT

Advice to parents surely constitutes the oldest category of content in parent education programs. The advice may concern the way in which parents handle a variety of child-rearing problems, without implication that these are linked to any developmental sequence or age period. In recent years, of course, as conceptions of developmental norms grew, much of the advice has consisted of modes of handling different stages of development of children.

Giving advice in parent education goes back, by inference, to the earliest times. The earliest historical records, as reviewed in the Appendix, show that advice antedates presentation of purely factual information, observations of children, or other types of content. The fact that Pratt (26) in 1935 stated that parent group leaders were beginning to feel that they should go beyond simply teaching parents the principles (norms) of child development and should furnish parents with instructions in dealing with these, may indicate that from 1920 to 1935 or so the emphasis in certain circles of parent education was upon presentation of developmental norms *without* accompanying advice, that is, the type of content treated in a previous section. However, that this was not representative of this period for parent educators on the average is suggested by other data mentioned below.

The many studies (5, 9, 15, 30, 33, 35, 38, 41) of advice given to parents are of recent date. These studies deal with the content of parent education programs from late last century to the present, and in one the analysis goes back to the beginning of the eighteenth century. The historical materials provide the basis for our consideration of two questions about "advice" in parent education programs. These are: changes in the actual content of the advice over time, such as changes from strictness to permissiveness; and changes in the style in which advice is given, such as changes from rigid rules to suggestions or "hypotheses" for parents to test. Each of these will be considered in turn.

The information on changes in advice is confusing. The different studies have dealt with different kinds of parent education activities such as mass media or group discussion. Some have dealt with major trends, while others have emphasized the publication of influential books which antedate periods yet to come. However, changes in the advice given to parents can be reviewed as follows.

Sunley's work (35) is the only one which deals with child training advice in parent education literature back to 1820. Sunley points out that prior to that date, advice was imported from England in pamphlets and books. He points out that early advice stressed the importance of the mother as an influence on the child's personality, the contention being that personality was determined by early childhood, that the father's role in the child's upbringing was small, and that the mother should do the disciplining. Mothers were urged to breast-feed their children; they were advised to allow self-scheduling of feeding; total weaning was to occur somewhat earlier than now recommended, namely, from eight to twelve months of age; and (what would now be an anachronism) drugs and alcohol were used to quiet the infant, but laudanum specifically was considered inappropriate to use. Apart from these relatively permissive feeding practices the advice is for strictness. Toilet training was to be started early, and mistakes were considered disgusting; dirt was to be avoided; in the area of infantile and later sexuality, masturbation was to be controlled since it was considered a ruinous practice.

Crying of a child was to be unanswered, the arguments being that crying was good for the child's lungs and that it was desirable to let him "cry it out" to break his will; if crying was responded to, the child would learn to cry even more.

In general, the latter practices stem from the Calvinist view that a child is born depraved and that parents must force absolute obedience and break his will to free him of his evil nature. However, Sunley points out that this advice reflected also the "hardening school," which in turn stemmed from Locke and Rousseau; the view was that parents should bring out the naturalness and manliness of the child, bring out his innate vigor to protect himself against the pitfalls of civilization. At the same time, there arose from unspecifiable sources in Europe the advocacy of a more gentle treatment, in which the child was viewed as fragile, as one who needed gentle discipline and kindly care, and who should be led and persuaded but not driven. Sunley suggests that according to his analysis by 1844 this point of view seemed to be making headway, and by 1860 had gained much influence.

The work which is concerned with subsequent periods is consistent in its results. In two fundamental studies Stendler (33) and Vincent (38) have made a content analysis of articles in infant care and child management appearing since 1890 in mass media such as *Good Housekeeping, Woman's Home Companion,* and *Ladies' Home Journal.* Stendler's work characterizes the 1890 to 1910 period as one of "sweet permissiveness," and the 1910 to 1930 period as one of rigid discipline. Vincent's results strongly support those of Stendler, his results showing that earlier recommended methods of infant feeding and discipline were that feedings should be "loosely scheduled"; that in 1920 a large group said feedings should be "tightly scheduled," and that the child should "cry it out," while in more recent years the great majority recommended self-regulation and mothering.

A third fundamental study of trends and advice has been made by Wolfenstein (41). The changes in advice were analyzed in the various issues of *Infant Care* published by the U.S. Children's Bureau in seven editions beginning with 1914 and appearing in

1921, 1929, 1938, 1942, 1945, and 1951. The changes analyzed pertain to the severity in handling five characteristics of child behavior: masturbation, thumb sucking, weaning, bowel training, and bladder training. Appraising the increase, decrease, or constancy of recommended severity in the issues of *Infant Care*, Wolfenstein obtains results which are on the whole in accord with those obtained by Vincent and Stendler. Table 1 in Wolfenstein's article is presented below.

Severity in the handling of:	From 1914 to 1921	From 1921 to 1929	From 1929 to 1938	From 1938–42 to 1945	From 1941–45 to 1951
Masturbation	Decreases	Decreases	Constant	Decreases	Constant
Thumb sucking	Constant	Decreases	Constant	Decreases	Decreases
Weaning	Increases	Increases	Constant	Decreases	Constant
Bowel training	Increases	Increases	Decreases	Decreases	Decreases
Bladder training	Increases	Decreases	Decreases	Decreases	Decreases

The results of these studies must be viewed as describing dominant trends and central tendencies in advice. They should not obscure the important fact that there were exceptions. Several examples can be given. First, while the onset of two decades of strictness in child care occurred about 1910, L. Emmett Holt's book, *The Care and Feeding of Children* (13), appeared in 1894. This book stressed the strict, routinized care of the child. The advice given was accepted by a majority of literate mothers for at least a generation, and must be viewed as a primary cause of this subsequent period of strictness. It is to be noted also that while John B. Watson's work in behaviorism attained professional significance during the 1920's and contributed to the intellectual change of the times, his *Psychological Care of Infant and Child* (39), which was directed to parents and stressed strict and routine child care, did not appear until 1928, when Freudian theory was well in its ascendancy.

As a contrasting example, from about 1910 several important organizations (such as Child Study Association of America) were stressing the importance of love, support, and an intelligent permissiveness in child care, based on the work of Freud, G. Stanley Hall, and other leaders in the clinical movement (some of whom lectured widely to parent educators during the first part of the twentieth century). This emphasis antedated by some fifteen to twenty years the decline of the period of strictness and scheduling mentioned above, and these organizations must be considered to have played a significant role in setting the new trend.

A third example is drawn from a generation later. Pratt (26) pointed out in 1935 that many parent educators then were advising that an indiscriminate permissiveness and free choice given to children would be detrimental to their adult character, thus showing that already a reaction to the uses of clinical theory was under way, which now is evidently in *its* ascendancy.

These three examples have dealt with precursors of later trends. Examples of the reverse situation, where advice common to an earlier period still persists, are also at hand. One parent education program in Ohio which has both a mass media and a general advisory service for parents, gives advice which seems indistinguishable from that appearing during the early 1920's, and advocates strict "conditioning" of overt behavior in a manner reminiscent of the Holt and Watson approaches. In sum, at any given time the analysis of content seems to show current emphases, as well as remnants of earlier times and precursors of things to come.

Why such changes over a seventy-five year period should have occurred in the advice to parents is considered by some to be an embarrassing topic for parent educators. Vincent (38) raises the question of how advice regarding child rearing can change over a period of three decades to represent almost opposite positions, and yet be promulgated as scientific findings. Some have argued that were it possible to demonstrate that such changes clearly reflected new scientific research findings on child development, the changes could be justified as improvements in the same way as are changes in other fields of practice, such as medicine and engineering. But this is doubtful in parent education; there is a less direct relation between changes in advice and advances in empirical research. As a result, parent education has been criticized in many quarters because of the many changes in advice regarding child-care practices.

This criticism seems to us to be in error, and to arise from a naive view of parent education. At least two points are relevant. One is that the objectives of child rearing may change over time: parents, and parent educators as well, may gain new conceptions of the desirable child and adult. Child-rearing practices and advice to parents naturally would change to accord with the new aims, so that the parents might use the methods which science indicates are the best for these aims. To expect advice to remain the same in spite of changing parental aims now appears as unwarranted. A second point is that even if aims do not change, advice might change over a period and still represent the best knowledge of a given time. It is in the nature of science to discover fresh truths, to supplant the old with the new belief which, though it may have a higher validity, is itself still subject to change, a step in the advance of knowledge. It is where advice claiming to arise from science does *not* change over a period that one should suspect it of being whimsy or dogma.

There have been several interesting analyses made of the relation between changing values, both in child rearing and in the wider culture, and the changes in advice to parents. Senn (32) points out that there is a considerable lag between research in child development and its subsequent influence on matters relating to children, especially parent education. He also states that practices in child care are never isolated from other important changes in this society. He suggests that the "impersonal" child-care practices of the 1910 to 1930 period were in large part the result of a scientific approach to human problems, with an associated "impersonality," which flourished at that time in fields such as the control of disease.

Sears, Maccoby, and Levin (29) point out that during the nineteenth century the responsibility for the expression of public beliefs and values belonged to the men of our society, and that the public beliefs and values about children, therefore, reflected both an aggressive male point of view toward youngsters and an abundance of male ignorance about them. The authors suggest that as women became better educated and more active in public affairs, political and otherwise, a change in the American value system followed. They point out that women know now (and knew earlier) a great deal about younger children and are strongly motivated to improve their child rearing. As women gained in influence, they demanded corrections in public values which had expressed only the male view; in particular, they sought to correct obvious defects in educational procedures, and in disciplinary customs in the home. Substantively, they urged recognition and tolerance of children's limitations and their developmental characteristics. The impact of this influence on the American value system evidently was not to bear fruit in child-training practices until the 1930's and thereafter.

Vincent, in interpreting the results of his study described above (38), points out that his data indicate that the period from about 1910 to about 1930 was "the age of the mother," in which the mother knew best and the baby was subordinate in terms of scheduling. In contrast, the period from 1935 to 1945 might be called the "baby's decade," where the mother becomes secondary to the baby's demands, for during the latter period there was an increased frequency of articles devoted to dangers of "psychological loss" to the child (lack of love, and the like), with no parallel increase of articles concerned with the mother. Of course, the "age of the mother" may have been just a by-product of the Holt and Watson views then dominant, in that the patterns of strict discipline and scheduling, advised for the good of the child, also worked out to the benefit of the mother.

A fourth explanation of changes in child care is concerned with the change from strict to more permissive patterns. Escalona (9) points out that public opinion of an authoritative kind believed in an orderly, strictly scheduled existence from early childhood on, that this was a highly rational approach reflecting the advances in the natural sciences which made it seem possible that perhaps bigger and better children could be produced. The author points out that this did not necessarily involve any aspects of affection, that scheduling or nonscheduling can be unrelated to the amount of affection shown to the child. The author then suggests that in more recent years our society has lost its earlier, naive sense of mastery over the world in which we live. This in turn has been reflected in changes in child-care patterns, for there has been a decline of the "technical mastery" approach to the child and an increased effort or willingness on the part of the adult to meet the needs of the younger child rather than master them and guide them. (9) Like Senn, this suggests that the more recent changes in child care reflect changes in the larger culture, rather than changes in the scientific knowledge of child-training procedures.

It should not be discouraging that changes in advice to parents have occurred. They reflect the improvement of current scientific knowledge, and also mirror changes in values regarding the desirable man. Even though it seems impossible to assess the relative influence of changes in cultural values versus new scientific findings regarding child development, one can hardly doubt that both have contributed to the changes in advice.

The second important aspect of advice as content is the manner in which advice is given. Our analysis focuses on the change from giving rigid rules to offering suggestions or hypotheses for parents to test. The continuing changes in knowledge and in theoretical explanations of child development spanning almost a fifty-year period have brought considerable humility to parent educators regarding their understanding of personality development in children, and the effects of parents on children. In Chapter II we have discussed the difficulties of the parent educator confronted with a continuous growth of knowledge regarding parent-child relations and personality development, which threatens his existing assumptions and theories. His solution must be to accept what now seems valid, on the basis of the best available evidence, and yet be prepared to change. This intellectual approach is now taken by most leading parent educators toward the advice they transmit to parents. In their programs there is a recognition of the changing nature of scientifically based knowledge, of the probabilistic character of any information given to parents, and therefore they make an effort to transmit advice to parents with some accompanying appraisal of the validity of the information.

Ojemann, whose research we have frequently cited, was the first to recognize that the solution to inadequate knowledge of child development was to present the knowledge to parents with accompanying probabilities of its effectiveness or validity. Over the past twenty-five years this point of view has developed to the degree where it supersedes earlier dogmatic positions dating from a generation or more ago. In Vincent's study (38), in which he analyzed 298 articles pertaining to feeding practices between 1920 and 1949, and ranked them according to the degree of dogmatism versus suggestiveness (the probabilistic character of the statements), the results show that for the period 1920 to 1924 some 65 per cent of the articles were dogmatic or absolute in their statements, and 10 per cent were suggestive, that is, provided alternatives. In contrast, for the period 1944 to 1949 the respective percentages were 17 per cent and 40 per cent. This clearly shows the shift from giving dogmatic advice toward a greater suggestion of alternatives.

There are still some who give "rules" or "laws" rather than hypotheses. A half-dozen years ago Weng (40) analyzed 76 pamphlets related to the feeding of infants, and found there is still "considerable room for improvement" in presenting advice. Some examples in the parent education literature are the following. In a recent article (10) in a magazine directed to parents of crippled children, a "primer for parents" is presented consisting of more than two dozen rules; for example, "food, shelter, clothing, and love are necessities; and the greatest of these is love." Another article (21) entitled "Nine Psychiatric Commandments" presents a list of rules which, it is alleged, if meticulously followed would do much to promote mental hygiene. Among the nine commandments are: "Mothers should not dominate fathers" and "Parents should not be concerned to an excessive degree with children's acts of elimination (bowel habits)."

At the beginning of the decade 1920 when the parent education movement in this country was moving toward the heights of its expansion, the aim was to have the newly established child development station produce information on desirable child-rearing practices, which would be directly transmitted as advice to the parent. The view of the parent was that he was an uncomplicated bit of machinery giving neither resistance nor difficulty, into which new rules, in the form of expert advice, could be put and then superior child-care practices produced. We have shown in Chapter III how this naive model of the simple rational man was soon demonstrated to be inadequate. In Chapter IV we have discussed some of the criticisms of the "rule-following" and the "loving and accepting" parents as practical working goals of parent education. Among the points made in these discussions are a few of special relevance to the effects of rigid rule-giving. These are mentioned again here. It has been argued that using "rules" as content in parent education has resulted in an increase in parents' dependency on professional students of human behavior, especially where the parent is detached from his original cultural milieu through social or geographic mobility. This dependency is usually accompanied by rigidity or inflexibility in child care, by a decrease in creativity and in spontaneity on the part of the parent. Where the advice involves affectional aspects of the parent-child relation, which are less easily controlled, if at all, by conscious effort, the additional result may be to increase feelings of guilt if one is unable to behave toward his child in accord with the best current advice.

The trend toward giving advice as suggestion and hypothesis should mitigate some of these effects. Where the effort is made to give advice with its probable validity indicated, one not only maintains his own scientific integrity, but cultivates in the parent himself an attitude of scientific inquiry. The parent reduces his dependency on experts; also he no longer rejects the best information available simply because that information turns out in some instances to be wrong. The newer form of advice seems to parallel the newer conception of developmental stages, where the stress is on variability around the norm. The objectives of transmitting advice in the form of hypotheses have been to provide the parent with a repertory of problem-solving skills which have a higher than usual probability of success (that is, higher than the folklore and precepts of cultural tradition), and yet which do not *promise* success; and to avoid giving the idea that the advice is based on final knowledge about child rearing, in turn reducing the likelihood that the parent becomes either inflexible or disillusioned about the value of child development research.

OTHER TYPES OF CONTENT

In the beginning of this chapter we proposed that the selection of content was regulated in significant part by the working goals of the program. The two most frequently used types of content, which we have discussed above, clearly correspond to the pursuit of certain of the working goals described in Chapter IV. The use of child development data as content is the means of achieving the working goal of the parent who has an "understanding of child development," and the use of advice as content is instrumental to attaining the goals of the "rule-following" parent and the "loving and accepting" parent.

What kinds of content are related to the other less common working objectives? For one of them, "the comfortable, relaxed, natural" parent, we have stated that there is no relevant content other than telling the parent that whatever he does is all right. The content of programs espousing this goal actually consists of material pertinent to some other goal or goals; for example, the program gives advice on toilet training or on home management.

For each of the three working goals which remain, there are certain kinds of content which are especially appropriate. Since we already indicated what these are in prior chapters, only a few words by way of review are needed here. Where the objective is to educate the parent about his effect upon the child, appropriate content is information on general personality development and functioning; that is, information similar to that acquired in a standard college level course in personality theory. Such materials have been used only infrequently, although aspects seem to occur in all programs. In this connection a few parent education programs have begun to use original research reports as content, with the parents in groups analyzing the implications of each for parental practice. A recently published *Family Life Source Book* (6), written for the general public and for educators who need nontechnical materials on family living, is of relevance, since it gives about 400 selections of original research reports sampled from 4,000 appearing over the past ten years. It is one of the few works, if not the only one, in parent education content which aims to present research directly without interpretation.

Where the working goal is to increase parents' "problem-solving abilities," few argue for training in logic or thinking itself. Most seek to broaden the parent's repertory of child-rearing techniques, and extend the number of child-care situations he has studied. The content of primary relevance to this objective is information on the experiences of other parents, and the ways in which they have handled different child-rearing situations. Ordinarily, this content occurs in conjunction with the method of parent group discussion. The parent acquires information regarding procedures for solving problematic situations and thereby gains from the other parents a variety of potential actions to add to his repertory. Often the parental discussion is accompanied by a presentation of beliefs of experts in child development about the matter. One way of developing this kind of discussion and elicitation of information would be to use case studies of parental responses to specific situations, much like the case-study approach in law and business education. This does not seem to have been widely used.

In certain programs the discussion related to problem-solving is not of child-care practices only but also of the attitudes and feelings which the parents have toward particular kinds of behavior or characteristics in their children, and toward different practices. The content thus includes parents' feelings and beliefs as well as their behavior. It is widely reported that parents gain satisfaction from discovering that they are not the only ones who feel guilty after striking their children, and so on. This has been referred to as "dilution therapy" and is taken as an indication that parents desire information about how their own feelings and behavior compare with the average. The use of this type of content is not necessarily restricted to parent discussion group procedures. In fact there is much to be said for broadening the base of materials by using published reports of parent behavior. The sample of parents represented by the members of the typical discussion group is very small and probably unrepresentative; published data usually are based on a better sample. For our own culture, the recent book (29) by Sears, Maccoby, and Levin cited earlier is exemplary. The book describes the child-rearing practices and attitudes of nearly 400 mothers around Boston, of primarily middle-class origin. It is nontechnical and presents content which is suitable for parent education programs. The use of published information need not be restricted to parents in this culture; one could, with profit, include data on child-rearing practices in other cultures, so as to further broaden the perspective one has on his own behavior.

When the primary program objective is the good "home manager," the distinguishing characteristics of the content used are that it deals not so much with the understanding of one's self, or of children, but rather with practically oriented information on running the home. Since we have discussed this matter at some length in Chapter IV, a few examples will suffice here. This content deals with how to occupy children's interest during periods of fatigue so as to lessen family tension, ways of getting the dinner dishes washed without quarreling, information on different kinds of toys, suggestions for occupying the child's time on rainy days, and how to avoid physical accidents.

All of these different aspects of content compete for the attention of the parent educator. However, the absence of adequate evaluation studies which deal with the relative effectiveness of different kinds of content means that choice of content in parent education must continue on the basis of theoretical allegations as to its merits. It is sincerely to be hoped that more bold and creative experimentation with classes of content can be undertaken by parent education programs in the years ahead, and that evaluative research to provide a scientific basis for the selection of content undergoes significant development.

REFERENCES

1. Aberle, David F., "Social System and Socialization" in *Conference on Cross-Cultural Research on Personality Development*, by David F. Aberle, Alfred L. Baldwin, John W. Whiting, Robert R. Sears, Daniel Miller, and William E. Henry. Kansas City, 1955, mimeographed.

2. Allen, Winifred Y., and Doris Campbell, *The Creative Nursery Center:* A Unified Service to Children and Parents. Family Service Association of America, New York, 1948.

3. Baldwin, Alfred L., "Differences in Parent Behavior Toward Three- and Nine-Year-Old Children," *Journal of Personality*, vol. 15, 1946, pp. 143–165.

4. Benedict, Ruth, "Continuities and Discontinuities in Cultural Conditioning" in *A Study of Interpersonal Relations*, edited by Patrick Mullahy. Heritage Press, New York, 1949, pp. 297–308.

5. Bruch, Hilde, "Psychiatric Aspects of Changes in Infant and Child Care," *Pediatrics*, vol. 10, 1952, pp. 575–579.

6. Byrd, Oliver E., compiler, *Family Life Source Book*. Stanford University Press, Stanford, Calif., 1956.

7. Dybwad, Gunnar, "How We Train for Leadership in Parent Education," *Children*, vol. 1, 1954, p. 10.

8. Erikson, Erik H., *Childhood and Society*. W. W. Norton and Co., New York, 1950.

9. Escalona, Sybille, "A Commentary Upon Some Recent Changes in Child-Rearing Practices," *Child Development*, vol. 20, 1949, pp. 157–163.

10. Fleischer, Ernest, Madeline Karl, and Marguerite Eversden, "An Idea for a Guidance Program," *The Crippled*, vol. 6, 1956, p. 27.

11. Gesell, Arnold, and Frances L. Ilg, in collaboration with Janet Learned and Louise B. Ames, *Infant and Child in the Culture of Today:* The Guidance of Development in Home and Nursery School. Harper and Bros., New York, 1943.

12. Hall, Calvin S., and Gardner Lindzey, *Theories of Personality*. John Wiley and Sons, New York, 1957, chap. 2.

13. Holt, L. Emmett, *The Care and Feeding of Children:* A Catechism for the Use of Mothers and Children's Nurses. D. Appleton and Co., New York, 1894.

14. Kawin, Ethel, *Middle Childhood*. University of Chicago Press, Chicago, 1957.

15. Langdon, Grace, and Irving W. Stout, *The Discipline of Well-Adjusted Children*. John Day and Co., New York, 1952.

16. Lemkau, Paul V., "Local Mental Health Services," *Annals of the American Academy of Political and Social Science*, vol. 286, 1953, pp. 116–125.

17. Macfarlane, Jean W., Lucile Allen, and Marjorie P. Honzik, *A Developmental Study of the Behavior Problems of Normal Children Between Twenty-One Months and Fourteen Years*. University of California Press, Berkeley, 1954.

18. Malinowski, Bronislaw, *The Sexual Life of Savages in North-western Melanesia*. Liveright Publishing Corporation, New York, 1929.

19. Mead, George H., *Mind, Self, and Society*. University of Chicago Press, Chicago, 1934.

20. Michigan State Department of Mental Health, *A Report of Some Aspects of the Effectiveness of the Pierre the Pelican Mental Health Pamphlets*. Lansing, Mich., 1952, mimeographed.

21. Mosse, Eric P., "Nine Psychiatric Commandments," *Medical Record*, vol. 160, 1946, pp. 547–549.

22. Mullahy, Patrick, editor, *The Contributions of Harry Stack Sullivan:* A Symposium of Interpersonal Theory in Psychiatry and Social Science. Papers presented at meetings of the William Alanson White Association. Hermitage Press, New York, 1952.

23. Ojemann, Ralph H., and associates, "A Functional Analysis of Child Development Material in Current Newspapers and Magazines," *Child Development*, vol. 19, 1948, pp. 76–92.

24. Ojemann, Ralph H., "Generalizations Relating to Child Development Involved in Intelligent Parental Guidance," *University of Iowa Studies in Child Welfare*, vol. 10, 1934, pp. 29–99.

25. Piaget, Jean, *Logic and Psychology*. Basic Books, New York, 1957.

26. Pratt, George K., *Three Family Narratives for Use in Parent Education Groups*, With a Discussion of the Problems of Study Group Leadership. National Council of Parent Education, New York, 1935.

27. Russell, David H., *Children's Thinking*. Ginn and Co., Boston, 1956.

28. Sears, Robert R., *Survey of Objective Studies of Psychoanalytic Concepts*. Social Science Research Council, New York, 1943.

29. Sears, Robert R., Eleanor E. Maccoby, and Harry Levin, *Patterns of Child Rearing*. Row, Peterson and Co., Evanston, Ill., 1957.

30. Senn, Milton J. E., "Changing Concepts on Child Care: A Historical Review," *March of Medicine*. New York Academy of Medicine Lectures to the Laity, No. 17. International Universities Press, New York, 1955, pp. 83–103.

31. Senn, Milton J. E., with Evan McLeod Wylie, "The Epoch Approach to Child Development." *Woman's Home Companion*, November, 1955, pp. 40-42 ff.

32. Senn, Milton J. E., "Fads and Facts as the Bases of Child-Care Practices," *Children*, vol. 4, 1957, pp. 43–47.

33. Stendler, Celia B., "Sixty Years of Child Training Practices," *Journal of Pediatrics*, vol. 36, 1950, pp. 122–134.

34. Strang, Ruth, *Reporting to Parents:* Practical Suggestions for Teaching. Bureau of Publications, No. 10, Teachers College, Columbia University, New York, 1947.

35. Sunley, Robert, "Early Nineteenth Century American Literature on Child Rearing" in *Childhood in Contemporary Culture*, edited by Margaret Mead and Martha Wolfenstein. University of Chicago Press, Chicago, 1955, pp. 150–167.

36. Thompson, Helen, "Physical Growth" in *Manual of Child Psychology*, by Leonard Carmichael. 2d ed. John Wiley and Sons, New York, 1954, chap. 5.

37. United States Department of Health, Education, and Welfare, *Health Services and Juvenile Delinquency*. Children's Bureau, Washington, 1955.

38. Vincent, Clark E., "Trends in Infant Care Ideas," *Child Development*, vol. 22, 1951, pp. 199–209.

39. Watson, John B., *Psychological Care of Infant and Child*. W. W. Norton and Co., New York, 1928.

40. Weng, Lorraine, "A Study of Lay Publications on Child Feeding," *Journal of American Dietetic Association*, vol. 28, 1952, pp. 927–932.

41. Wolfenstein, Martha, "Trends in Infant Care," *American Journal of Orthopsychiatry*, vol. 23, 1953, pp. 120–130.

42. Yu, Hsi Chi, *Survey of the Parent Education Movement in the United States of America and Canada*. Master's thesis, University of Toronto, Canada, 1948.

CHAPTER SEVEN:

The Choice of Methods

THE CHOICE OF METHODS in parent education has received more attention and stimulated more theory than any other topic. It will be a longer task to examine this body of theory than has been the case with other aspects of parent education. Our analysis and discussion of methodology is organized into three parts. We present, first, a brief overview of the different types of methods, along with some impressions of historical developments. Second, we consider the theoretical basis of selection between the major methods, that is, mass media, counseling, and group discussion. Last, for each of these major methods, we analyze the reasons for the selection of one or another of their variations.

AN OVERVIEW OF THE BASIC TYPES

The basic methods consist of three different types: mass media, counseling, and group discussion procedures. Other variants of method are best discussed as subtypes of these three major classes. Our overview of these basic types gives examples of their varieties, and illustrates their use by reference to specific educational programs.

Mass Media Methods

The phrase "mass media" customarily refers to methods of reaching a mass audience, such as radio, television, and pamphlets. However, in this chapter we use the phrase slightly differently in order to include such educational methods as lectures. Here mass media are seen as comprising all efforts directed to an *anonymous* audience, where the parent educator cannot know his clientele as individual parents. The mass media approach includes a wide range of educational activities.

1. Books. Books for parents about child care need little description. These books are written by the staffs of, or under the auspices of, organizations, as well as by individual authors. Examples of the first are recent books published under the auspices of the Institute of Child Welfare, University of Minnesota, and early books such as *Outlines of Child Study* from the Child Study Association of America. Commercial organizations such as Field Enterprises Educational Corporation, the publisher of the multi-volume series *Child Craft*, also are active in producing work of this type. The published works of Holt, Watson, and Spock are among the most notable examples of individually authored books for parents. In any given recent year the number of such books in print is estimated to be in the several hundreds.

2. Pamphlets. Pamphlets directed to parents are familiar to all. What needs to be stressed here is the overwhelming number of pamphlets sold or given away each year. Conservative estimates of parent educators are that the total number of copies distributed *each year* is in the neighborhood of 25 million.

Some contrasting examples of programs using pamphlets are the following. The commercial organization Science Research Associates publishes three major series of pamphlets, of which one is specifically prepared for parents. While these booklets cover many of the same areas as do other mass media, such as health of the child, questions about sex, and sibling relations, they are notable because some also deal with the topics of helping youth choose careers, overcoming prejudice, guiding the gifted child, and others infrequently included in other publications.

The Child Study Association of America publishes pamphlets notable because of their consistently high professional quality. While their advanced intellectual level may make them unsuitable for parents of limited education, they gain the distinction of setting standards for pamphlet preparation in certain other parent education organizations.

Another program is that of the Louisiana Society for Mental Health under the direction of Loyd Rowland. This program uses a series of pamphlets (*Pierre the Pelican*) in letter form, which are mailed to parents of newborn babies within the state. Some 12 million pamphlets of this type have been distributed during the past ten years and more than 10 per cent of all parents of first-born children in the United States have received the series through various state health departments or other public health groups. This pamphlet series is notable for the reason stated in Chapter V: since the age of the child is known from birth records, the mailings can be timed to anticipate the occurrence of a given developmental stage, with the hope that the parent is thus educated and prepared for its onset, rather than having to seek such education because of anxiety or failure *after* the developmental stage has occurred.

Under government auspices the outstanding examples are the publications of the Children's Bureau (Department of Health, Education, and Welfare) and the publications of the state extension services of the Department of Agriculture. These are important because of their tremendous distribution; they probably have influenced the greatest number of parents. Publications of the former include the well-known *Infant Care:* Your Child from One to Six, and about 20 more, including a series for parents of children with special disabilities. Publications of the state extension services number about 500 different titles. The reason for this large number (and resulting duplication) is that each state extension service must write its own materials for distribution rather than purchase and distribute existing materials.

3. Magazines and Newspapers. The extent and variety of magazine material for parents is shown by the following examples. *Parents' Magazine*, a commercial venture, has been a notable financial success. Its current circulation is almost two million, and it is recognized by professionals as having acceptable content. *Baby Talk, Your New Baby*, and *Baby Care Manual* each has a distribution of about half a million. They differ from *Parents' Magazine* in laying greater emphasis upon the physical care and safety of the infant and young child. The magazine of the National Congress of Parents and Teachers, the *National Parent-Teacher*, is available through subscription to the more than nine million members of the National Congress. It carries guides for discussion groups, special articles, and regular features prepared by experts in a variety of fields relating to child development.

The magazine *Child Study*, published by the Child Study Association of America, is notable for the same reason as the organization's pamphlets, namely, its consistently high professional quality. Each issue is usually devoted to a specific topic such as prejudice, children's reading, and the like. Although the circulation of this magazine is quite limited compared to the others mentioned, its high standards are important.

Other magazines carrying significant parent education material include *Ladies' Home Journal*, *Family Circle*, *Woman's Day*, and the defunct *Woman's Home Companion*.

Parent education materials in newspapers appear in both local and nationally syndicated columns, which have an immense, if incxactly known, readership. Indeed, even the number of such columns has yet to be enumerated, but their number is great. Examples of well-known columns are those of Dorothy Barclay in the *New York Times*, and the syndicated column of Frances L. Ilg and Louise B. Ames of the Gesell Institute.

4. Plays. The presentation of plays dealing with family or parent-child themes has had a limited but recognized use as an educational method. Ordinarily, such plays are used in conjunction with subsequent group discussion. The plays which have had greatest use have been prepared by one group in the main, the American Theater Wing Community Plays. Many, but not all, of these plays deal with family problems.

An outstanding example of the use of plays is the program of the Division of Mental Hygiene of the state of Ohio. The Division maintains several traveling repertory companies which are available to any organization in the state, if the latter is willing to provide both an audience of forty or more and a discussion leader for subsequent group discussion. This has been widely used in the state.

5. Films. Although films had been used in parent education for some time, it was not until after World War II that they became an important parent education method. Today films ordinarily are used in accompaniment with other methods, primarily that of group discussion. Their audiences do not equal those of published materials; nevertheless, films have been viewed by an impressive number of persons. For example, statistics indicate that during 1957 some one hundred thousand persons from the state of Kansas saw mental health films. A substantial proportion of these films, certainly the majority, were devoted to family and parent education programs, rather than to services for the mentally ill.

Examples of the organizations producing film are the National Film Board of Canada; universities, such as the University of Oklahoma, which have their own film division; the Mental Health Film Board in New York City; and, as a commercial enterprise, the McGraw-Hill Text Films. Films are sponsored and distributed through state departments or some divisions of state departments of health, education, mental hygiene, or mental health; through local mental health associations, public libraries, and university divisions, such as the New York University Film Library and Columbia University's Center for Mass Communication.

6. Lectures. Lectures as a method of parent education have been used for a long time and they play a significant role in many parent education programs and occur in a variety of contexts. The usual pattern of use of lectures is for an organization, such as a local parent-teacher association, to ask a speaker to present materials in the area of parent education. Most often the lecturer is obtained from one of the many organizations involved in parent education. University extension services, local mental health associations, and various local social work agencies will provide speakers upon demand to groups interested in this topic.

An innovation here is the production of tape recordings of lectures, running from fifteen to thirty minutes in length, on a variety of topics. These are made by the Institute of Child Welfare, University of Minnesota, and the Department of Extension Teaching at Cornell University (13). The tapes are available to organizations with parent education programs to provide the basis for subsequent group discussion and serve much the same function as a personal appearance lecture in parent education programs, with the "question and answer period" replaced by group discussion.

7. Radio and Television. Radio never has had more than minor usage as a mass media method in parent education, in spite of the considerable attention it received in the 1930's (26). Few parent education programs established then have lasted. However, notable among the enduring noncommercial programs is one under the direction of Alice Sowers, presented in connection with the University of Oklahoma. Currently on commercial stations there are from time to time radio discussion programs in parent education, and on WTIC (Hartford) there is a fifteen-minute lecture program, answering questions sent in, which is conducted by a private school headmaster. This serves to underscore the absence of larger programs.

Turning to television, there are two types of commercial programs. One has the primary objective of educating parents; for example, in the past several years Benjamin Spock presented such a program. The other type has entertainment as its aim, but has relevance for parent education because family life is the theme. In certain locales, interested members of parent-teacher associations watch a program together (for example, "Father Knows Best"), and then discuss its implications for child rearing.

Noncommercial parent education programs have been presented under auspices of the Metropolitan Educational Television Association (New York City) whose discussion series "Problems of Everyday Living," included parent education. Major universities, such as the University of Minnesota, televise courses in child development; parents can enroll in the course by correspondence for university credit, and the enrollment has been substantial, numbering in the many thousands. The University of Southern California televised a course in child development with an estimated audience of one hundred thousand persons (28). A similar program at the University of Colorado consisted of nine thirty-minute sessions on child development. The presentation was sponsored by the University and the Colorado Congress of Parents and Teachers (66).

8. Screening, Reviewing, and Distributing Mass Media Materials. A very important aspect of the use of mass media as a parent education method is the work done by organizations active in parent education which do not deal directly with parents as consumers, but rather serve as suppliers to parent education organizations. The functions performed by these organizations are to screen the good from the bad in current materials, for example, books, films, and pamphlets from among the many being published; to provide reviews of books, films, and plays for organizations so that they then can choose those they want; and to procure and distribute materials on a cost basis to parent education organizations.

Notable among these is the Mental Health Materials Center, which operates primarily in the area of pamphlet materials and films. Parent education is an important aspect of its program. The Center, for example, distributes packages of materials which include pamphlets and information about films six times a year to a number of subscribers. Twenty-five hundred persons or organizations subscribe. They include perhaps 40 per cent of all family service associations in the country, and of the 2,500 subscribers, about 25 to 30 per cent are church educational organizations. The Center also fills special orders for materials which in number far exceed subscription materials. For example, the Division of Mental Hygiene of the state of Ohio may order 20 thousand of a given item at a time; some other organizations may purchase 150 thousand copies of a pamphlet.

The screening and reviewing of materials at the Mental Health Materials Center is done by a group of highly trained and respected consultants, who ordinarily would not be available to the smaller parent education organizations. The result is to raise the general quality of mass media materials used in parent education as a whole by a more careful screening.

A number of other organizations are active in the screening, reviewing, and distributing process. The educational division of the National Association for Mental Health provides these services, selecting through its panel of consultants materials for distribution to its many member organizations. The Association for Family Living in Chicago and the St. Louis Mental

Health Association are active in selecting pamphlets and in making them available. With respect to books, the Child Study Association of America regularly publishes a list of selected books for parents, classified and annotated. Selective lists of children's books constitute another important enterprise: active organizations are the American Library Association, the Child Study Association of America, and large city public libraries, which usually have their own lists.

Individual Counseling Procedures

Individual counseling ranks second to mass media and ahead of group discussion in the number of parents it reaches. Counseling is regularly associated with the practice of a number of professions of widely varied background. It follows that the same term "counseling" may be used to refer to activities which are quite different. One important context in which parent counseling occurs is that of health services; for example, pediatric or general practice counseling, and public health and visiting nurse consultation. Another significant setting for individual counseling is the schools. Counseling occurs at the elementary and secondary school level in connection with conferences with teachers, often centering around report cards, or is done by guidance counselors, psychologists, and social caseworkers who are employed by the school system. At the kindergarten and preschool level these programs are significantly greater.

Counseling is offered to parents as a service by educational, religious, and social welfare organizations as a service in its own right. For example, the Institute of Child Welfare, University of Minnesota, has a parents' consultant service. The Child Study Association of America has a short-term counseling program. Some family social work agencies offer counseling in addition to therapeutic services. Clergymen and other church related personnel are in a strategic position to counsel, and do carry on individual counseling to a significant extent.

Compared to the distinctions between mass media methods, which parallel the different types of physical transmission of information, or the distinctions between types of group discussion procedures, based on variations of size, leadership, content, and others, there has been little theoretical attention given to the classification of different counseling procedures.

Most of the work on counseling has dealt with the distinction between education and therapy, which we have already discussed in detail in prior chapters. Therapeutic counseling, of course, does not belong in an educational program. While there are some organizations in which actual therapeutic counseling occurs under the guise of parent education, this is because of the naivete of the personnel in such organizations. In leading pediatric counseling (e.g., 39), and in counseling in service organizations (48), as in most programs, counseling is used only for those parent-child relations which the counselor believes will respond to education. Educational counseling is thus of necessity limited in goal, in scope, and in depth in contrast to therapy.

Another distinction between types of counseling has been made which is based on how the content is introduced. The difference is whether the counselee comes voluntarily for the specific reason of obtaining counseling (for example, in family agencies) or whether the counseling occurs in connection with other routine services and thus is not sought for its own sake. Examples of the latter are counseling in connection with school participation, as in the cooperative nursery school where the nursery schoolteacher is in continuing contact with the parents, and to a lesser degree in other nurseries and in day-care centers.

A third distinction, perhaps of minor importance, is made between the number of sessions, especially whether it is a single or continuing series of counseling sessions. However, for both the second and third distinctions, the theoretical importance of such classifications has not been adequately spelled out; in the former the implication is that there are differences in parent motivation, while in the latter there are implications for the amount of change that can be produced.

Types of Group Discussion Methods

Group discussion procedures used in parent education must be distinguished from two other methods of producing change in people through group participation. One of these is group therapy, and since the education-therapy distinction was clarified before, no more need be said here. The second seeks to improve people's competence in working with others by focusing on their behavior in groups, making them conscious of the role they are playing, and of the motives they have. This is sometimes referred to as training in "group dynamics." The difference between this and parent group discussion procedures is discussed by Frank (21) and is put succinctly by Auerbach in her very important theoretical paper (3, pp. 1–2) as follows: "We are focusing specifically on the experience of parents meeting under skilled professional leadership in small discussion groups. . . . The attention of the members is not focused directly on the group process or the roles they play in it. While there is reason to believe that if they learn to function more effectively in a group, they may function more effectively in other human relations; their primary purpose in coming is to become better parents, not better group members." It is the former aim which is the function of the parent discussion group and the latter aim, that is, becoming better group members, which belongs to training in "group dynamics."

The group discussion procedures themselves can be classified according to a number of characteristics of group *structure* and group *process*. Considering *structure* first, there are differences in the composition of groups regarding sex, age, education, intellect, and culture, as well as the actual homogeneity or heterogeneity of a given group in regard to these characteristics. Programs vary in terms of their choices of group composition, such as having parents of children of a similar age versus children of different ages, or having the groups composed of fathers and mothers in contrast to mothers only. Group structure also includes several "administrative" matters such as how large the group should be, and the desirable number and length of meetings.

Turning now to group *process*, one aspect of process is the same as that discussed for individual counseling, that is, how the content is introduced. The differences here are among the most significant in group discussion procedures. In some organizations, such as the Child Study Association of America, the content is derived from the interests and concerns of the participants; it is developed through parents sharing their knowledge and their experiences with their children, with the leader helping the group to look at the different aspects of the topics under discussion, and adding information as necessary. In other educational programs the discussion centers on content introduced through a mass media procedure, whether a lecture, a film, a play, or the like, as is the case in the St. Louis Mental Health Association and the Association for Family Living. In some programs, such as the Parent Education Project of the University of Chicago, the content comes from previously prepared study outlines and readings which provide the basis for discussion. In other organizations, such as cooperative nursery schools, it is direct observation of one's own children in interaction with other children that provides the basis for subsequent group discussion, although this mode of introducing content is more frequently used with individual counseling. Still others, as in certain local parent-teacher association programs, generate content for discussion through using role playing of parent-child episodes.

A second fundamental aspect of group process involves the qualifications and training of leaders and the leadership techniques utilized. There are programs using leaders with professional backgrounds (clinical psychologists) but with no special training in group discussion leadership, as in the program of the Child Guidance League in Brooklyn, New York. Others use as discussion leaders persons who are trained as leaders but who do not necessarily have a professional background. These include programs of the Parent Education Project and the St. Louis Mental Health Association described above. Organizations using trained leaders differ in the amount of training they deem necessary, providing a further differentiation. Another type of parent education program uses leaders with a professional background who also have been trained with regard to content and leadership skills, for example, the Child Study Association of America. There seems to be no organization of recognized standing which uses as a group discussion leader a person who has neither professional background nor some training in leadership techniques, although this may occur in some organizations with limited resources and understanding.

Historical Changes

At the present time there are no data which permit any conclusive statements about changes in methodology. The data could be obtained but the task of preparing comparative statistics is a formidable one and probably the question is not important enough to make the effort worthwhile. As a consequence, the few paragraphs which follow on historical changes are based upon informal statements by a number of prominent parent educators who have been active in the field over the past generation.

The first observation is that there seems to have been only a few new techniques developed. The White House Conference report (72) a generation ago discussed the parent education methods of lectures, group discussions, radio programs, films, supervised observation of children, nursery school participation, individual counseling, and printed material. To these have been added television (66), role playing in conjunction with group discussion (54, vol. 62), and a few other minor innovations, for example, joint meetings of children and parents (24). However, even the method of joint meetings of children and parents had been discussed by Lindeman and Thurston (45) as early as 1931.

Some time ago (55) it was said that parent education seems to have devised no special methods of its own, but rather has drawn its techniques from other fields as they have developed. Goller (23) has shown how this was true in the case of group discussion procedures, with parent education drawing on group methods in the fields of adult education, therapy, social work, and others. Perhaps it is necessarily the case, since parent education is less a profession in its own right than a general means of influence employed by practitioners from a variety of professional backgrounds, and therefore reflects the professional methods of all, with great diversity as a consequence.

In regard to changes in methods, a recent critical appraisal of organizations serving families (19, p. 128) has said that their programs have moved from moral exhortation, to individual counseling and therapy, to procedures adapted to work with groups. This does not seem to have been the case in the parent education field. The survey by Witmer (73) of the methods used by major parent educational organizations some twenty-five years ago indicated that the largest percentage of organizations by persons in the field suggest that the use of study groups has been part of the parent education movement throughout its span of professional life, and as indicated in the Appendix, the earliest records dating from 1830 involve study group procedures. Caution has been suggested by some in interpreting Witmer's data, who say that the current discussion group procedures are advanced far beyond the study groups of these earlier years. Even granting this, the fact is that group methods have been part of parent education long before their vogue in adult education and other fields.

Change in the relative emphasis given to different methods seems to have gone in the direction of greater use of group procedures, with auxiliary content, such as films and plays, and with a corresponding decline in lectures. Recent volumes of the *Proceedings* of the National Congress of Parents and Teachers (54) indicate that the number of child study groups in the local member associations varies from under 20 in the smallest state to between three and four thousand groups in one of the large states; the large state has over 150 thousand members enrolled in such child study groups. The recent volumes of these *Proceedings* indicate that the child study groups are making increasing use of films and skits and that the parent-teacher association programs in general are decreasing their use of lectures and films and readings alone without discussion.

THE BASIC CHOICE: MASS MEDIA, COUNSELING, OR GROUP DISCUSSION

The rational choice of methods from the variety named above should maximize the attainment of the goals of the program. One selects methods judged most likely to achieve the working aims of the program, given certain classes of content to be transmitted and certain clientele to be reached. It follows that since many programs differ considerably in their working goals, clientele, and content, they would choose different methods on the grounds that some are more suitable for their kind of content (for example, mass media for factual information), or for their kind of clientele (for example, individual counseling for persons who need immediate and specific help).

Actually, the choice of methods by educational programs has not been logical or scientifically based. One reason advanced for this is that realistic limitations of method may arise from characteristics of the program, such as problems of space, money, and personnel. But it has been pointed out (13) that no program need want for excellent free printed material, films, or other media. Also, it is possible for numbers of nonprofessional persons to obtain brief training in group leadership, for example, from state education departments. It must be granted, however, that the unavailability of professional personnel may force a program to use lay leaders for discussion groups, and make it impossible to carry on individual counseling.

Still, the fundamental source of nonrational selection of method is something else. It is the virtual absence of data on the effectiveness of different methods, on how useful they are in achieving the variety of objectives, under different conditions of content and clientele. In the absence of scientific knowledge relating means to ends, the choice of means often depends on hunch, inspiration, imitation, or other similar factors. One effort to overcome this has been to rely on research on the effectiveness of these different methods in other fields of endeavor (such as public health education, or wartime propaganda). This research has been drawn into the vacuum and used to justify choice of one or another method in parent education. But theory and research drawn from allied fields can at most provide hypotheses about the efficiency of methods in parent education. The hypotheses then need to be tested in studies conducted in parent education itself, since there are a number of fundamental differences between parent education and other social change endeavors and the results may not be the same. For example, it is questionable extrapolation of findings to move from the results of studies of *ad hoc* problem-solving groups (27) consisting of college sophomores who meet once, to groups of parents who meet in a continuing group where the goal is diffuse, even different for each participant, and the orientation need not be one of "problem-solving."

Most likely certain methods *do* have greater efficiency when used with certain kinds of content and certain kinds of persons (23), but in parent education this has not been clearly demonstrated. The facts are that the choice of methods to be used, given certain aims, content, and clientele, is at best based on trial and error experience and common sense, and at worst on fadism and unthinking perpetuation of tradition.

In the sections which follow, the task is to review the theoretical arguments regarding the choice of methods and to appraise examples of the evidence which exists in other fields and the degree of its relevance.

The Use of Mass Media

In the arguments regarding the use of mass media, one may distinguish four foci of interest. The first of these is the straightforward and unchallenged observation, favoring the use of mass media, that of all techniques of education they have the lowest cost per capita of delivering units of information.

The second point concerns the motivation of parents reached through mass media. On the one hand, the advocates of mass media point out that such media are able to reach into the home and influence parents who do not participate in either counseling or discussion groups; they are more likely to reach parents not reached by the other two methods. No one seems to have contradicted this. However, the point is often made that the parents reached by mass media techniques are those with a low level of interest or motivation, so that even though they are exposed to mass media, the influence upon their behavior is negligible since they are not motivated to look at the material, to read it, or to accept the information. One can hardly deny that parents who have taken the initiative to seek counseling, or to join discussion groups to study child rearing, have demonstrated a level of motivation higher than those who have not made such efforts. There are several contrary criticisms, however; one is that many parents *have* taken the initiative in obtaining mass media material; have written for pamphlets, bought books, and the like. Even where the education is unsolicited, for example, booklets given free, other points are made. One of these is that research (64) shows that motivation may become so high that it interferes with attention and learning, and that a more moderate level of motivation is more conducive to learning. Thus, it may be that for the average parent the written word or picture falls upon fertile ground. In the absence of data in parent education regarding the relation between levels of parent motivation and learning, one should not conclude that if a parent does not join a group program, or seek counseling, his motivation is too low to learn anything.

Another contrary criticism regarding motivation is that parent motivation should not be viewed as a general and diffuse thing but as quite changeable through time and between different child-rearing situations. At any given time a parent may be strongly motivated to get information about one aspect of child care but unmotivated about another. As we have pointed out, Loyd Rowland of the Louisiana Society for Mental Health takes this view in distributing the *Pierre the Pelican* pamphlet series. Knowing the age of the children involved, the content is made to coincide with concerns of parents typical for children of that age. Moreover, for the printed materials, in contrast to lectures, television, and radio, another point follows. Even if pamphlets and books reach the parent at times when the content is of little interest, they may be retained so that when a specific interest in a subject matter does arise (because of maturation of the child or other changes in the family situation) the parent can turn to the material with a high level of motivation (1, p. 140). The humor in the familiar example of the parent "looking it up in the book" has masked its significance; namely, that the motivation represented by the effort of looking it up is indicative of a fertile ground for learning from the printed material. The use of mass media to provide a repository of information that the parent can turn to when needed would seem to be an important function.

The third focus of interest for theories of mass media is their relative effectiveness with different kinds of content. A common argument is that mass media may be suitable for transmitting factual information or the simple home management type of principles, but are ineffective in transmitting attitudinal, motivational, or value material. We have stressed that there is a virtual absence of research data comparing the effectiveness of different methods of education of parents. The one experimental study by Schaus is reviewed in Chapter IX. It reports that more information is learned from participation in group discussion procedures than from listening to lectures.

The research data which are cited on the comparative values of mass media and other techniques come instead from other fields. These studies need not be reviewed here, for excellent reviews are available. In Hovland's appraisal (29) he concludes that face-to-face communication is almost universally reported to be more effective than is radio. Bond's review (9) of the data from studies of the past twenty years, as well as her own research, indicates that the discussion techniques produce greater change in attitudes and behavior than do mass media techniques (usually lectures, sometimes printed materials). The data show further that even excellent mass informational programs often fail, because they tend to reach only those persons with preexisting favorable attitudes and fail to reach the very persons for whom the campaign is intended, that is, the uninterested. However, one notes there also are examples of the ineffectiveness of excellent group discussion and counseling programs.

There has been so much reliance (certainly beyond what is justified) upon Lewin's study of changing food habits (44) to support the use of group discussion procedures in parent education as well as in other fields that it deserves special mention. A few years ago Bennett (7) in a study similar to Lewin's obtained results which suggest that this prior research had confounded the group discussion versus lecture comparison with a variable that might be described as commitment to change versus noncommitment to change, and that "commitment" was being asked of subjects more frequently in a group discussion than in the lecture situation. In her findings she reports that two factors, namely, group discussion and public commitment, were found to be *nonessential* in changing behavior; and that two other factors, an individual commitment to change and a conception that there was a group consensus regarding attempt to change increased likelihood that the individual himself would change.

In general, one might say that while the data favor the arguments regarding the lesser effectiveness of mass media in changing the more emotionally toned characteristics of the adult personality, the definitive experiments have yet to be made. The advocates of mass media frequently respond by granting the conclusion that there are limitations on the changes which mass media produce, but argue that one can be content to efficiently transmit factual data and simple unemotional child-care practices, because it has yet to be shown that deeper changes in parent attitudes and motivation are more important for children's emotional health. And, even if this is shown to be true, the argument still remains that the low cost of producing gains in knowledge makes even this less important change worth accomplishing.

The fourth and final focus of theories of use of mass media is the allegation that they cause misunderstandings, increase anxiety which cannot be worked through, result in maladaptation of ideas to the parents' specific situations, and other undesirable consequences. It is pointed out that discussion of parent-child relations can create a great deal of affect (49); that the use of films can increase the tenseness and anxiousness of an audience (4); that the use of methods where materials cannot be adapted to known resistance of parents, to their needs, or to their initial level of understanding, results in errors and misunderstandings (26). Many have concluded that mass media materials should be accompanied in every case by the opportunity for discussion which permits the elimination of errors, the dissipation of anxiety, the adaptation of the materials to the parent's specific situation. Early efforts in this direction were the use of question periods following lectures, but here only a few at best could have their questions answered, and even then one must assume that the surface meaning of the question was all that was intended. More modern programs make use of group discussion following films or lectures, or in conjunction with the study of written materials.

There seem to be no counterarguments to this probable defect in the use of mass media except one, yet that is a powerful one; namely, that there has not been any systematic scientific demonstration that mass media, more than other methods, increase parental anxiety, misinformation, and rigid application of ideas.

The Use of Counseling

The use of individual counseling as a parent education method had somewhat the status of a *fait accompli*, since it was a natural part of the interaction of parents with persons in various professional contexts. The parent's relations with the clergyman, the pediatrician, and the general practitioner, the pediatric and the public health nurse, and, of course, the kindergarten and elementary schoolteacher, have provided natural settings in which parental questions regarding the child and counseling on the part of the professional have inevitably occurred. Some critics have raised the question of whether it is desirable to permit this *fait accompli* to continue; of whether it is the proper role for the clergy and pediatricians to counsel the parents in regard to, respectively, the nonspiritual and the nonphysical aspects of child care. But examinations of the problem find ample argument in favor of this natural counseling procedure, and most effort has thus taken the form of clarifying the theory regarding counseling, and of improving the educational skills of these professional persons, so that a greater advantage might be taken of this natural situation.

Each method has its strong advocates. For counseling, Baruch (6, p. 39) states: "Individual conferences constitute probably the most important method in parent education." It has been held that counseling can only approximate the values of mass media in some respects, but can equal or surpass them in others; and that while it may be inferior to the use of group discussion in some matters, it is superior to it on other counts. The various issues involved might be stated as follows.

With respect to efficiency in reaching parents (the matter of cost per capita), it is pointed out that though counseling is clearly more costly than mass media techniques, nevertheless much of the counseling occurs in the context of other professional services already paid for, so that there is little additional cost for the professional to carry on parent education.

With respect to restrictions on content, it appears that in contrast to mass media, there are none for individual counseling. It was noted that many hold that mass media serve well in the role of presenting factual information, but not affective materials. Individual counseling not only should do as well in presenting facts, but is a face-to-face interaction situation which research from other fields indicates is more effective in changing attitudes and motives.

Regarding possible undesirable consequences of the kind alleged to occur from the use of mass media, individual counseling is able to correct misinformation, to help alleviate anxiety, and to adapt content to specific parental situations. Some would say that it must be inferior to group techniques in this respect, because the counselor alone does not have so much background in parental needs and experience as do the group members with their combined resources. We return to this matter in the following section.

The more important theoretical considerations in the use of counseling have focused on the characteristic motives of parents in a counseling situation. There are several points to consider. First, counseling like mass media may be addressed to parents with relatively little interest when the counseling occurs in connection with some other professional service such as routine health checkups. If it seems that the parent may profit from counseling, the physician may undertake this, whether the parent is "motivated" or not to have asked for advice. A parallel therefore exists to the situation in which the relatively uninterested parent is exposed to content presented by mass media. In the less frequent case, where the counseling occurs as a primary service and where the parent must take the initiative to obtain counseling, as in some family organizations and in independent institutions like the Child Study Association of America (48), the motivation of the parent must be quite high; probably higher than that of parents participating in discussion groups. An interesting study would be to compare the results of counseling under the two conditions of low and high motivation just described.

A second important point is the following. If parent motivation *is* variable in strength and nature, if it is a concern with specific situations at certain times rather than a constant concern with the general area of child rearing, counseling provides the opportunity for meeting this variable interest. The parent is able to obtain counseling on a specific subject at the time when his motivation is high; for example, the parent can discuss his problem with a physician or a teacher. This parallels the case for mass media, where he can turn to printed material when the need arises, and contrasts with the discussion group situation, where the interests of the group may not coincide with his specific concern of the moment.

A third point regarding motivation is that many parents are so reserved or timid, or have interests they feel are so personal, that they cannot discuss them in a group context (17). This in no way means that these concerns are therapeutic problems and consequently beyond the realm of education. Rather it is to say that some individuals are embarrassed about discussing some aspects of their family life and their feelings about their children, and thus find them not suitable for group presentation. In such cases, the more intimate counseling situation would provide a more effective method of education. This point would gain in importance if further research shows that a large number of parents feel more comfortable in a one-to-one professional-client counseling relation for discussions of their children than they do taking part in discussion groups with other parents.

The Use of Group Discussion Procedures

The greatest amount of existing theoretical work on major parent education methods concerns the use of group discussion procedures. The focus of much of it is the superiority of group procedures over mass media, especially printed material. The understanding of individual counseling has benefited from the analysis of group procedures, for the two have many points in common.

It is not clear why the greater interest in group procedures exists. Perhaps the use of group discussion requires considerably more effort than does individual counseling, and is substantially less efficient in the ratio of effort to number of persons reached than are mass media, so that it may appear to require special justification as a method. In addition, the emphasis on group discussion may have arisen in response to research on motives and attitudes during the 1930's, and the development of clinical theory, especially from 1920 on, both of which raised a number of questions about the effectiveness of impersonal methods such as books and lectures, and thus led one to look for new techniques.

Most of the theory regarding parent discussion groups has been borrowed from other fields and applied to parent education (23). Important sources used by parent educators include Cantor's *Learning Through Discussion* (11) and books by Leigh (41) and by Pigors (60); work in the therapeutic field by Moreno (51) and Slavson (62) also was influential.

Some of the arguments against the use of discussion groups have been mentioned in connection with counseling or mass media procedures. One is that the per capita cost of instruction is highest for discussion group procedures. Another is that the discussion group technique teaches a small and highly selected segment of the population of parents. Parents in discussion groups are self-selected in terms of motivational characteristics which at the present time are unknown. It seems likely that their general level of interest in child care is higher than that of other parents, although as pointed out earlier, the most highly motivated may be too anxious to come to such discussion groups. Parents are also self-selected according to sociability and willingness to talk over somewhat personal matters in a public situation. A third criticism is that the typical discussion group, no matter how the matter for discussion is introduced, does not deal with the interests of all members in a group at the same time, but rather those of the majority. The level of interest of some specific members may thus be low. This is to say that the discussion group procedure is not so adaptable to the changes in area of motivational concern of the parent as is a repository of mass media materials to which the parent can turn in time of need, or an individual counseling procedure available on demand.

On the other side are important arguments favoring group discussion. One is that group discussion, even while remaining educational, while staying at the conscious level and not actively seeking to deal with parent anxieties or defenses, nevertheless can reduce anxiety and hostility and relax the defenses so that significant changes in attitude and feelings occur. This results from participation in free discussion with other parents about child rearing, which permits the parents to make full expression of their feelings under nonpunitive conditions. Through airing these concerns and having them accepted by others, and listening to other parents express the same kinds of concern, beneficial results occur. The parents see their own feelings as being less deviant, as being nothing to be ashamed of, as being shared by a host of parents, so that if they are normal parents they are able to confront their feelings directly for the first time and deal with them in a constructive way. Freed of tension in the group setting, the parents then are better able to consider changes in child-care practices (3, 49, 50, p. 34, 56). In addition, the active participation and involvement in the discussion, shown in other fields (29) to enhance learning, probably also contribute to a more significant change.

Another favorable point made for the use of discussion groups is their alleged superiority in enriching each member's repertory of solutions to specific child-rearing situations, since these solutions emerge in the group discussion and represent the varying success and failure of a number of parents in child care; and since the discussion helps each parent to see several sides to the issue, including the child's. It has been noted, however, that this characteristic of group discussion need not be unique, since a mass media publication easily could illustrate a variety of superior applications of a general child-care principle, so that the parent's resources are as greatly enriched as if he drew upon the experience of members of a discussion group. Proponents of group discussion respond that while this may be true, it still does not permit a detailed spelling out, in verbal interchange, of various approaches to what may be a person's unique family situation.

Another and related argument is that group discussion is a superior means for reaching a solution to any specific child-rearing problem presented by a member, in that the resources of many parents can be drawn upon (e.g., 12). This point of view has been given extreme statement. For example: "Evidence is quite conclusive that the best thinking occurs in small groups; probably a group of five is an ideal size." (16, p. 22) However, considerable evidence on group versus individual problem-solving (46) indicates that this statement and this general point of view are not necessarily true. The superiority of group or individual problem-solving depends on a large number of variables such as the level of skill of the group members and the type of problem. While at first glance it appears that the efforts of the parents to handle a specific child-care situation would be improved by discussing it with others, the evidence implies that for some parents this would be a waste of time since their own solution might be superior to any which is recommended by the group.

There are arguments favorable to the use of groups which have received considerably less examination, and are mentioned here in order to complete the picture. It is suggested, for example, that although in parent discussion groups the emphasis is on content rather than mode of participation, participation in a discussion group with a democratic and tolerant leader may stimulate members to behave toward their children in this democratic way (3, pp. 6–7). Also, participation in discussion groups may help to free them from timidity in expressing their own opinion, so that they become more expressive in their relations with their children. This view assumes, of course, that more democracy and expressiveness are desirable in the parent-child relation.

An additional point is advanced by Foote and Cottrell (19, pp. 132–133), who point out that discussion groups serve as an example of "quasi-families," which may have an important function where the actual family has failed, or where it is not supportive of the aims and understandings of the parent. The group may provide support in maintaining his current child-rearing practices in the face of family opposition or support in undertaking changes if this is the wiser choice. The fact that this often produces conflict of parent and parent educator with other members of the family has already been discussed in Chapter III.

To summarize this section, there are no research data which indicate the effectiveness of the different methods and choice must be made instead on the basis of theories outlined above. The care with which organizations choose their methods varies greatly. In some cases, for example, the Child Study Association of America, multiple methods are used because theory indicates separate advantages for each. These also may be complementary, as in referrals of parents from discussion groups to counseling, and the reverse, depending on their interests and needs. In other instances, multiple methods are employed in duplicative effort with little analysis of their separate functions or of the advantages that might follow. The indiscriminate use of a variety of methods also must reflect the lack of specification of goals in certain programs.

If the future brings more research comparing the outcomes of different methods of parent education, and if there is a clarification of aims of parent education programs, it would then follow that more careful choices of methodology could be made, and also that greater specialization among parent education organizations could occur.

THE SPECIFIC CHOICES: VARIATIONS WITHIN EACH METHOD

Choices Among Mass Media Procedures

It is surprising to find no handbook, manual, or primary theoretical work regarding the preparation and use of mass media materials in parent education. Such manuals or handbooks, or even full book-length analyses, exist for other methods. This is true even though they have been less studied, on the whole, than mass media. There is no question that the full analysis of the use of mass media in parent education would be especially valuable.

There are two ways to look at the variations within mass media procedures. One is in terms of the different media themselves. The other is in terms of the characteristic ways in which content is presented, such as emotional versus logical appeals, the use of positive versus negative statements, and so on. Unfortunately, few examples of programs using one or another variation can be given, because many programs do not make such a differentiation, and for others the data have not been reported.

Considering first the choice among the various media themselves, there is little research in parent education to guide one in his selection, and no comprehensive discussion of their merits in the parent education literature. As we have said, however, the research from other fields is large in volume. For example, Hovland's comprehensive review (29) of studies of effectiveness indicates that an oral presentation (radio, lecture, or other such type) is more effective in changing opinion than printed material; and that films seem to be about equal to "an instructor" in bringing about gains in factual knowledge and concepts. Whether such conclusions would be true in the field of parent education remains to be seen. For example, regarding the superiority of oral presentation, recall that in the field of parent education the printed material often is kept in reserve until it becomes relevant to the parent's current interest, at which time it might be more influential than the same data presented orally at an earlier time when the motivation level was low. Certainly research on different effects of mass media in parent education is needed and this point is discussed at length in Chapter IX.

Another aspect of choice between the media themselves is not their effects but rather whom they reach. What audience is best reached by books and magazines in contrast to television, or by films in contrast to lectures? Hovland points out that studies conducted in other fields tend to be confidential, since they have been made by commercial organizations, and that many suffer from poor sampling procedures and designs. There seem to be no data within the field of parent education itself. It will be recalled that in Chapter V data were given on parents reached by the different major methods, for example, mass media versus discussion groups, but that there were no comparative studies of variations within a given method. In sum, in the absence of empirical information regarding audiences reached, decisions about mass media continue to be regulated by matters of cost, expediency, and personal conviction.

Turning now to variations in mass media which concern characteristics of the communication they give, a number have been identified in experimental research. While only a few can be mentioned, those so noted are considered important for the field of parent education and could be given more attention in program planning.

One concerns the type of appeal made by mass media material, emotional versus rational. Existing research data (29) indicate no consistent superiority of effect of one or the other procedure. However, the theory and research regarding the type of appeal to be made in mass media have their roots in the study of propaganda, and return us to the ethical questions raised in Chapter IV. Were studies to show that even under some conditions, emotional appeal rather than appeal to evidence produced effects held desirable by the parent education program, would this justify its use? Is the appeal to emotion consonant with the achievement of ends held by some parent education programs of increasing the independence and rationality of their clients?

A second characteristic of the mass media communication which has been mentioned in parent education, and on which work has been done in related fields, concerns whether the communication should be positive or negative in tone. Again, the research data (29) are mixed in their indication of the superior effectiveness of one or the other approach. In parent education there has been a clear change from a strong negative emphasis of a generation or more ago to a positive emphasis. This is exemplified by the criteria of acceptability used for the text of the publications of the United States Children's Bureau. One reason advanced for the historical use of negative statements is that the parent educator at first believed he knew that certain things were wrong, without knowing what to suggest as substitutes. As Lemkau and others (42) point out, this left the process of finding out what is right to the creative capacities of the reader.

The theoretical argument for this change has been that negative statements such as "do not do x, because" aroused the parents' apprehension concerning events which could occur. The belief is that most parents who read, view, or hear the communication already have a comparatively high level of motivation and do not need to be further aroused by frightening statements or warnings. Moreover, research by Janis and Feshbach (35) shows that if anxiety (fear) rises too high then the communication is not attended to. In total, this suggests that positive statements to parents already strongly motivated may be the most effective, leaving open the possibility that the negative approach is necessary where this motivation does not exist; that is, statements positive and negative in tone can be used according to the characteristics of the recipient.

A third aspect of the mass media communication, and the one receiving most attention from parent educators, concerns the intellectual level of the communication, assessed in such terms as the reading ability required to understand the pamphlet. It has been called to the attention of parent educators (68, p. 16) that the mothers of the nearly sixteen million children under five years of age in this country include nearly five million with a grammar school education, or less, and nine million who have completed only one to four years of high school. It follows that users of mass media methods must make their material readily understandable.

Two studies of about a generation ago show the printed material of that time to have a high intellectual level. Witmer (73, p. 48) cites research showing the material then was probably too difficult for more than half of the parent clientele. Ojemann (57) shows that some three-fourths of the material he sampled required ability beyond high school. Several things point to a change toward simplicity, at least in printed material. A study by Weng (71) in 1952 analyzed some 75 national and state pamphlets relating to the feeding of infants and preschool children. The analysis of the reading level of a subsample of 44 pamphlets showed

80 per cent to be at the seventh- or eighth-grade level and the remaining 20 per cent at the ninth or tenth grade, or above. Deliberate efforts to make sure the readability is adequate for the
audience are made by some; for example, the *Pierre the Pelican*
series is pitched at the sixth-grade level and others (e.g., 20) aim
at the sixth-grade level also. It is reported that the Children's
Bureau aims its written material at the tenth-grade level, or in
some instances at the twelfth. While the material directed to an
eighth- or tenth-grade level no doubt is suitable for the greatest
number of parents, it still is somewhat too difficult for the
poorly educated groups, and too elementary and unchallenging
for the better educated parents. Organizations with a large national mass media program and with widely representative clientele have no other course. Organizations with a more specialized
clientele, or definable subgroups within a general clientele, can
make a better adaptation of the material to the parents' educational level. Among the organizations which tailor their mass
media materials to fit the more extreme groups is the Play Schools
Association (New York City), which is one of the few to have
among its parent clientele a number with very limited education.
As a consequence, some of the written material prepared by the
Play Schools Association for use in its programs consists of third-
grade-level paragraph stories. In contrast, the Child Study Association, which is oriented toward the well-educated parent, prepares pamphlet material which is excellent for such parents but
generally is regarded as being too demanding for the average
reader.

As a final example of variations in mass media procedures
from which the parent educator should choose, consider the matter of "order of presentation" of material in the communication.
Much experimental research has been done and some of the generalizations supported by the research data have been set forth in
a recent publication as follows: "When two sides of an issue are
presented successively by different communicators, the side presented first does not necessarily have the advantage. . . . When
contradictory information is presented in a single communication, by a single communicator, there is a pronounced tendency

for those items presented first to dominate the impression received. . . . Presentation of information relevant to the satisfaction
of needs after these needs have been aroused brings about greater
acceptance than an order which presents the information first and
the need-arousal second. . . . Placing communications highly desirable to the recipient first, followed by those less desirable, produces more opinion change than the reverse order." (30, pp. 130–
136)

The parent educator will recognize that these facts present a
dilemma, since once again the findings are couched in terms of the
effectiveness of different ways of persuading a recipient to one's
point of view. Where the aim is not to persuade but to educate,
and in educating to familiarize the parent with different points of
view, how is the communication prepared so as to avoid giving
undue emphasis to some particular position on an issue?

Choices Among Individual Counseling Procedures

The work available on educational counseling consists almost
entirely of descriptive manuals for certain counseling programs,
with some suggestions for improvement of their procedures. At
the beginning of this chapter we noted that the materials presented in these manuals raised few significant issues and described
few differences in counseling practice. Compared to the analysis
of types of mass media and group discussion procedures, the analysis of educational counseling is still at a superficial level. A basic
reason is that educational counseling first has had to clarify its
distinction from therapy, and this has drawn effort away from
analyses of variations in educational counseling procedures themselves.

It follows that any experimental research on the effects of different types of parent education counseling is also nonexistent.
There have been some evaluative studies of counseling in other
areas, which are reviewed in the chapters on counseling in the
Annual Review of Psychology (2) for recent years. These studies constitute an important source of hypotheses for the parent educator.
In addition, the Dollard and Miller analysis (14) of the therapeutic counseling situation in terms of learning theory would

interest the educational counselor because it reveals the contrast with his own procedures. It must be remembered, however, that the theory and results of these studies cannot be directly generalized to educational practice with parents, because the latter is different.

There are only a few reports of parent counseling methods which provide sufficient data for analysis. Baruch (6, chap. 5) presents some long and illuminating protocols of individual counseling sessions of parents in a school situation. Blum (8) has described the educational counseling practices of pediatricians in New York City well-baby clinics; the subjects were 19 physicians and 81 mothers with babies ranging from three weeks of age to two years. Among other findings Blum reported that of the physicians' comments to the mothers, some 68 per cent were neutral, 29 per cent positive, and 3 per cent negative. But the reassuring comments concerned the baby; the reassurances made directly to the mother about her role performance did not occur frequently. Some 75 per cent of these physicians' comments were self-initiated, and 25 per cent were responsive to the mothers' statements. The inference, therefore, is that the mothers' participation is small and that the physicians tend to lecture mothers rather than counsel them. Korsch (39), in a recent article of outstanding value, has described in detail the theory and practice of pediatric counseling as formulated over a number of years by David Levy in the Attitude Change Project under his direction. This approach, which we discuss later, seeks to alleviate the shortcomings of the counseling process as reported by Blum.

The serious theoretical analysis of different types of educational counseling is only now beginning. The half-dozen or so most important theoretical works on educational counseling are centered around counseling in the school situation, in medical settings, or in independent agencies. With respect to counseling of parents by educators the books by Leonard and associates (43), and Langdon and Stout (40) are significant works. In the area of medical services to children the articles by Solnit and Senn (63), by Korsch (39), and the monograph of the American Public Health Association, *Health Supervision of Young Children* (1), are representative of the high quality of work done in this connection. The theoretical article by McClure and Schrier (48), describing the educational counseling service of the Child Study Association of America and its underlying assumptions, is an important contribution to our understanding of counseling procedures.

In these works on the counseling of parents various ideas regarding method are advanced. These include the proposal (48) that counseling should appeal to the parent's strength, rather than work through parent weaknesses; and the emphasis in the Attitude Change Project (39) on utilizing and improving the parent's already thought-out approach to a problem because it will have elements of adaptation to the mother's personality and environment, and thus be more realistic than many new solutions which the pediatrician might suggest. However, ideas such as these have not been developed to the point where they are significant issues in the area of counseling. There is only one which has received sufficient use as a basis of differentiating between counseling programs to warrant more detailed attention here. This is the way in which the content or subject matter of the discussion is introduced.

The differentiation according to source of content developed naturally from the occurrence of counseling in different professional settings. The variations in mode of introduction of content are large. One significant type of program includes counseling services where parent participation is self-initiated and voluntary. This occurs most often in family service organizations. In such programs, an example being that of the Child Study Association of America, the initial introduction of subject matter is by the parent in reference to his self-perceived difficulty with respect to the child; the parent educator does not observe the child or originate the discussion of certain aspects of child care prior to this.

A second type of counseling program is in the familiar professional setting where both the parent and the parent educator have had the opportunity to observe the child; for example, the teacher observing a child in school and the parent at home. The point is that both parent and counselor have a basis for introducing content into the counseling session, and both are justified in initiating the first conference, rather than just the parent, as above. The medical and educational contexts are the most frequent ones in which this occurs.

There is an important class of counseling situations which might be viewed as a subgroup of the one just mentioned, but differs from others in that both the parent and the educator view the child in the identical context. In medical settings, the familiar case is that of the "rooming-in" situation in which the mother and newborn baby are in the same room during her stay in the hospital. This program has been fully developed in New Haven in connection with Yale University and has been described in a series of articles (33, 34, 38). Joint observations of the mother's care of the baby provides a basis for counseling.

This same type of counseling is developed to a much greater extent in cooperative nursery schools (65). In these schools the parents (almost always mothers) observe their children and also work in the school and participate in teaching, under supervision. Both their own actions with the children and observations of their own and other children provide material for a discussion between mother and parent educator, who is usually one of the nursery schoolteachers. The cooperative nursery schools also use discussion group procedures, as noted in the next section, but their more common educational method is counseling. This type of education is argued for as meritorious because it provides the opportunity for actual practice under supervision, and for demonstration by others (70, pp. 48–49; 19, p. 38). Also the point has been made long ago (e.g., 69) that supervised observation of one's own children helps one gain objectivity about developmental stages. But others object to this mode of introducing content for counseling because it subjects the mother to a conflict between her roles as a student and as a mother, and may increase self-consciousness in her performance as a parent to a point where really detrimental effects occur for the parent-child relation.

Katharine Whiteside Taylor has led the development of cooperative nursery schools in this country, and has fully described the schools and their role in parent education (65). Cooperative nursery school programs also have been analyzed in other publications (31, 58, 67). Like many other types of counseling, this was the natural outgrowth of a specific situation, here a cooperative endeavor originally undertaken for predominantly other purposes. At present in some programs the counseling is viewed as the most important reason for establishing the cooperative nursery school.

Each of the aforementioned types of counseling has its adherents, although there exists no research basis for choosing one in contrast to another; that is, there are no facts concerning which parents are reached, and with what effects, by these different counseling practices. There are a number of assumptions which demand attention here. The further theoretical refinement and classification of types of educational counseling, going beyond the excellent beginnings made by Senn, by Schrier and McClure, by Korsch in describing Levy's project, as well as research on the correlates of different counseling procedures, are important ventures for the future.

Group Discussion Procedures

The theory and analysis of group discussion procedures is substantially further advanced than is true for mass media or counseling methods. As stated earlier this is due partly to the fact that the use of discussion groups required a theoretical justification, for it had neither the naturalness of counseling, nor the low cost and high saturation efficiency of mass media. Its greater attention also came from the fact that work in parent education was stimulated by the sizable theoretical literature regarding group process which developed in the adult education, group psychotherapy, and other fields during the past generation. However, actual research evaluating the effects of different group methods is almost nonexistent; at present the research on consequences does not permit one to choose between the several variations on a scientific basis. Instead, each draws its supporters on the basis of theoretical argument or practical experience.

A number of excellent manuals of procedure for parent discussion groups are available (12, 13, 15, 18, 22, 36, 53). Some such as Cheavens (12) are practically oriented, while others such as

Goller (22) go into a careful theoretical analysis of the use of parent groups. Some of the basic issues dealt with in these volumes already have been considered, for example, the education-therapy issue. Other fundamental aspects of discussion group procedures to receive attention here can be grouped under two major headings, group structure and group process.

1. Group Structure. Several aspects of discussion groups which are logically classed as properties of group structure have received attention. One of these concerns the composition of the group in terms of the homogeneity or heterogeneity of members. There are many variables on which group members may or may not be homogeneous, such as sex, age, education, intellect, cultural background, age of children, motives for attendance, existing factual knowledge of child development, personality traits such as general anxiety level, and degree of prior acquaintance, to name but a few that have been mentioned in the literature. Note that the issue raised here is *not* the characteristics of persons who should receive education. Rather the question here concerns the proper mixture of individuals with different kinds of characteristics to enhance the effectiveness of the group discussion procedure.

Studies comparing the effects of a homogeneous with a heterogeneous grouping, holding other matters constant, would seem in order. In the absence of scientific data regarding the effects of different degrees and kinds of homogeneity, one can do little more than cite some of the arguments. It has been pointed out that group homogeneity increases the possibility of developing a cohesive group, of being able to orient the content and method toward a common audience, for example, persons who are equally interested in the same subject matter. Another argument favoring the homogeneous group is that in its opposite, the heterogeneous group, the content must be reduced in difficulty to the lowest common denominator, to the lowest ability level present. In favor of the heterogeneous group are the arguments that through heterogeneity there is greater opportunity to examine cultural value differences in child care, and to draw upon a greater variety of child-care practices so that each parent's knowledge is increased, and also his understanding of the range of variability between individual parents and how he himself compares with others.

A second structural aspect concerns the size of the group considered most desirable. It is hard to say whether the differences between educators constitute a small or a large amount of disagreement. One educator (36) suggests that a group of 25 is ideal. Another (25) suggests 20 to 30 is good. A third (22) states that the range may be from 8 to 22 with about 15 being the most desirable. Still a fourth (12) indicates that between 15 and 25 is usually thought to be ideal. These recommendations and preferences are based on experience, but apparently no one has systematically described the concomitants for the group process and for the parents themselves of using various sized groups. Such data might be available in existing protocols of groups now stored in the files of different parent education organizations, and if so, the facts deserve analysis.

The number and length of meetings have also received attention. In actual practice, discussion group sessions seem to last from forty minutes to more than two hours, and the groups hold from two to more than a dozen meetings, with usually an interval of a week between each meeting. The arguments favoring sessions about an hour and a half in length are that fatigue develops after this length of time, but that if shorter sessions are used, every group member may not have a chance to participate actively and to become involved in the discussion, and also that fruitful development of content is impossible. The arguments favoring a number of consecutive sessions, without lengthy intervals between them, are that it takes time for a group to develop the ability to function and learn together (18) and also that a series of meetings, rather than one, provides the opportunity to organize new knowledge and to develop a consistent point of view. That is, the parent has the opportunity to test new ideas in normal day-to-day life, and then discuss the experience in subsequent group sessions.

2. Group Process. There are three important characteristics of group process to which parent educators have given some attention. These are: the source of content and the way it is introduced to the discussion group, the type of interaction between members, and the role of the leader. Regarding the first, the use of a discussion group instead of individual counseling considerably widens the variety of ways in which content comes into the discussion.

One view is that all content in the discussion should come from the parents themselves. Goller (22) distinguishes between the type of program carried on by the Child Study Association of America, in which the time is devoted to discussion by members of their current questions and experiences relating to their children, and the study discussion group program, in which the discussion may be based on prior reading or on the use of a prepared outline (36). It is customary in the first for the leader to introduce content when there are materials directly relevant to the subject under discussion by parents and where they otherwise would not receive attention. The use of parents' questions as the basis for discussion rests on the assumption that people learn more rapidly when the material being studied is directly relevant to their own experiences and needs, and that the discussion of each other's experiences by members of the group provides precisely this kind of material. The contrary arguments are that parents do not have sufficient experience and intellectual resources to provide the content necessary for a sound educational program, and moreover, that in any case the leader will introduce a sizable amount of material, so it should be formally planned for. Another argument (e.g., 1, p. 139) grants the value of parents' discussion of their own experiences, but holds no harm is done by increasing the amount of information which can be used in the parent discussion, and that a combination of sources may be desirable.

Content is also provided for the group discussion from parental observation and participation in various nursery schools and preschools for children. We pointed out the importance of the cooperative nursery school programs in providing the locale and material for individual counseling and noted they were also associated with parent discussion groups (e.g., 32, p. 10). For example, in the state of California the cooperative nursery school movement, nursery school centers, and the child-care center programs for working mothers all have programs of parental participation and/or supervised observation with related discussion groups.

The use of films (and to a lesser extent plays) as sources of content for discussion groups has increased in frequency (4). Many organizations use the method of films and subsequent discussion; the leader, if a professional person, may make the material apply to specific situations raised by the group, may help to work out conflict in the group's interpretation of the film, and may answer questions; if the leader is a trained but nonprofessional person, he usually regulates the discussion but does not introduce or interpret content.

Other familiar modes of introducing content include the use of assigned reading. This is stressed more frequently in programs associated with universities, notable examples being the Parent Education Project of the University of Chicago and the several programs of the Institute of Child Welfare, University of Minnesota (37, 13). Kawin, pointing out that what the groups talk about is important as well as "how it is discussed" maintains that few groups can be successful without accepting responsibility for studying.

While public lectures have declined in importance as the method of parent education, some modern equivalents have come to take their place. We refer to radio addresses, television programs, and something newer, the tape recordings of professional lectures on child development topics produced at the University of Minnesota and at Cornell University (13). Many organizations which have a discussion group program use lectures or related methods as a source of topical information for the group's discussion. For example, parents enrolled in a child study course by radio at the University of Minnesota (28) are asked to listen as members of groups and then discuss the material under the guidance of the leader they have chosen.

Role playing has been given some attention as a possible focal point for a group discussion and as a means of generating subject matter to be discussed. The Family Study Center of the University of Chicago introduced role playing as an experimental technique in certain parent education aspects of its program and the National Congress of Parents and Teachers in its general manual of group educational procedures (53) suggests the use of role playing. The arguments in its favor vary. Eckert states: "The interplay of spontaneous thought and feeling give new insights and understanding, particularly to those who play the roles." (16, p. 18) But a comprehensive review (47) of the effects of role playing indicates that no such change has yet been demonstated. The National Congress (53) states that where the issue is one which contains a delicate or difficult problem in human relations, role playing can be of great value. It does not state why, however, and there is always a possibility that role playing arouses too much unforeseen emotion and is too revealing of people's feelings for the group to handle adequately in its later discussion. Many argue that role playing is more suitable for therapeutic than for educational programs.

Still other techniques for introducing and eliciting content have been used by organizations. The Play Schools Association (25) has been especially creative in its work with the less educated population, using hand puppets, cartoons, and "props" such as baby bottles to provide a focal point for the discussion and to bring about a freer and simpler association of ideas in the child-care area.

The second aspect of group process which requires consideration is the type of interaction between members viewed as desirable. The problem has been to select the type which will bring about the greatest learning by group members. Consonant with the general assumption that participation in an interaction situation (indicating, as it does, a greater involvement and level of motivation) is conducive to greater learning, the one characteristic of interaction which is often recommended as desirable is equality of participation by group members. The publications which mention this (e.g., 12, 49) advocate attempts by the leader to equalize the participation in the discussion. Even though we have found no exception to this viewpoint, there should be parent educators who would challenge this assumption since the relation between equality of participation and overall learning by group members is still unknown.

The impressive development of experimental research on small groups by sociologists in the past ten years or so (27) has resulted in studies describing many characteristics of group interaction.

These include cohesiveness, solidarity, morale, efficiency, and many others. Complete classification systems for interaction have been developed, the best known being that of Bales (5). With only a few exceptions, these studies in the experimental tradition have been concerned with *ad hoc* problem-solving groups. Only rarely has the researcher been interested in the differences in learning which occur in members of the group. The question remains, therefore, of whether any of the interaction characteristics studied in these experiments have relevance for parent discussion group interaction, where the interest is in learning. In sum, while the student of parent discussion groups could not help profiting from reviewing the classifications used in the experimental small group literature, it remains to be seen if these are the relevant dimensions of interaction in parent groups, or whether new characteristics, perhaps quite different, must be conceptualized for this particular type of group.

The third and last issue regarding group process is the role of the leader. There are two aspects of leadership behavior which are of fundamental importance in group discussion procedures. Note that we do not discuss here the personal characteristics and training of group leaders, this being deferred to the next chapter. Rather our emphasis is on aspects of the leader's behavior toward the group. The first question regarding leadership is whether the role of the leader should be to keep the group "task oriented," working toward the completion of previously established agenda, or whether his role should be to let the discussion run freely according to the members' interests, acting as leader only in such matters as trying to equalize the participation of members in the discussion.

There are arguments by parent educators to favor both positions. The planned agenda tend to be used more frequently by programs where the content is based on outside study, such as in the *National Parent-Teacher's* group discussion outlines. Often a set of questions about a topic that members have studied is used as a guide to orderly discussion, much as might be the case in an advanced college class. The programs using the flexible agenda are more often associated with independent organizations and with mental health associations, and more frequently draw on the parents' resources for content, with the leader contributing as needed. As Cheavens says (12), the group should decide what the discussion topic should be, and the leader should not play an active role in demanding that the group adhere to the topic but should recognize that as the discussion wanders and a new topic is discussed, it will gradually swing back to the original issue. Of course, it is a moot point of just how active "too active" is, and how much the leader should strive to relate the various aspects of the ongoing discussion to each other. Many advocate a role for the leader which stands between the extreme of autocratic leadership on the one hand and leaderless group discussion on the other, but just where has not been made sufficiently clear.

The arguments favoring free discussion rather than adherence to planned agenda are that freedom permits the individual to relate the material to his own experiences through these explorations (12). Also, it makes it more feasible for the group members to arrive at their own solutions. In addition, by permitting the members to express their own immediate concerns, their level of interest in the subject matter is kept high and greater learning results. The arguments favoring the planned agenda are that the discussion of child-rearing materials in parent discussion groups is largely an intellectual process which does not need "involvement," or require the expression of individual emotional characteristics, and therefore that the use of agenda is desirable. Significantly more material can thus be covered in an orderly and systematic fashion than if unrelated problems were discussed. Many have advocated a more moderate position, in which the group is primarily responsible for the selection of content but the leader keeps the group members from irrelevant considerations and strives to relate different points of discussion to the main topic chosen by the group.

We know of only one study in parent education itself of this matter of task orientation in groups. In a doctoral thesis by Schulman (61) 66 parent discussion groups were analyzed. Significant differences were found between noncontinuing groups (where the group and leader had no definite plans to continue during the year succeeding the study) and groups which planned to continue. The pertinent difference was that the program of the continuing groups was better planned and arranged than that of the noncontinuing groups, and the leadership of the former was more defined and active. What this means, however, is open to question. Perhaps there was a compounding of types of leadership techniques with personal characteristics such as training or professional background of the leaders, so that the results are ambiguous. It may mean that members of the less planned groups were less satisfied and hence did not plan to continue during the succeeding year; or it may mean that they were more satisfied and felt that they learned enough so that they did not need to continue.

Studies of classroom teaching reviewed recently (10, chap. 6) show that students desire more opportunity for the expression of personal or idiosyncratic interests, and are more fond of the teacher who permits this, even though in task-oriented classes they learn significantly more, and have more respect for the teacher who leads the class in this way. However, it must be added that classroom learning is of set subject matter, while learning in parent discussion groups in a free discussion situation is not, often varying in substance for each individual member.

One other aspect of the task orientation versus free discussion contrast is seen in research on types of leadership in experimental studies of small groups. This research (27, 59) shows that in *ad hoc* problem-solving groups two leaders naturally develop, and are often unrecognized by themselves. One leader keeps the group oriented toward the task, and the other attends to the emotional or expressive concerns of the group members, that is, helps to maintain group morale and personal satisfaction. The implications for parent education are these. The contrasting roles which have been advocated for the parent group leader, namely, permitting the group a wide range of topics of their choice, and holding the group to the task at hand, correspond to the two roles discovered in experimental small group studies. But in parent education there is but one leader, and so it appears that he may have to assume both roles, to fulfill both functions. Perhaps this is the middle-of-the-road position advocated by some parent educators. But can one do this successfully? If the leader handles only one function, such as task orientation, does a member of the group assume the other role to lend a balance and complete the picture? If we analyze the contributions of the two most active members of a parent discussion group, what might be the roles assumed by these participants in terms of the above dichotomy? Perhaps too much is expected from a parent group leader, and that actually two leaders should be provided for each parent group, one whose task it is to be agenda-oriented, and the other whose task it is to make sure of some free discussion, with consideration given to members' interests and feelings.

The other aspect of the leadership role to receive attention is the degree to which the leader should act as an expert, as a resource for the group. Variations in using the group leader as an expert range from one extreme in which the group leader introduces the content for the discussion in the form of an outline, a report on research, or a brief lecture, and continually introduces expert factual knowledge as it is relevant during the discussion; to the other extreme in which nonprofessional persons are used who disclaim any knowledge in the area of child development and whose role is only to assist the group in discussion procedures. The middle-of-the-road practice has been to use persons of professional background who elicit by their leadership the knowledge and experience of the group members, who seek to involve the members in the problem and to bring to bear on the solution their own personal data, who encourage the parents' own problem-solving, but who supply information as needed to fill gaps in parent experience.

The arguments favoring the leader taking the role of expert in child development include: group members wish to learn factual information; they want to learn it from experts rather than lay persons like themselves; the most efficient way of teaching is to have the group leader knowledgeable in the area; and, especially, discussion by group members having no expert guidance may lead to so serious a compounding of ignorance on a particular topic that conclusions damaging to the child can be drawn from the discussion. At the other extreme are arguments that the wish of parent educators is to avoid creating dependency on experts, to increase the personal resources of parents in the form of creativity and problem-solving ability, and that this is achieved by avoiding the role of expert; and even, as some have proposed, that programs should use nonprofessional leaders so that there is no possibility of their playing the role of the expert.

The more moderate position seems to be coming into favor among most parent educators. Advocates of this position criticize the extreme "nonexpert" position just referred to, on the grounds that it often degenerates into a leaderless group where the leader becomes simply one more parent; that research from small group studies (27) indicates that tension and lack of effectiveness occur in leaderless groups; that there are many situations in which the leader cannot remain passive and achieve good results. For example, where the majority of the group overwhelm one or two members with their point of view, but the minority is factually correct, it is the leader's obligation to try to impart a wise point of view.

Criticisms of the opposite position, the leader as expert, date from many years ago (e.g., 52). The contention was that to involve parents in the subject matter, to keep their motivation and attention level high so that learning proceeds, to encourage them to adapt the materials creatively to their own situation, demand that the leader should avoid taking the role of expert and instead should encourage parents to utilize their own problem-solving resources in discussions of child rearing. As Auerbach has stated (3, p. 4): "If the group is to provide an opportunity for the members to build on their own ego-strengths by sharing their experiences in a way that offers them wider choices, new or strengthened ways of behavior and feeling in response to new understanding, then the leader's role is not that of a therapist or an instructor or an 'authority' but of someone skilled in the art of helping the group members to think for themselves." In the moderate view, when the leader is faced with a direct demand for information from group members, or with a situation in which certain members of the group obviously are reaching false conclusions, a professionally trained person can introduce content either in his role as an expert or by referring to authoritative sources. In like manner, the lay leader in this situation can refer to publications of the lay type, that is, pamphlets known to the group members which introduce perhaps cautionary or contradictory materials; however, often he simply has to postpone discussion of a question until the additional information can be obtained from an expert. As Auerbach sums up the situation, "faced with such a demand, the leader in a group education program may do a variety of different things, depending on his evaluation of the situation. He may turn the question back to the group with a simple 'Well, what do you (or you all) think?' Or he may see the demand as one which calls for further information which the group cannot draw from its own experience; this he may then introduce, not as his own opinion, but as varied data from reputable sources. In so doing, he may also introduce conflicting material, showing controversial differences in interpretation. He may, if he feels this will be helpful, give his own personal opinion, identifying it, however, as that and not posing it as the answer to be accepted by the members, but rather as another point of view to which they can react. But, whatever he does, he must use this situation to direct the thinking of the group back to its proper focus and to the goal of the group—namely, the development of their ability to find their own answers, answers that may or may not be acceptable to the other members but that are right for *them*." (3, pp. 4–5)

In concluding this latter part of our consideration of methods, it can be seen clearly that there is a serious lack of research data which would permit a sensible selection of methods to reach different program aims. The great need for evaluation research in which the experimental design includes variations in types of method such as homogeneity of members, group size, length of sessions, ways of introducing content, types of leadership, and others, has been exemplified by the speculative characteristics of the preceding analysis.

REFERENCES

1. American Public Health Association, *Health Supervision of Young Children.* The Association, New York, 1955.

2. *Annual Review of Psychology.* Annual Reviews, Inc., Palo Alto, Calif., vols. 1–10, 1950–1959.

3. Auerbach, Aline B., *Parent Groups in Education.* Presented in Symposium on "Parent Groups in Education, Psychotherapy, and Group Work" at Annual Meeting of American Orthopsychiatric Association, New York, March, 1954, mimeographed.

4. Auerbach, Aline B., "Varieties of Purposes and Methods in Film Discussion Meetings," *Mental Hygiene*, vol. 41, 1957, pp. 396–403.

5. Bales, Robert F., *Interaction Process Analysis:* A Method for the Study of Small Groups. Addison-Wesley Press, Cambridge, Mass., 1950.

6. Baruch, Dorothy W., *Parents and Children Go to School:* Adventuring in Nursery School and Kindergarten. Scott, Foresman and Co., Chicago, 1939.

7. Bennett, Edith B., "Discussion, Decision, Commitment, and Consensus in 'Group Decision,'" *Human Relations*, vol. 8, 1955, pp. 251–273.

8. Blum, Lucille Hollander, "Some Psychological and Educational Aspects of Pediatric Practice: A Study of Well-Baby Clinics," *Genetic Psychology Monographs*, vol. 41, 1950, pp. 3–97.

9. Bond, Betty Wells, *Group Discussion-Decision.* Minnesota Department of Health, Minneapolis, 1956.

10. Brim, Orville G., Jr., *Sociology and the Field of Education.* Russell Sage Foundation, New York, 1958.

11. Cantor, Nathaniel, *Learning Through Discussion.* Human Relations for Industry, Buffalo, New York, 1951.

12. Cheavens, Frank, *Leading Group Discussions.* Hogg Foundation for Mental Health, University of Texas, Austin, 1958.

13. Cummings, Pearl T., Dan C. Overlade, and Dale B. Harris, *A Guide for Leaders in Parent and Family Life Education.* Institute of Child Welfare, University of Minnesota, Minneapolis, 1955.

14. Dollard, John, and Neal E. Miller, *Personality and Psychotherapy:* An Analysis in Terms of Learning, Thinking, and Culture. McGraw-Hill Book Co., New York, 1950.

15. Duvall, Evelyn, and Sylvanus Milne Duvall, *Leading Parents' Groups.* Abingdon-Cokesbury Press, Nashville, Tenn., 1946.

16. Eckert, Ralph, *Handbook on Parent Education.* Bulletin of the California State Department of Education, Sacramento, vol. 19, no. 5, 1950.

17. Elliott, Harrison S., "Philosophic Attitudes Implied in Counseling Procedures," *Parent Education*, vol. 2, 1935, pp. 3–5.

18. Family Life Education Department of Kansas City, Missouri, Public Schools, *Parent Education Handbook*. Curriculum Bulletin No. 96, June, 1955.

19. Foote, Nelson, and Leonard S. Cottrell, Jr., *Identity and Interpersonal Competence:* A New Direction in Family Research. University of Chicago, Chicago, 1955.

20. Ford, M., and E. E. Hartman, "Measuring Reader Comprehension of a Preschool Pamphlet," *Public Health Reports*, vol. 69, 1954, pp. 498–502.

21. Frank, Lawrence K., *The Place of the Mental Hygiene Clinic in a Group Work Agency*. Address given at New York State Welfare Conference, New York City, November 16, 1954, mimeographed.

22. Goller, Gertrude, *When Parents Get Together:* How to Organize a Parent Education Program. Child Study Association of America, New York, 1955.

23. Goller, Gertrude, "Use of the Small Discussion Group in Parent Education," *Social Work*, vol. 2, 1957, pp. 47–53.

24. Governor's Conference on California's Children and Youth, *Big Town Meeting*. California State Printing Office, Sacramento, April 4–5, 1956.

25. Grossman, Jean Schick, *How to Use Hand Puppets in Group Discussions*. Play Schools Association, New York, 1952.

26. Gruenberg, Sidonie, *The Use of Radio in Parent Education*. University of Chicago Press, Chicago, 1939.

27. Hare, Paul, Edgar F. Borgatta, and Robert F. Bales, *Small Groups:* Studies in Social Interaction. Alfred A. Knopf, New York, 1955.

28. Harris, Dale, "Courses for Credit," *American Psychologist*, vol. 10, 1955, pp. 593–596.

29. Hovland, Carl I., "The Effects of Mass Media of Communication," *Handbook of Social Psychology*. Addison-Wesley Publishing Co., Cambridge, Mass., 1954, vol. 2, chap. 28.

30. Hovland, Carl I., and others, *The Order of Presentation in Persuasion*. Yale Studies in Attitude and Communication, vol. 1. Yale University Press, New Haven, Conn., 1957.

31. Institute of Child Study of the University of Toronto, *Twenty-Five Years of Child Study*. University of Toronto Press, Canada, 1951.

32. Institute of Child Study of the University of Toronto, "Parent Education in the Nursery School" in *Proceedings of Parent Education Conference, September, 1956*. University of Toronto Press, Canada, 1956, pp. 9–11.

33. Jackson, Edith B., and Genevieve Trainham, editors, with assistance of members of the Rooming-In Committee, *Family Centered Maternity and Infant Care*. Josiah Macy, Jr. Foundation, New York, 1950.

34. Jackson, Edith B., and Ethelyn H. Klatskin, "Rooming-In Research: Development of Methodology of Parent-Child Relationship Study in a Clinical Setting," *The Psychoanalytic Study of the Child*. International Universities Press, New York, vol. 5, 1950, pp. 236–274.

35. Janis, Irving L., and Seymour Feshbach, "Effects of Fear-Arousing Communications," *Journal of Abnormal and Social Psychology*, 1953, vol. 48, pp. 78–92.

36. Kawin, Ethel, *A Guide for Child-Study Groups*. Science Research Associates, Inc., Chicago, 1952.

37. Kawin, Ethel, *Parenthood in a Free Nation*. Parent Education Project, University of Chicago Press, Chicago, 1954.

38. Klatskin, Ethelyn H., Anton N. Lethin, and Edith B. Jackson, "Choice of Rooming-In or Newborn Nursery," *Pediatrics*, vol. 6, 1950, pp. 878–889.

39. Korsch, Barbara Maria, "Practical Techniques of Observing, Interviewing and Advising Parents in Pediatric Practice as Demonstrated in an Attitude Study Project," *Pediatrics*, vol. 18, 1956, pp. 467–490.

40. Langdon, Grace, and Irving W. Stout, *Teacher-Parent Interviews*. Prentice-Hall, Inc., New York, 1954.

41. Leigh, Robert D., *Group Leadership*. W. W. Norton and Co., New York, 1936.

42. Lemkau, Paul, Benjamin Pasamanick, and Marcia Cooper, *The Implications of the Psychogenetic Hypothesis for Mental Hygiene*. Paper presented at the 1953 Annual Meeting of the American Psychiatric Association.

43. Leonard, Edith M., Dorothy D. Van Deman, and Lillian E. Miles, *Counseling with Parents in Early Childhood Education*. Macmillan Co., New York, 1954.

44. Lewin, Kurt, "Group Decision and Social Change" in *Readings in Social Psychology*, edited by Theodore M. Newcomb, Eugene L. Hartley, and Eleanor Maccoby. 3d ed. Henry Holt and Co., New York, 1958.

45. Lindeman, Eduard C., and Flora M. Thurston, *Problems for Parent Educators*. National Council of Parent Education, New York, 1931.

46. Lorge, Irving, David Fox, Joel Davitz, and Marlin Brenner, "A Survey of Studies Contrasting the Quality of Group Performance and Individual Performance, 1920–1957," *Psychological Bulletin*, vol. 55, 1958, pp. 337–372.

47. Mann, John H., "Experimental Evaluations of Role Playing," *Psychological Bulletin*, vol. 53, 1956, pp. 227–234.

48. McClure, Dorothea, and Harvey Schrier, "Preventive Counseling with Parents of Young Children," *Social Work*, vol. 1, 1956, pp. 68–80.

49. Meyer, Marguerite S., and Edward J. Power, "The Family Caseworker's Contribution to Parent Education Through the Medium of the Discussion Group," *American Journal of Orthopsychiatry*, vol. 23, 1953, pp. 621–628.

50. Milbank Memorial Fund, *The Elements of a Community Mental Health Program:* Papers Presented at the 1955 Annual Conference of the Milbank Memorial Fund. The Fund, New York, 1956.

51. Moreno, J. L., *Who Shall Survive?* Rev. ed. Beacon House, Beacon, N. Y., 1953.

52. National Congress of Parents and Teachers, *Parent Education:* The Third Year Book. The National Congress, Washington, 1932.

53. National Congress of Parents and Teachers, *New Hope for Audiences.* The National Congress, Chicago, 1954.

54. National Congress of Parents and Teachers, *Proceedings* of Annual Convention. The National Congress, Chicago, vols. 1–62, 1897–1958.

55. National Society for the Study of Education, *Twenty-Eighth Year Book:* Parts I and II, Preschool and Parent Education. Public School Publishing, Bloomington, Ill., 1929.

56. Neubauer, Peter B., "The Technique of Parent Group Education: Some Basic Concepts," *Parent Group Education and Leadership Training.* Child Study Association of America, New York, 1953, pp. 9–15.

57. Ojemann, Ralph H., "The Reading Ability of Parents and Factors Associated with Reading Difficulty of Parent Education Materials," *University of Iowa Studies in Child Welfare,* vol. 8, 1934, pp. 9–32.

58. Osborn, D. Keith, "Play Group: An Experience for Parent and Child," *Merrill-Palmer Quarterly,* vol. 2, Spring, 1956, pp. 139–142.

59. Parsons, Talcott, and Robert F. Bales, in collaboration with James Olds, Morris Zelditch, Jr., and Philip E. Slater, *Family, Socialization and Interaction Process.* The Free Press, Glencoe, Ill., 1955.

60. Pigors, Paul, *Leadership or Domination.* Houghton Mifflin Co., Boston, 1935.

61. Schulman, Eveline D., *Analysis of Characteristics of Sixty-Six Parent-Child Study Groups in Nine Maryland Counties During 1954–1955.* Doctoral dissertation, University of Maryland, College Park, 1957.

62. Slavson, Samuel R., *An Introduction to Group Therapy.* Commonwealth Fund, New York, 1943.

63. Solnit, A. J., and Milton J. E. Senn, "Teaching Comprehensive Pediatrics in an Outpatient Clinic," *Pediatrics,* vol. 14, 1954, p. 547.

64. Taylor, Janet A., "Drive Theory and Manifest Anxiety," *Psychological Bulletin,* vol. 53, 1956, pp. 303–326.

65. Taylor, Katharine Whiteside, *Parent Cooperative Nursery Schools.* Teachers College, Columbia University, New York, 1954.

66. Terrell, Glenn, "Television Instruction in Child Psychology," *American Psychologist,* vol. 13, 1958, p. 484.

67. Treat, David B., "The American Cooperative Nursery: A New Folk Movement," *Understanding the Child,* vol. 25, 1956, pp. 2–3.

68. United States Department of Health, Education, and Welfare, *Health Services and Juvenile Delinquency*. Children's Bureau, Washington, 1955.

69. Wagoner, Lovisa C., "What the Mother May Learn Through Directed Observation of Her Child" in *Parent Education*, edited by Richard Olding Beard. University of Minnesota Press, Minneapolis, 1927.

70. Wall, William D., *Education and Mental Health:* A Report Based Upon the Work of a European Conference Called by UNESCO at the Musée Pedagogique in Paris, Nov.-Dec., 1952. UNESCO, Paris, 1955.

71. Weng, Lorraine, "A Study of Lay Publications on Child Feeding," *Journal of American Dietetic Association*, vol. 28, 1952, pp. 927–932.

72. White House Conference on Child Health and Protection, Section III: Education and Training, Committee on the Family and Parent Education, *Parent Education:* Types, Content and Method. Century Co., New York, 1932.

73. Witmer, Helen L., *The Field of Parent Education:* A Survey from the Viewpoint of Research. National Council of Parent Education, New York, 1934.

CHAPTER EIGHT:

Selection and Training
of Personnel

IN THIS CHAPTER the questions to be considered are, first: What characteristics and knowledge are believed to be desirable for parent educators, and how are these derived from the means and ends of parent education? Second, What are the important types of programs of selection and training?

CHARACTERISTICS AND KNOWLEDGE HELD TO BE DESIRABLE

Characteristics

In the works in parent education devoted to the selection and training of personnel, the great bulk of attention has been given to matters of desirable knowledge and skills, rather than to traits which the individual should have. This may reflect the opinion that the work of the parent educator requires knowledge gained by training rather than any particular set of personality characteristics. However, it might also be evidence of a lack of attention to the job specifications of the parent educator, and to the possibility that there might be optimal characteristics of intelligence, tolerance, nurturance, marital status, or others which should be used as criteria for selection. To say that one sees parent educators of many different personalities doing a good job is not an adequate answer, because the criteria of job success are vague, and the personality differences and variability in social background of the educators may be more apparent than real.

When characteristics are mentioned it is only in passing, so to speak, while the author is preparing for discussion of the more important matters of knowledge and training. Moreover, it is only discussion group leaders who are mentioned. For example, several persons have raised the question of the relative desirability of men or women as group leaders or counselors (e.g., 33), especially when the clientele are fathers instead of mothers. Friendliness and emotional maturity (25) have been suggested, as have humility, ingenuity, a happy home life of one's own, and awareness of the needs of one's community (16). Some programs for parents of children with special disabilities such as mental retardation choose as counselors (after further training) parents of similar children, on the grounds that they have a greater understanding.

Many times the desirable traits are implicit in the selection procedure used in obtaining candidates for leadership or other kinds of training. Thus, the Parent Education Project of the University of Chicago takes persons recommended by their local organizations, on the assumption that they have already demonstrated the personal characteristics necessary in a good leader; the Child Study Association of America in selecting its trainees take those recommended by their superiors in their organizations.

Insofar as research goes, there are only beginning efforts in this direction represented by a report of a study by the Child Study Association (14) which points out that nurses with high initial test scores on "authoritarianism" seemed less able to profit from a leadership training course than the other nurses. Certainly more work in following up this and other leads in the literature is desirable.

Knowledge

Almost without exception the statements of what the parent educator should know, the facts and skills he should possess, have been made about leaders of parent discussion groups or counselors of parents. The analysis of what desirable knowledge would be for the mass media specialist has received almost no attention in parent education. This neglect reflects the general lack of interest which we have noted before on the part of parent educators in theoretical work on mass media.

Before we consider the existing work in parent education, at least a few paragraphs on the area of mass media seem warranted because of its neglect elsewhere. It would be valuable to know who the persons are that prepare mass media material for parents. What is their professional background? It appears that the standards of selection in most organizations implicitly demand a high level of professional knowledge. This is seen clearly in the printed materials of several programs: for example, the care with which commercial organizations such as Parents' Institute prepare the materials; the way in which the Children's Bureau materials are carefully reviewed by panels of experts; the working and reworking of materials in the *National Parent-Teacher* for accuracy; the employment of notable experts in the field of child development by commercial magazines; all attest to the fact that the organizations believe the individual who is preparing mass media materials should be professionally informed in the area of child development and parent-child relations.

There are contrary cases, it is true. Television programs are put on without responsible attention being given to the competence of the educators in the area of content, and publications are prepared in many local community organizations in which the content is quite poor.

Another kind of knowledge believed desirable for the mass media specialist is how to prepare materials in intelligible, effective form. The parent education curriculum of the Institute of Child Welfare, University of Minnesota, includes in its training methods some work in writing for mass media. But this must be a rare thing. The common solution has been not to require the parent educator to possess writing skills, but to hire professional writers who work collaboratively with these experts in content. This reflects the case where in group leadership a lay leader may be competent to lead a group but relies on experts for content; and it contrasts with the common case where the group leader is expected to know both content *and* method. Certainly one needs to clarify standards of knowledge needed in the use of mass media, and relate the standards to program objectives.

We turn now to consideration of the knowledge expected of group leaders and counselors. Kerckhoff (27) has reported on a study using personal interviews with lawyers, clergymen, physicians, and social workers, randomly selected in the Detroit area, concerning the qualifications which marriage counselors should possess. His results show that the subjects in each group emphasize their own academic training as being the desirable qualification; each subject felt his own profession to be the best qualified to do the counseling. The situation in the field of parent education seems better than the state reported by Kerckhoff as existing for marriage counseling, although there is room for improvement in the theoretical sophistication with which standards are chosen.

In a report (13) of a workshop in 1954, attended by representative parent educators from 16 states, the following kinds of knowledge and ability were stated as desirable for a group leader: knowledge of parents' concerns about their children; a basic understanding of people; the ability to recognize underlying emotions; the ability to handle the anxiety of others; the ability to identify with the parents; the ability to accept differences comfortably; expertness in appropriate educational techniques; knowledge of one's own limitations; the ability to keep discussion moving; reliable information on child development and parent-child relations; awareness of his own personality needs and how these influence role performance; the effect of his own activity on his community customs and social values; an awareness of the individual ego needs of parents; a sensitivity to group atmosphere and structure; the ability to see what elements in group experience can be used constructively; the ability to prevent destructive developments; the ability to establish an atmosphere for tolerance of differences; the ability to keep discussion relevant to the purpose of the program; the skill to protect the group as well as individual members; the ability to protect absent family members from being exposed; the ability to show where material is interrelated and to help parents carry over material to their own lives.

Clearly some order must be brought out of this chaotic assemblage of skills and information. The various components seem classifiable under the familiar headings of content and method; but even this classification does not permit us to discuss all of these, only the most important within each class.

1. Knowledge of Content. The content viewed as desirable to know ranges from none at all in certain programs to the equivalent of several years of graduate study and more in others. The latter is seen in the following statement of kinds of information relevant to the practice of parent education (5, 6, 17): "1. Knowledge of the development of children in normal family living with particular emphasis on the similarities and differences in their stages of growth and patterns of physical and personality development; 2. awareness of the effect of parenthood on husband and wife individually and in their interrelation; 3. appreciation of factors making for mental health and a diagnostic awareness of them, since the basic goal of parent education is to build on strength in the individual parents; 4. cultural factors affecting patterns of family living and the readiness of the parent objectively to review such patterns." (17) These will be seen as drawing respectively on the major disciplines of child development, sociology of the family, abnormal psychology, and cultural anthropology.

In actuality, the training in content which parent educators do receive ranges from two-day workshops in child development; through two-week training sessions in selected areas of child development, as in the Parent Education Project of the University of Chicago; through 14 day-long sessions with supervised field work, as at the Child Study Association; through the Master's degree in home economics, and the M.D. degree in pediatrics or psychiatry, or the Ph.D. degree in child development itself.

Whether or not the parent group leader needs to have no knowledge, some, or substantial knowledge of content is usually debated as the issue of lay versus professional leaders. Goller (22) has developed a helpful classification of parent group leaders in terms of their knowledge of content and their knowledge of method (discussed later), which clarifies the points involved. Goller points out that a *lay* leader is a person who is not a member of a particular profession, and who has had little or no training in method, while the *trained* leader is one who also is not in a profession, but who has had extensive training in working with groups of all kinds. The *professional* leader is a member of a particular profession such as psychology or social work, and the *trained professional* leader is one who combines both professional training and training for parent group leadership. In this section, while we are discussing content, the important distinction is between the nonprofessional (both lay and trained) and the professional person (trained or untrained).

In Chapter VII we pointed out that the lay versus professional leadership issue is intertwined with the issues of whether the leader is to serve the group as an expert, and of the degree to which he must introduce content into the group discussion. The research on the effects of leaders with different knowledge, under different conditions, is negligible. The few studies (reviewed in Chapter IX) comparing different procedures in leadership show that "experts" transmit more information, that is, produce greater improvement in parent knowledge, than do "nonexperts"; and that the use of a psychologist versus a psychiatrist and a "group-oriented" versus "leader-oriented" method does not result in appreciable differences in effects produced. These data are not enough to permit scientific standard setting, hence the specification of needed knowledge of content is much a matter of opinion. If the parent education program holds that the group leader should be able to serve as an expert resource to the group, and/or to introduce content for the group discussion, it follows logically that the leader must know content, at least in the areas to be covered by the group. If one holds that the leader should never take this expert role, and never introduce content into the discussion, then it would not seem to make any difference how much training in content the leader had.

In spite of this observation, the use of lay leaders is criticized on the grounds that it is impossible for the leader not to become involved in matters of content; for example, in the repercussions of the effects of films on the group (31, 37, p. 35), or in the disagreements between group members where he cannot avoid being cast in the role of expert, and that, therefore, all leaders should have knowledge of content in the relevant areas (42, p. 3;

50, p. 15). The counterargument is that if the discussion of the group follows planned agenda, taking account of lay leader limitations rather than engaging in expressive free discussion, the leader is unlikely to meet situations for which he is unprepared.

One other argument sometimes advanced in favor of using lay leaders is that there simply are not enough professional persons interested in parent education activities to meet the parent demands (25, 56) and, therefore, nonprofessionals should be used. The contrary opinion, of course, is that there is little merit to this argument, since it is better not to engage in parent education than to use parent educators who may be incompetent for the task.

A reasonable approach to specifying the kinds of knowledge which the parent education leader should have would be to make the specifications accord with the aims and methods of the program. The variety of existing programs in parent education suggest that many differences in the selection and training of personnel might be justified, since each type of program logically might demand different skills. While we return to this general idea at the end of the chapter, the application to leadership training can be pointed out here. Lindeman and Thurston (33, p. 9) many years ago pointed out the desirability of classifying problems for discussion, indicating that some are suitable for all parent educators, regardless of training, but that some problems require considerable professional background in order for one to provide discussion leadership. Such a specification of problems points to a possibly more efficient use of variety of background in information which exists among parent educators.

It appears that the specification of what a parent educator should know is indeed related to characteristics of the program and in logical ways. Those persons stressing the use of lay leaders (e.g., 16, p. 4; 26) are associated with parent education programs in which the content is introduced on the basis of lectures, films, or previously assigned studies; where the leader is responsible for keeping the discussion moving smoothly, but is not viewed as an expert; and where the discussion itself is planned to follow fairly routinized or structured agenda. In contrast, advocates of the use of professional persons as leaders seem associated with programs where the emphasis is on content being built around the immediate interests of the group members, where the leader has the resources to introduce factual material when pertinent, to direct or influence the discussion toward content which has been overlooked, and where the discussion itself proceeds freely rather than being oriented toward the completion of set agenda. The latter is the type of group discussion advocated by organizations such as the Child Study Association of America.

It follows that the specification of the knowledge of content needed by a discussion leader might not logically fit the program characteristics. This does not seem to be the case where the professional leader is used in a program for which the lay leader is suitable, as described above, because the professional leader should be able to operate effectively in either type of group discussion procedure. But the other relation between training and program, namely, where a lay leader is used in the program where the discussion is unstructured, or otherwise makes demands upon him which he is not ready to meet, seems an unjustified use of the personnel. In summary, as long as the dimensions of different programs are fairly understood, the differences between the advocates of lay and professional leaders become somewhat clearer, and the possibility that there may be merit in the arguments from both sides becomes somewhat easier to understand.

2. Knowledge of Methods. Two matters loom large in the area of methodology and have received much attention in theoretical work in parent education. The first is the degree to which the parent educator must learn to distinguish between education and therapy as methods of influence. We have stated some of the criteria which might be used in making this distinction in Chapter I. Yet in that chapter we stressed that this was a working distinction, that probably education and therapy are distinguishable only as ends of a continuum. The boundaries of the two are indistinct, and in any specific case it is difficult to describe a procedure as one or the other.

Many insist that the educator should learn the distinction and practice it, because if he is untrained in therapy he may unwittingly cause much trouble for his clientele when he becomes involved inappropriately in their important defenses and unconscious motives. But there is a puzzle here, for most persons who are trained to make the distinction are also trained to practice therapy, so perhaps for them the distinction is unnecessary. It may be this which has led some professional parent educators to say that the distinction is unimportant.

The solution appears to be this: if one maintains that the educator should learn the education-therapy distinction, then lay personnel and members of professions without psychotherapeutic training are the groups in critical need of training to make the distinction, for they are incompetent to practice therapy and hence must be able to see when they have reached the limits of their skills. The trained therapist will already know the difference, but this may be less important; indeed, he may wish to utilize his clinical skills at times in dealing with parents (although arguments against this are cited below). The one stricture here is that he not call the latter parent *education*, which can only confuse the issue.

The foregoing discussion has assumed that it is desirable to distinguish between education and therapy. Yet this assumption itself is sometimes challenged. Thus, it has been argued that when the educator is a lay person, and when the content is introduced in standard form and the discussion proceeds according to closely planned agenda, few if any personal matters are raised in the discussion or addressed to the leader. It is known that he is no expert, and the content in any case has been selected to avoid stimulating questions involving unconscious matters. It is argued that there is no more need for the educator to be able to apply this distinction than for leaders of other adult groups, for example, the labor mediator or the teacher of a bible study class, since in none of these instances does the discussion significantly involve neurotic or unconscious areas.

The contrary argument, often associated with programs where there is freer discussion, with more likelihood of unconscious factors coming to the fore, is that it is imperative for the parent educator to recognize the education-therapy distinction and apply it to the group discussion. The leader must avoid situations in which group members are excessively defensive, on the theory that effective learning does not take place under conditions of high anxiety. When anxiety does appear, the leader through his acceptance and impartiality attempts to reduce threat and to encourage a free expression and exchange of ideas. If a member then expresses a concern which appears near the surface, which seems potentially to be under conscious control, the leader looks for a way to help the group bring it out. But if the concern appears to be a deep one, springing from unconscious motives, the leader works to avoid its expression and moves on to other matters. In particular, if the parent shows resistance, an inability to profit when educational methods are employed, the leader is aware that motives may be present which are not appropriate for group discussion. It is just this ability of the leader to recognize when he is confronted with areas of unconscious resistance which is recommended by some as a necessary skill (35).

A closely related matter, really a by-product of acquiring the ability to distinguish between education and therapy, is the suggestion that parent educators should be able to recognize in both the children of the parents involved in the program (on the basis of the parents' description) and in the parents themselves the indications of emotional stress. This provides a basis for the educator to determine whether the situation is appropriate for educational service, or demands referral to therapeutic services where further diagnosis and treatment can be initiated. In this way the parent educator along with his primary educational function can serve a secondary but critically important screening function; he thereby provides the frontline diagnostic service so desperately needed in preventive work in mental illness.

These are difficult tasks to accomplish, and granted that they are necessary there can be little doubt that special training is required, for these are not natural skills. Consider an example of a mother in a discussion group who becomes so involved that she breaks down and cries in front of the group (29). Those who argue for training point out that it would be almost impossible for the untrained person to differentiate between crying indicating a release of tension over something which is under conscious control and crying expressing a conflict which lies much deeper and of which the mother is unconscious. One must avoid being overconcerned where the matter is simple, an error which Meyer and Power (36) suggest is often the case, and at the same time not underestimate the significance of certain symptoms.

The second important issue in knowledge of methods is the amount of instruction (both in theory and practice) which the parent educator needs before practicing individual counseling or leading parent discussion groups. It appears that there is much less variation in the amount of training in methods which parent educators have than was true of content. There is little disagreement in the field regarding necessity for at least some training in the educational procedure to be used, although there still may be some who maintain that such teaching "comes naturally," or is an "art." (43)

Many of the arguments stressing the need for training in parent education methods are directed to members of professions who have their own "methods" and who already know "content." But the arguments stress the point that knowledge of content does not carry with it knowledge of methods in education, a point reminiscent of the observation made so frequently of the college instructor who is competent in the area of content but who may be an ineffective teacher because he has had no training. The targets of this argument have frequently been members of the clinical profession, to whom it is pointed out (10, p. 106) that the special skills of the therapist are not the same as those of the educator, and the therapist should not conclude that his training in therapy will make him competent as an educator.

Apart from these statements emphasizing the need for training and directed toward persons outside of parent education, the differences of opinion among parent educators themselves center more on the amount of training held to be desirable. As we have said, the variations are not so wide as was true for knowledge of content, but still they seem to range from one extreme of lay leadership in which the discussion leader training may be to read a pamphlet or two (16) to the trained leader, professional or nonprofessional, who has had graduate training in counseling or discussion techniques and practice under supervision (e.g., 5).

Probably a common core of training (25) would include instruction in the philosophy and techniques of good group discussion, an understanding of the various types of programs which groups can use, and an understanding of the different roles that leaders can take. In general, the remaining differences are associated with differences in program aims and procedures, as was true with regard to knowledge of content. Where materials are introduced in the course of discussion, and the way of developing them is free and discursive rather than organized and systematic, obviously more demands are made upon the leader and a greater knowledge of educational methods is specified as desirable.

SELECTION AND TRAINING IN DIFFERENT PROFESSIONAL SETTINGS

Our objective now is to look briefly at the selection and training for parent education which goes on in different professions such as medicine. There are eight important groups of persons engaged in parent education in this country which are discussed in this section: family life educators; medical personnel, especially pediatricians and general practitioners; nurses, especially members of visiting nurse services and public health services; clinical personnel, including psychiatrists, clinical psychologists, and social workers; home economists; clergymen and religious educators; teachers, a broad term amplified in the paragraphs below; and finally "parents," referring to parents with no professional connections, but who have received some training in content and method and who serve as organizers and group leaders.

Like other topics in this book, this one of selection and training deserves the attention of a whole volume; but we cannot do more here than give examples of selection and training for each group, and try to relate them to each other so that one is able to gain a better grasp of the whole.

For every profession which engages in parent education one can ask several questions about the training its members receive. Under what auspices do training programs usually operate? (For example, are they under university or college auspices, or under some other private or public organizations?) Who are the persons who train the parent educators in the different programs? How adequate are the programs in their instruction in the areas of content and method?

Family Life Educators

The term "family life educator" designates persons trained for a career devoted to the education of family members in a number of roles, whether they be husband-wife relations, parent-child relations, or others. Their training and work includes parent education as one of the major categories of family life education.

Family life educators are with few exceptions trained in university departments of child development, family life education, psychology, and sometimes in home economics. Many of these training programs date from the decade of 1920, and were established in conjunction with the child research centers founded by grants from the Laura Spelman Rockefeller Memorial. Many have maintained their importance on the national scene, with outstanding training programs now located at the State University of Iowa, the University of Minnesota, at Cornell University, at Teachers College, Columbia University, as well as at several other institutions. Family life educators also have been trained in less formal ways, some having come up through the ranks of parent education organizations, obtaining their training from the teaching and supervision of the older personnel in the institution.

Most family life educators receive training which is sound with respect to both content and method. An important aspect of their training in method is that the trainees often have the opportunity for supervised field work, either as a counselor or as a discussion group leader of parents. This experience is of limited quality, to be sure, for sometimes the supervision is only by fellow students instead of mature instructors, and the field work itself is short compared to the field training in other professions such as medicine, social work, and psychiatry. Nevertheless, it is unusual in parent education.

Family life educators play a significant role in American parent education because they are the only group for whom parent education is not just an auxiliary aspect of some other profession, such as medicine, or an avocation as is true on the part of many persons. The family life educator frequently makes a substantial portion of his living through the practice of parent education, and has received on the average much more training in both content and method than other persons in parent education programs. They are therefore called upon in many instances to provide leadership in parent education, and to institute training programs for members of other professions who wish to launch parent education activities. We return to the place of the family life educator in the overall scene in the last section of this chapter, where we deal with professional aspects of parent education and probable developments for the future.

Clinical Personnel: Psychiatrists, Clinical Psychologists, and Social Workers

Clinical personnel are grouped together here because they have in common not only training in the clinical aspects of child development, but also the need for additional training in educational methods which goes beyond their professional training in therapeutic procedures.

Psychiatrists, of course, hold medical degrees and have been trained in medical schools by other psychiatrists in departments of psychiatry. Many of the psychiatrists engaged in parent education have specialized in child psychiatry. Even these, however, in their training are exposed to practically none of the experimental literature on the normal aspects of child development. Fortunately some departments of psychiatry are now introducing more of these research data to accompany the training in clinical content.

The clinical psychologist customarily holds a Master's or a Ph.D. degree and has been trained in universities within departments of psychology by other psychologists. Of all of the groups which we consider here the clinical psychologists receive the most extensive training in the experimental child development research literature, and also are trained in clinical literature on child development and on parent-child relations. It is true that there is variation in training programs in the amount offered of one or the other of these bodies of content, but in general the clinical psychologist has a broader knowledge of content than the other professional persons mentioned here.

Neither of these two groups receives training in methods suitable for parent education. Their training for therapeutic counseling and for leadership of therapeutic groups does not equip them to engage in educational practice because the latter is different. Indeed, in training programs for these clinical personnel even the distinction between education and therapy may be unrecognized or glossed over. It follows that members of these professions would need additional training in methods if they are to participate in educational programs.

Social workers have yet to enter the field of parent education practice in the numbers that one would expect, in light of their training and professional objectives. It is true that leading social work organizations and their publications have recognized parent education as a significant aspect of social work practice. Important publications on the topic include those by the Family Service Association of America (19) and by the Welfare and Health Council of New York City (54), now the Community Council of Greater New York. The influential *Social Work Year Book, 1957* (45) discusses family life education as one of the definite areas of social work; the journals *Social Casework* and *Social Work* have carried a number of articles on parent education; the National Conference on Social Welfare in recent years has held a number of sessions on family life education and parent education at its annual meetings. This interest notwithstanding, social workers have not actively moved into the field of family life education or parent education to the extent that one would expect.

In regard to their training in content, Auerbach (4) has pointed out that social workers have an unusually good background for parent education. They are familiar with the psychodynamic approach to human behavior; they have had training in child development and family relations (although primarily with a clinical rather than an experimental orientation); and have been trained in the recognition of pathology in the individual and family behavior. Moreover, many are now sensitive to wide variations in cultural values, especially where children are concerned.

Social workers, however, as is true of the other types of clinical personnel, need training in educational methods. Often this is difficult for them to attain. Some idea of the training in methodology which is required for social workers, and probably for many other personnel coming into the field, can be gleaned from the analysis of the training program of the Child Study Association for social caseworkers and group workers. In describing this program Auerbach (4) points out that the Association has come to recognize that each of the professions, including the social workers, with whom it has had close contact in its training program has characteristic strengths, but each has needed some additional help in focusing on the needs of parents and in learning how these needs could be met in groups. The caseworkers in particular, while alert to the readiness of their clients to move in new directions, needed help in recognizing the normal as well as the pathological, needed training in leadership skills, and required education in seeing and working through the parents' strength rather than through individual pathology. The group workers needed help in focusing the parents' discussions toward understanding of themselves and their children, rather than in emphasizing the achievement of group consensus toward social action, or in improving the interpersonal relations of members within the group context.

Home Economists

Home economists receive their training in college or university settings from professionals who have had graduate training in home economics or related disciplines. Many of the home economists who later become active in parent education programs have not had training beyond the undergraduate level and thus differ from many of the family life educators and the clinical personnel referred to above.

At the graduate level the training of home economists includes a significant amount of study in child development and family life, including supervised practice in infant care. However, the emphasis is almost wholly on experimental research data with probably insufficient attention being given to training in clinical theory and data (51). Where the home economist has had only undergraduate collegiate training, the adequacy of knowledge of content is doubtful since the formal training in child development or parent-child relations usually consists of no more than a course or two.

In neither the graduate nor undergraduate program does the home economist receive sufficient training in counseling with parents or working with groups, except in some unusual instances. This training would have to be acquired at a later stage if the home economist is to meet the standards of counseling and group leadership held by the significant parent education programs in this country.

Teachers

The training of teachers, occurring as it does in schools of education and teachers' colleges, exposes them to a wide range of academic disciplines. Each of them, such as sociology, anthropology, child development, and educational psychology, has something to contribute toward preparation for parent education activities.

Many teachers receive good training in the growth and development of young children, although for the profession generally it is of variable quality. One difficulty is that in many places the courses may be taught by instructors who were trained in education and who have had no need to keep up with the experimental child development or clinical literature, so that their course materials tend over time to become obsolete. Another shortcoming which many note is that the training of teachers is not adequate with respect to the emotional needs of children and the recognition of disturbance or maladjustment in the child (30, p. 448).

Teachers evidently are receiving better training in this latter regard, for Beilin's excellent review (8) of teachers' competence in making clinical judgments shows increasing congruence between clinical and teacher judgments in a number of studies over the past twenty-five years.

Training in methods of parent education varies considerably from one institution to another (48). A number provide courses specifically addressed to the relation of the teacher to parents, and use some of the excellent texts in this area such as Hymes' *Effective Home-School Relations* (23), and Strang's *Reporting to Parents* (47). New programs are under way of particular significance for the role of the teacher in parent education. For example, the New Jersey Department of Education, with support from the Grant Foundation, is adding staff members to provide consultant services to child study groups, and to work toward establishing programs in teachers' colleges in the state which will train graduate students so that they can coordinate child study programs in local school systems. In universities such as the University of Minnesota where there are separate departments or programs of parent education, the students from schools of education may take the parent education courses on techniques and methods of working with parents, even as the child development content is acquired in their own school or department.

If other sources of training are unavailable, the teacher may participate in one of a variety of in-service training opportunities such as special summer programs, workshops, or institutes. An outstanding program of this kind is offered by the University of Maryland (11). Much of the leadership in making such in-service opportunities available has come from Hazel Gabbard (20, 21) of the Office of Education, U.S. Department of Health, Education, and Welfare.

Medical Personnel

About two-thirds of all children are attended by physicians in general practice, which makes them, along with pediatricians, the persons with medical training most likely to become involved in parent education. How are they prepared in the regular course of their medical training for this possible involvement in parent education? First, with respect to knowledge it must be recognized that the information on children presented in the medical curriculum is one-sidedly concerned with physical development. It is true that recently many of the leading medical schools have developed active departments of psychiatry, and there is an increase in the extent to which psychiatric teaching is included in all four years of the medical school curriculum (15). The exposure of the medical student to psychiatric theory helps to counterbalance the emphasis on physical maturation of children, but leaves his training seriously inadequate because the psychiatric knowledge gained is still slight, and even this represents only one approach to the study of emotional development. The information on child development and parent-child relations which the average pediatrician and general practitioner learn includes little on the areas of social and cognitive development in children, or on the experimental studies in the area of emotional development. For example, in a major textbook of pediatrics (41), out of 1,619 pages of text there are about a dozen pages on mental and emotional development and three times as many on psychological disorders, mainly speech problems.

Training in methods of parent education is virtually absent. Some relevant observations may be given by members of the departments of psychiatry in connection with their teaching but most psychiatrists themselves are untrained in parent education. In some degree skill in the education of parents also may be obtained informally through discussion with, and observation of, one's professors in medical school in connection with the performance of their services. However, the lesson which is learned may just as often be a bad as a good one, since there is no reason to believe that the medical school faculty is especially skilled in the education of parents. It seems ironic that training in methods should be so inadequate among medical personnel, for they are the group who probably have more actual experience in dealing with parents during the course of their training than any of the others; yet this experience is not utilized as an opportunity for supervised training in educational practices.

Some fundamental changes seem to be taking place in the roles of the pediatrician and the general practitioner and one result may be a further development of the education of parents as an aspect of their medical practice. While this is discussed in more detail at the end of the chapter, we mention it here because we believe these changes to be the cause of the current ferment and experimentation in medical training programs. At least this seems to be the case for the pediatrician. There is increased recognition of the deficiencies in training, especially in the area of educational counseling methods, and recent reviews of the arguments on this topic include the outstanding article by Korsch (28) and the earlier paper by Kanner (24). Influential publications stressing the need for improved training include those of the American Public Health Association (1) and of the U.S. Department of Health, Education, and Welfare (50).

Experimental programs with the objective of increasing the medical student's knowledge of family dynamics and of ways of counseling family members include those in which a medical student "adopts" a family at the prenatal visit and then follows the family during his four years at medical school; these programs exist at Pennsylvania, Western Reserve, Harvard, and other medical schools. With specific reference to pediatrics, the Grant Foundation is supporting several experimental projects: Benjamin Spock is directing a three-year study exploring methods of casework most suitable for child care and investigating the ways in which medical advice can be of most assistance to parents; and Milton Senn at Yale is preparing for publication the materials developed in his experimental training programs for pediatricians and general practitioners over the past years, with a special emphasis on developing methods which the nonpsychiatric physician might use in leading parents (46). Another notable program of training designed to alleviate the shortcomings of the traditional medical curriculum is that under the direction of David Levy in New York City (28). The Commonwealth Fund has provided support for another experimental program of this same general order at the State University College of Medicine in Syracuse, New York. It is to be expected that in the future these programs of training will have a significant influence upon the competence of medical personnel to carry on programs of parent education.

Nursing

The nursing specialties which in the natural course of their professional performance are most closely associated with parent education activities are the obstetrical, pediatric, and public health fields of specialization. The training which nurses receive in the ordinary course of their education does not include enough information on child development, especially in the areas other than physical growth, to meet the standards of many parent education programs. In regard to training in methods, the ordinary nursing education contains little or no instruction in matters pertaining to individual parent counseling or the leadership of discussion groups. This is true even though the field of nursing is one in which a situation similar to that in the medical profession occurs; namely, there are opportunities for supervised field experience but these are not emphasized in training in educational methods.

The result is that members of these nursing specialties usually require further training after graduation to enable them adequately to perform significant roles in parent education programs. This deficiency in nurses' training has been recognized for some time and there are several important efforts in the field of nursing which have as their objective the provision of better parent education training. Notable among these are the several programs sponsored by the Children's Bureau in conjunction with different universities in the United States. These joint efforts, for example, at Teachers College, Columbia University, the Boston University School of Nursing, and at the University of Chicago (9) provide a special curriculum at the level of the Master's degree. Most enrollees among nurses have been trained as pediatric nurses but some public health nurses may enter these training programs. An important emphasis is on training in content germane to parent education programs, that is, child development and clinical information on the personality of the child as well as his physical maturation. To some extent this emphasis on content is becoming a recognized part of nurses' training programs even at the undergraduate level.

These programs still do not provide extensive training in parent education methods even though some members may take courses in departments of family life education or family agencies. The recognition of the inadequacies of nurses' training in the area of methodology also has led to experimental training programs designed to remedy the situation. Probably most significant among these is a program of the Child Study Association of America training nurses and nursing supervisors in parent group leadership skills (and child development content), which is sponsored by the Division of Health Services of the Children's Bureau and the New York State Department of Health. This full year's training course includes supervised experience in the field (2, 3). A program of a similar kind, run by the Child Study Association in conjunction with Region VII of the Children's Bureau, the Maternal and Child Health Division of the Texas State Department of Health, and Texas Woman's University, recently has been completed (14).

The full descriptions of these many experimental projects, as well as the research evaluations of the effectiveness of some of these programs such as the one in Texas mentioned above, are just now beginning to be published and made available to the field as a whole. It is to be expected that they will have a significant influence upon nurses' training in relation to their role in programs for the education of parents.

Clergymen and Religious Educators

In an article of almost a generation ago Fahs (18, p. 21) urged recognition of the importance of the religious leader in individual counseling of parents, and urged recognition of the consequence also; namely, that training of clergymen and religious educators should provide more adequate education in the field of counseling and group leadership.

Fah's first point seems now to have achieved general acceptance. The present shows a marked contrast to the situation she described twenty-five years ago. This is seen in many places, for example, the large mass media programs of the leading religious denominations involving magazines, pamphlets, and books, and directed to improving mental health through parent education; the increased degree to which seminaries and other training institutions now include courses in the field of mental health; the recent establishment of the Academy of Religion and Mental Health which has as a broad objective joining the knowledge and experience of religion and the sciences in the effort to improve mental health.

However, Fahs' second point that improved training was necessary has yet to gain equal recognition. Many hold that the training which clergymen and religious educators receive is inadequate with respect both to content and educational methods, when compared with that training believed desirable by personnel in the parent education field. The fact thus remains that in spite of interest in mental health and the pursuit of such objectives through parent education members of religious organizations require further training.

The recognition of this need for more training than is received in the ordinary course of professional instruction has led to certain significant programs. The Board of Christian Education of the Presbyterian Church in the United States of America, through their Office of Family Education Research has completed a major study, soon to be published, of the types of family life educational counseling which parents wish to receive from their ministers, as well as other important information. The study also gives major consideration to the role of the minister in parent education and gathers information on the kinds of training and information he feels he needs in this aspect of his role. It certainly would be desirable if research of this kind were undertaken in connection with the other professional groups mentioned previously. Among the examples of training programs is one sponsored by the Protestant Council of the City of New York. This is a three-year experimental program, conducted for the Council by the Child Study Association, which provides for a number of ministers and directors of religious education a training program similar to that described just previously for nurses, but adapted to the special needs of this group.

Parents

A substantial number of the personnel of parent education programs will consist of parents who have had no special professional training in any of the fields already mentioned. However, these parents have received training, of widely varying amounts to be sure, in both content and method. The programs for training parents to work in the field of parent education seem to occur in connection with almost all the professions mentioned up to this point.

Mental health associations at both the community and state levels may support significant programs of training. Many of these have been mentioned before. They include, for example, the well-known programs of the St. Louis Mental Health Association, and of several Texas communities, including Fort Worth, El Paso, San Antonio, and Austin (12). Another important kind of program occurs under the auspices of colleges or universities, or sometimes in connection with state departments of education. Ordinarily this program consists of workshops for parents, especially those which emphasize training in leadership techniques. Among institutions carrying on this training are the University of Minnesota, the Institute of Child Study of the University of Toronto, the Merrill-Palmer School, the University of Denver, Vassar College, and Cornell University (16, 56). Other programs are conducted under the auspices of cooperative nursery schools (48). Still others are related to special programs of parent education as exemplified in the group leadership training program offered in connection with the Parent Education Project of the University of Chicago (26).

Probably the best-known program of training of parents is that of the National Congress of Parents and Teachers (38, 39). The Congress, through its state and local members, now provides for leadership training institutes in almost 40 states. After World War II the demand of members for more and better parent education brought about an expanded program of training. The program emphasized training in leadership procedures through workshops running a minimum of five days, and usually longer. This program was established initially for a five-year period following the war, but continues today in vigorous fashion in almost all states.

The degree of training in these many places varies considerably both in length and in relative emphasis upon content or method. Most programs of training for parents emphasize method rather than content, and take the form of one- or two-week workshops rather than longer programs. However, one must include programs of organizations such as the Montreal Mental Hygiene Institute, which offers a two-year course of study and seems little different from the typical family life education graduate program referred to previously.

The role which trained parents take in an educational program is usually consistent with the kind of training they have received. In general, the effort has been to recruit lay leaders into the ranks of parent education by drawing upon parents without professional background and providing them with brief courses of leadership training. These personnel have little knowledge of content and have little choice over the curriculum of the educational program. Instead they are provided with the skills necessary to take a role as discussion leader. Some of the parents recruited through such training programs do, indeed, go on to take further work in universities and to this extent join the ranks of family life educators. Most, however, remain at the level of limited training in methodology and serve parent education programs as adjunct personnel to the professionals of the community.

DISCUSSION AND CONCLUSIONS

In the Appendix we point out that in the historical development of parent education there has been a gradual increase in the number and variety of organizations which utilize parent education as a means of achieving their objectives. Members of numerous professions have come to realize that the education of parents provides a method of change which may enable them to achieve their aims. In part also, the increased use of parent education may have resulted from the solving of certain pressing problems in these other professions, so that with new-found leisure the members of the professions are able to turn their attention to the achievement of positive goals. It has been pointed out that the significant increase in time now at the disposal of the pediatrician and general practitioner since the development of antibiotics enables them to deal with less pressing matters than the immediate physical health of their patients. The same may be said to be generally true with respect to the nurse and the teacher. Still another influence leading to the greater use of parent education among these professions has been the recognition that members of these professions have a strategic relation with parents in the course of their professional practice, and constitute a channel of influence which should be utilized. This has long been pointed out with respect to nurses (44), physicians (34), and nursery school- and elementary schoolteachers (52). For these several reasons, therefore, there has been an increase in parent education as part of the regular and legitimate professional activity of the different specialists noted above.

It is possible that there has been a corresponding decrease in the number of family life educators who give a significant part of their time to parent education; in any event it is probable that at least these have not increased proportionately to either the number of parents in this country or to the increase in interest in parent education among members of other professions. One report a generation ago (40) pointed out that parent education was then too new and undeveloped to have many workers among its ranks especially trained for its services. The fact is, of course, that no clear-cut and separate profession of parent education has emerged and it is doubtful if there are any more, or indeed as many, persons being specifically trained in the field as there were some time ago.

Witmer in her report in 1934 (55) endeavored to find out who were the parent educators. No answer to the question could be given then, nor can it be given at present because we lack accurate statistics. However, she reports her impressions gained from the survey, which were that the important distinctions of that time were between the trained family life educator and the lay or parent recruit; the distinction between the family life educator and other professionals using parent education (such as pediatrics today) was as yet unimportant. In a survey (56) made in 1948 Yu found that statistics presented at the 1930 White House Conference on Child Health and Protection showed that about two-thirds of the administrative personnel and others with important responsibilities for parent education programs had Ph.D. degrees in the areas of psychology, education, or child development, that is, in those fields of knowledge which in the main provide the core curriculum for the family life educator. Although we have no statistics, it is highly doubtful that so large a percentage of leaders in parent education today would be from these fields; instead the percentage most likely would be reduced because of the addition of personnel from medical, clinical, and other educational fields.

In the years ahead it seems very likely that there will be continued and substantial growth in the provision of parent education by those persons who come directly into contact with parents by virtue of their professional role, such as the pediatrician, general practitioner, the teacher, the clergyman, and the others named here. We recognize that there has been resistance to changing their role in this way on the part of some professional bodies. Most likely this resistance will continue in the years ahead. This is particularly the case among medical personnel and certain bodies in the clinical groups, for example, psychiatric social workers. One reason is that prestige has been associated with the handling of the sick or disturbed; some pediatricians would resent the fact that they cannot treat illness but must deal with improvements in what appear to be already healthy persons; some social workers, in like manner, achieve professional prestige when allowed to work with seriously disturbed persons, much as the pediatrician achieves recognition when he deals with rare and possibly fatal illnesses among children. However, resistance of some notwithstanding, it seems likely that the training in the professions mentioned above will be expanded so as to include training in both content and method related to parent education, so that members are equipped for the practice of this newly recognized portion of their professional service to the public.

When it comes to the future of full-time specialists in parent education, one can only speculate. Perhaps it will turn out that their primary function is not to deal directly with parents, since they do not have strategic professional contexts in which to carry out education, but instead to serve as teachers of parent education to other professional groups, and to provide leadership in developing research and theory in the field of parent education. Certainly this would justify the cost of their lengthy specialized training, customarily the equivalent of a Ph.D. degree in psychology or child development. It would justify also their full-time support by organizations with significant parent education programs, no matter what profession was involved. This would include institutions such as the Children's Bureau, universities with centers of child development research, university departments of family life education, as well as religious, nursing, medical, and educational organizations which could make use of specialists in the education of parents.

One cannot say whether this development will actually take place. Some parent educators point out that members of the different professions will want their own members to provide the instruction rather than a person trained in some other discipline such as family life education. Or perhaps parent education will become so significant a part of the practice of one or another profession that it becomes identified as the professional property, so to speak, of that group. Some believe that there is a trend in the direction of parent education taking its place in time in schools of social work. Others have pointed out that it is the province of public health personnel to deal with this matter. Indeed, the possibility of a gradual change from private to public sponsorship of mental health programs in this country might be a significant factor. If mental health programs eventually come under the auspices of public groups, as is now the case with physical health, then one can envisage at the community level the existence of professional personnel whose concern is the mental health of the community, much as there is now a public health officer. The current private work of mental health associations, family service organizations, and related programs might eventually come under this program. The Grant Foundation even now is providing fellowships at the Harvard University School of Public Health for advanced training in community mental health for those professional persons wishing to specialize in this at the graduate level. The program aims at providing personnel competent in administration, research, and teaching to administer community health programs. Eventually such public programs would be large enough to warrant the employment of specialists in mental health education for parents, namely, the full-time parent educator.

Leaving now these few paragraphs of speculation, we turn to some conclusions as to what is needed in respect to selection and training of personnel. Certainly research is needed on the effects upon parents of using personnel with different training. To what extent does training in counseling, in group leadership, in preparation of mass media, in child development content and parent-child relations, improve the effectiveness of educational programs (32, chap. 3)? The other aspect of research is the evaluation of the effects of different types of training upon the parent educator. Studies in related fields (e.g., 7) suggest that training in group discussion leadership produces significant improvements in the students; however, whether this research is applicable to parent education or not is unknown and almost no effort has been made to evaluate the changes resulting from training programs in parent education. We noted earlier that some of these reports are to be published within the next year or two and that at least one preliminary report (3) on the training of nurses suggested that the effectiveness of the training depends in part on the personality characteristics of the student, in that the data suggest a negative relation between authoritarian attitudes on the part of nurses and the amount of improvement they show during the program. Informal observations like these serve to underscore the fact that much of the theory underlying training and selection at the present time is borrowed from other fields, and has not been validated in parent education itself.

A second conclusion is that better resource materials for use in training programs are very much needed. This is not so much the situation with respect to the area of content, where there are excellent summaries of research materials, but certainly is true with respect to training in methods; there are no standard works on preparation of mass media; the work in counseling theory includes but a handful of analyses; the work on group leadership procedures is almost wholly borrowed from other fields of activity. It would be especially valuable to have more concrete materials on educational counseling and on group discussion consisting of actual protocols of a verbatim nature, so that the student can become acquainted with the kinds of situations he will encounter in his role as parent educator.

Our final point is probably the most important. It is the need for increased communication between members of different professions who are active in parent education. We have described the variety of personnel active in parent education, and given some idea as to the many aims and methods involved in their programs. This diversity arises because parent education is a procedure employed by many different professions. Persons engaged in parent education owe their primary professional allegiance to various professional organizations, such as the National Council on Family Relations, American Orthopsychiatric Association, American Psychological Association, American Psychiatric Association, Adult Education Association, and the National Association of Social Workers, to name but a few. The picture is further complicated by the fact that a large number of activities in parent education are carried on by both commercial and lay organizations, rather than professional groups, although they may have professional staff members.

The variety of programs and professional settings is impressive, but the result is detrimental to the professionalization of activities in parent education. The most immediate consequences are the absence of a national professional group of parent educators, and the absence of professional journals devoted primarily to parent education. In regard to the first point, the one national meeting which is closest to fulfilling the function of national meetings of existing professional bodies is the annual Institute for Workers in Parent Education, held by the Child Study Association. However, although of high quality, the Institute is small considering the total number of parent educators and lacks representiveness. In regard to the second point, the materials pertaining to parent education are published in the professional journals sponsored by the professional societies of the authors. The result is that instead of one or two key journals carrying materials on parent education, there are some 50 journals which must regularly be canvassed for articles pertaining to professional activities and problems in parent education.

A result of there being no national organization or professional journal is that communication between parent educators of different backgrounds, and indeed sometimes between those of the same background, is ineffective. Identical research may proceed in two different localities without either group's having knowledge of the other; training programs are conducted which are quite similar, but with no sharing of information between the organizations. Indeed, it is the absence of communication that accounts for the "discovery" of parent education as a "new method" by some persons in the field of mental health, and the fact that such persons proceed with extreme naiveté in ignorance of the long tradition of parent education. Moreover, this lack of communication leads to many instances of duplication of effort in the same geographic area, resulting in confusion and often undesirable competitive situations between parent education programs. With respect to training, efforts should be made to recognize the unity of all the programs established to train members of these different professions in the practice of parent education. At present, responsible personnel in different professions still proceed as if none but their own group had given thought to the question of training for parent education; materials in pediatric training may make negligible use of the work already done with respect to teacher education, while training of social workers may give little attention to the significant materials developed in connection with the training of home economists.

Another effect of inadequate communication is that standard-setting for parent education programs and training is difficult, if not impossible. Parent education is an activity requiring special skills over and above those of any given profession, and the remarkably varied conceptions of such skills arise in part from the absence of professional integration.

This is not to imply that some single standard of training should be developed and applied to all individuals. On the contrary, what increased communication could accomplish is a greater familiarity with the work going on in other settings, leading one to develop his own theory and to clarify his conception of the different roles to be filled in parent education, and the different training which each of these may require (22). Moreover, it would lead one to develop a more adequate theory of training for his own profession. For example, in the important work of Korsch (28) describing a program of training in individual counseling for medical personnel, cognizance is taken of the specific role of the pediatrician and the realistic limitations upon his time and type of interaction with parents. The important theoretical work of the Child Study Association (5) on training for group leadership gives special recognition to the professional settings in which different types of personnel must work, and seeks to establish training programs which fit these professional roles. At the very least, if a group is acquainted with the work going on in other professions with respect to training, it must enrich its insight into its own strengths and weaknesses for parent education, and bring about a more judicious statement of theory underlying its training program.

It seems doubtful that the problem of professional integration of parent education will be solved through a natural convergence of interests, as is normally the case. Persons engaged in parent education prefer to attend the national meetings of their respective professional groups and to write for their respective journals for the usual reasons of prestige and reward. It is to such groups also that their financial support is given. In retrospect it is apparent that the integration offered by the National Council of Parent Education stemmed primarily from outside financial support, rather than from contributions made by the members as is customary in professional societies. When this support was withdrawn, the membership was not able to carry the organization.

It seems strongly indicated that parent education needs the equivalent of a professional clearing house, some means of distributing information among parent educators in different professions. Much might be gained through the establishment of a continuing conference of the leaders of the major training programs in this country, with such a conference having the objective of establishing and maintaining standards for the selection and training of individuals involved in the education of parents.

Both our analysis and the historical development of parent education have indicated that this activity probably cannot be supported in the same manner as in other professional groups because of the allegiance of parent educators to various professions. Since the success of the National Council of Parent Education came from support by foundation rather than membership funds, it may be that an equivalent type of clearing house could only operate if supported by foundation or other types of non-membership funds.

REFERENCES

1. American Public Health Association, *Health Supervision of Young Children*. The Association, New York, 1955.

2. Auerbach, Aline B., "Public Health Nursing and Parent Education: A Pilot Project of Training for Parent Group Leadership," *American Journal of Public Health*, vol. 45, 1955, pp. 1578–1589.

3. Auerbach, Aline B., "New Approaches to Work with Expectant Parent Groups," *American Journal of Public Health*, vol. 47, 1957, pp. 184–191.

4. Auerbach, Aline B., *Training of Professional Persons for Work in Family Life Education*. Paper presented at the 86th Annual Forum, National Conference on Social Welfare, May 26, 1959, mimeographed.

5. Auerbach, Aline B., and Gertrude Goller, "The Contribution of the Professionally Trained Leader of Parent Discussion Groups," *Marriage and Family Living*, vol. 15, 1953, pp. 265–269.

6. Auerbach, Aline B., and Marion F. Langer, "Training for Parent Group Leadership" in *Parent Group Education and Leadership Training:* Three Reports. Child Study Association of America, New York, 1953, pp. 16–22.

7. Barnlund, Dean C., "Experiments in Leadership Training for Decision-Making Discussion Groups," *Speech Monographs*, vol. 22, 1955, pp. 1–14.

8. Beilin, Harry, "Teachers' and Clinicians' Attitudes Toward the Behavior Problems of Children: A Reappraisal," *Child Development*, vol. 30, 1959, pp. 9–25.

9. Blake, Florence, *The Child, His Parents and the Nurse*. J. B. Lippincott Co., Philadelphia, 1954.

10. Board of Education, City of New York, *The Bureau of Child Guidance in the New York City Schools:* A Survey. The Board, New York, 1955.

11. Brandt, Richard M., and Hugh V. Perkins, "Research Evaluating a Child Study Program," *Monographs for the Society for Research in Child Development*, vol. 21, 1956, pp. 1–96.

12. Cheavens, Frank, *Leading Group Discussions*. Hogg Foundation for Mental Health, University of Texas, Austin, 1958.

13. Child Study Association of America, "Parent Education: Its Ends and Goals," *Workshop Reports:* Proceedings of the 1954 Conference for Workers in Parent Education. The Association, New York, 1954, pp. 17–32.

14. Child Study Association of America, *Report on Training of Nurses for Leadership of Parent Groups:* An Experimental Project in Parent Education. The Association, New York, 1958, mimeographed.

15. Coleman, Jules V., "Workers in the Field of Mental Health," *Annals of the American Academy of Political and Social Science*, vol. 286, 1953, pp. 81–91.

16. Cummings, Pearl T., Dan C. Overlade, and Dale B. Harris, *A Guide for Leaders in Parent and Family Life Education*. Institute of Child Welfare, University of Minnesota, Minneapolis, 1955.

17. Dybwad, Gunnar, "How We Train for Leadership in Parent Education," *Children*, vol. 1, 1954, p. 10.

18. Fahs, Sophia Lyon, "Parent Counselling in the Practice of Various Professions: The Religious Leader," *Parent Education*, vol. 2, 1935, pp. 20–21.

19. Family Service Association of America, *Scope and Methods of the Family Service Agency:* Report of the Committee on Methods and Scope. The Association, New York, 1953.

20. Gabbard, Hazel, *Working with Parents*. Bulletin No. 7, Office of Education, Government Printing Office, Washington, 1948.

21. Gabbard, Hazel, *Preparing Your Child for School*. Pamphlet No. 108, Government Printing Office, Washington, 1949.

22. Goller, Gertrude, *When Parents Get Together:* How to Organize a Parent Education Program. Child Study Association of America, New York, 1955.

23. Hymes, James Lee, Jr., *Effective Home-School Relations.* Prentice-Hall, New York, 1953.

24. Kanner, Leo, "The Development and Present Status of Psychiatry in Pediatrics," *Journal of Pediatrics*, vol. 11, 1937, pp. 418–435.

25. Kawin, Ethel, *A Guide for Child Study-Groups.* Science Research Associates, Inc., Chicago, 1952.

26. Kawin, Ethel, *Parenthood in a Free Nation.* Parent Education Project, University of Chicago Press, Chicago, 1954.

27. Kerckhoff, Richard K., "Interest Group Reactions to the Profession of Marriage Counseling," *Sociology and Social Research*, vol. 39, 1955, pp. 179–183.

28. Korsch, Barbara Marie, "Practical Techniques of Observing, Interviewing and Advising Parents in Pediatric Practice as Demonstrated in an Attitude Study Project," *Pediatrics*, vol. 18, 1956, pp. 467–490.

29. Korsch, Barbara, Lewis Fraad, and Henry L. Barnett, "Pediatric Discussions with Parent Groups," *Journal of Pediatrics*, vol. 44, 1954, pp. 703–717.

30. Krugman, Morris, "Education's Debt to Orthopsychiatry," *American Journal of Orthopsychiatry*, vol. 23, 1953, pp. 445–453.

31. Lemkau, Paul V., "Local Mental Health Services," *Annals of the American Academy of Political and Social Science*, vol. 286, 1953, pp. 116–125.

32. Lemkau, Paul V., *Mental Hygiene in Public Health.* McGraw-Hill Book Co., New York, 1955.

33. Lindeman, Eduard C., and Flora M. Thurston, *Problems for Parent Educators.* National Council of Parent Education, New York, 1931.

34. Mercer, Mary E., "Mental Health Consultation to Child Health Protecting Agencies" in *The Elements of a Community Mental Health Program.* Milbank Memorial Fund, New York, 1956, pp. 47–56.

35. Merrill, Pearl, *Training for Parenthood.* Child Guidance League, New York, 1955.

36. Meyer, Marguerite S., and Edward J. Power, Jr., "The Family Caseworker's Contribution to Parent Education Through the Medium of the Discussion Group," *American Journal of Orthopsychiatry*, vol. 23, 1953, pp. 621–628.

37. Milbank Memorial Fund, *The Elements of a Community Mental Health Program:* Papers Presented at the 1955 Annual Conference of the Milbank Memorial Fund. The Fund, New York, 1956.

38. National Congress of Parents and Teachers, *New Hope for Audiences.* The National Congress, Chicago, 1954.

39. National Congress of Parents and Teachers, *Proceedings* of the Annual Convention. The National Congress, Chicago, vols. 1–62.

40. National Society for the Study of Education, *Twenty-Eighth Year Book: Parts I and II, Preschool and Parent Education*. Public School Publishing, Bloomington, Ill., 1929.

41. Nelson, Waldo Emerson, editor, *Mitchell-Nelson Textbook of Pediatrics*. 5th ed. W. B. Saunders Co., Philadelphia, 1950.

42. New York State Citizens' Committee of One Hundred for Children and Youth, *The Four Million*. Albany, 1951.

43. Pratt, George K., *Three Family Narratives for Use in Parent Education Groups*, With a Discussion of the Problems of Study-Group Leadership. National Council of Parent Education, New York, 1935.

44. Rand, Winifred, "Parent Education Opportunities of the Public Health Nurse," *Parent Education*, vol. 1, 1934, pp. 3–6.

45. *Social Work Year Book, 1957*. National Association of Social Workers, New York, 1957.

46. Solnit, A. J., and Milton J. E. Senn, "Teaching Comprehensive Pediatrics in an Out-Patient Clinic," *Pediatrics*, vol. 14, 1954, pp. 547–556.

47. Strang, Ruth, *Reporting to Parents:* Practical Suggestions for Teaching. Bureau of Publications, No. 10, Teachers College, Columbia University, New York, 1947.

48. Taylor, Katharine Whiteside, *Parent Cooperative Nursery Schools*. Teachers College, Columbia University, New York, 1954.

49. United Parents Association of New York City, *City Parent*. The Association, New York, 1957.

50. United States Department of Health, Education, and Welfare, *Health Services and Juvenile Delinquency*. Children's Bureau, Washington, 1955.

51. United States Department of Health, Education, and Welfare, *Experiences with Infants in the Preparation of Home Economists:* Report of a Conference Called by the Children's Bureau and the Office of Education. Government Printing Office, Washington, 1955.

52. Wall, William D., *Education and Mental Health:* A Report Based Upon the Work of a European Conference Called by UNESCO at the Musée Pedagogique in Paris, Nov.-Dec., 1952. UNESCO, Paris, 1955.

53. Whiteside-Taylor, Katharine, "Parent Education Through Preschool Groups," *The Councillor*, Baltimore Council of Social Agencies, vol. 18, 1953, pp. 4–8.

54. Welfare and Health Council of New York City, *Group Methods in Casework Agencies*. The Council, New York, 1955, mimeographed.

55. Witmer, Helen L., *The Field of Parent Education:* A Survey from the Point of View of Research. National Council of Parent Education, New York, 1934.

56. Yu, Hsi Chi, *Survey of the Parent Education Movement in the United States of America and Canada*. Master's thesis, University of Toronto, Canada, 1948.

CHAPTER NINE:

Evaluating the Results

IN THIS FINAL CHAPTER the most difficult problem of all awaits analysis: the problem of evaluating the effectiveness of parent education programs in achieving their aims. Evaluation of the effectiveness of the work of an individual or of an organization always carries a threat in that the results may publicly reveal inadequacies. It is natural that many seek to avoid evaluation and react to it with anger and with defensive statements, holding that their work has such subtle and complex effects that they are not measurable. In addition, evaluation research of a scientific kind is extremely difficult to carry out successfully because of the variety of logical and experimental errors which the researcher may make. Hence, our consideration of evaluation in parent education requires the utmost care and detail.

First we discuss the effects which should be studied, as for example, parent attitudes, mental illness, or the like. Next is a discussion of which parent education programs or which parts of such programs should be evaluated; for example, should the study be of variations in method, in content, in clientele, or what? Attention then is given to the types of evidence necessary to provide an adequate scientific evaluation. After these matters have been discussed, we turn to a detailed analysis of the available research. Finally, we discuss the conclusions that can be drawn from the current state of evaluation research in parent education.

WHAT EFFECTS SHOULD BE STUDIED?

The choice of the effects to be studied (the dependent variables to be appraised) in an experimental evaluation must proceed at several levels of generality. First, the broad aims of the educational program will determine the kind of effects with which the evaluation should be concerned. In earlier chapters we have stated that the overall aim of the majority of parent education programs is to improve the mental and physical well-being of children by altering the parents' behavior through education. Hence, the ultimate criterion of effectiveness of a program must be some characteristic of children, rather than of their parents. In addition, we have stressed that the majority of programs are now directed to the mental health of the child, rather than his physical health, since the latter aim has been achieved to a remarkable degree in this country during the past century. Hence, these aims determine that the criterion of effectiveness should somehow represent the child's mental health rather than his physical health.

Given this broad category of evaluative criteria, there is a further classification which follows from the theory underlying parent education programs and which serves as a basis for classifying the actual evaluation studies made in this field. Parent education shares in common with other action programs some theory of the sequence of events leading from exposure to the program to eventual changes in the child. This sequence of effects, with each class of effects being potentially usable as a criterion in evaluation studies, is frequently viewed as follows. First, there are changes in a parent's factual information (knowledge); subsequently, changes in motivation or attitudes or feelings ensue; these in turn are manifested in changes in the parents' overt actions. As a result of changes both in the parents' motives, attitudes, and feelings, and in their overt behavior, the child's behavior and attitudes are altered in some measurable way. The validity of the assumptions involved in this view of the causal sequence is still much a matter of speculation. If we had more basic research clarifying such causal sequences, the task of program evaluation would be much simpler.

Most evaluation studies have used as criteria changes either in parents' information or in their attitudes or feelings, while in fact other elements in this causal sequence, such as direct measures of the child's mental health or of parents' overt behavior, might better be used as criteria of effectiveness of programs. Each of these will be considered briefly below.

First, with respect to direct appraisals of the child's mental health as a criterion of effectiveness, one faces the question of using rates of incidence of mental illness. The difficulty in using incidence rates, whether for children in evaluating a parent education program, or for adults in evaluating other kinds of programs directed to reducing mental illness, is that the rates are influenced by a number of factors other than the program being evaluated. The actual tabulation of frequencies of mental illness may be considerably removed in time and in sequence from the educational program, thus permitting these other factors to occur. The research on rates of mental illness (e.g., 15, 26) has pointed out that rates can change radically when new definitions are instituted, either legally or by the public itself; when there is an increase in treatment facilities such as available hospital beds; and also because of other factors. Thus, an educational program for parents might be effective in reducing the true incidence of mental illness in children but the frequency of such mental illness expressed in rates might increase owing to improved diagnostic facilities in the community.

There is another point to consider: a program could be effective in improving the mental health of initially *healthy* children by virtue of education of their parents without in any way preventing or reducing illness in incipient or already sick children. This is to say that a parent education program might be efficient in promoting mental health but not in reducing or preventing mental illness, and that attention to the rates of mental illness as currently measured by hospital admissions or diagnoses would not reflect the increase in the well-being of children who never were disturbed enough to be counted in the establishment of rates.

These considerations have led the thoughtful parent educator to look not at rates but at other characteristics more directly indicative of the child's personal well-being. This involves the crucial problem of stating the characteristics of a mentally healthy child. We have pointed out the difficulty that parent educators and others in the mental health movement have had in attempting to specify characteristics of mental health (35). Especially is this a problem when the definition is to be used in a research venture, where general and diffuse statements will not do. If the achievement of aims is to be evaluated scientifically, the descriptions of mental health or definitions in terms of some solitary global trait such as "adjustment" make mental health impossible to measure, and hence place it beyond the realm of research operations. What is needed is a conception for research purposes which views mental health as composed of a variety of characteristics. This permits one to isolate those worthy of study, whether they be a child's causal approach to life, social desirability to others, the relation between his real and his ideal self-image, his feelings of self-worth, or the like. Of the evaluation studies which we discuss subsequently in this chapter, very few have taken as a criterion of effectiveness some characteristic of the child. This procedure is used by Ojemann and his colleagues (48, 50), and also in the St. Louis study (54) evaluating parent discussion groups. The difficulties involved, plus the ease and availability of other criteria, have led the evaluator back toward earlier events in the sequence which relates the educational program to the child's mental health.

Thus, attention has been given to the appraisal of change in the parents' overt behavior as an indication of the effectiveness of educational programs. Where overt parent behavior has been used as a criterion, the data regarding the behavior usually have been collected by asking the parents to describe what they do. The procedure varies from brief descriptions of handling feeding problems (12) to comprehensive reports on the child-care practices used throughout a whole day (59). This procedure has been criticized by many observers on the grounds that the parents' description of their behavior may bear little resemblance to what they actually do. Attempts to solve this problem by making objective observations of the parents' behavior also have met with criticism. One line of approach has been to visit the home as an observer (e.g., 4, 5, 8) but such efforts have been few in number.

Some contend that the effects of the observer in the family are probably just as distorting as the alleged distortion which occurs in parents' self-reports. Another approach has been to bring parent and child together and give them some contrived task over which they can interact, either in the home (e.g., 62) or in the laboratory. Whether this is more or less artificial than the others is difficult to say. One recent report has shown that parents' self-reports and direct observation of the kind described in the laboratory situation may elicit about the same kind of description of the parents' behavior.

Other researchers have dealt with parent attitudes, motives, and the like, or straightforwardly with changes in parents' factual information. Fewer problems arise here with regard to the validity of the data, although one can question whether parents' self-reports on attitudes and feelings are valid in the sense of representing those they have when the child, rather than the researcher, is present. There is very little information on this point. One recent study (11) finds that mothers' self-reports of certain attitudes are more closely related to their children's aggressive behavior than are the children's beliefs about what the mothers' attitudes are. In any event, while the validity of attitudinal and factual tests may be greater, they suffer from being more distantly removed from the ultimate criterion variable, namely, the child's mental health.

Whereas the question of selection of criteria was discussed above in terms of the probable validity of the data obtained, the matter to be considered now concerns the strength of the relationship between the criteria, such as "improved attitudes" and the child's actual mental health.

What is the validity of the assumed sequence of events relating education to changes in the child's mental health? The importance of this is clear. The studies to be reviewed indicating increases in information, the numerous studies attesting to an improvement in the parents' attitude or in behavior, are simply irrelevant to the issue of the child's mental health unless it is demonstrated independently that these changes are in fact instrumental in promoting mental health. Indeed, a contrary assumption to that of a causal relation between, say, information and mental health is simply that there is no such relation, and that we might improve the information of the general public on human development a hundredfold and not influence in the slightest the mental health of children. It is imperative, therefore, in the selection of criteria for evaluation that one consider the validity of this assumed causal sequence.

Looking at changes in overt behavior which have been shown to result from parent education programs, what evidence is there that such changes are related to the child's health? Obviously, one cannot question the principle that a parent's relations with his child influence the latter's mental health. The great bulk of clinical literature stemming from and including the work of Freud supports this principle, although with the reservations given in Chapter II. Consider, however, what the several studies on the changes of parent behavior, to be reviewed subsequently, have shown; for example, increases in self-demand feeding, in casual instruction of children in sexual matters, in general permissiveness in child care. Consider the results of the *Pierre the Pelican* evaluation studies, indicating that parents may improve in their handling of several matters: in asking the child's permission to use his things for the new baby, in providing the baby with a separate room, and in the frequency with which the father changes the diapers, among others. Do we know from research studies that these characteristics of parent behavior promote or inhibit the mental health of the child? There is little evidence. While it may seem valid that casual instruction in sex matters helps the child develop a healthy attitude, this is still a hypothetical relation. This is true for the others also: the causal relation between these and the child's mental health remains an open question.

In the area of attitudes, motives, and feelings the situation is hardly better. Some of the studies discussed subsequently report favorable changes on the Minnesota Multi-phasic Personality Inventory after educational programs. One can question, however, whether parents with MMPI profiles indicating poor adjustment also produce undesirable emotional characteristics in children.

There is little information on this point, although there are data from another field which are suggestive. Crawford (18) compares pupils of three poorly adjusted teachers with those of three well-adjusted teachers as determined by the MMPI. A test-retest of the children with Rogers' test of personality adjustment reveals that during the year the pupils change in the direction of the teacher's adjustment. Those pupils with poorly adjusted teachers significantly decline in adjustment. The reverse is true for the pupils of the well-adjusted teachers.

Other studies have shown improvement on a test of parental attitudes developed by Shoben (58). Shoben originally validated the test by the method of known groups and included in the scale 85 items which discriminated between mothers of problem and nonproblem children. However, the mothers were not from the same social class background, and recent research (39) shows that only a few of the original 85 items discriminate between mothers of problem and nonproblem children *within the same social class*. It appears that the original findings resulted in part from the greater frequency of problem children among a lower-class population. In regard to other attitude changes which have been demonstrated in the studies of parent education (for example, changes toward more developmental approaches, changes toward more acceptance of one's self), for all of them it can be said only that while there is a certain validity to be assumed between such changes and the mental health of the child, unfortunately this has yet to be clearly demonstrated.

Turning to factual knowledge, there seems to be no study which relates the amount of knowledge that a parent possesses to the mental health of his child. Recent work (63) shows, at least when mass media are used, that teaching factual information is easy in the area of mental health, but that it is comparatively difficult to change people's feelings or attitudes. It does not follow, therefore, that changes in factual information produce either changes in attitudes, or subsequent improvement in the child's mental health. This would seem to demand research attention. It has been pointed out (e.g., 48) that factual knowledge often is imparted in a way that makes it difficult to translate into attitudinal or behavioral changes, so that it may remain useless information. Others might argue that gains in factual knowledge from educational programs should not be treated lightly, for it may lead to important consequences, and that parent education has demonstrated its usefulness if it can show an increase in parents' factual knowledge. Clearly what we need here is some work correlating factual information with parental attitudes and behavior, and children's health.

What criteria, then, should be used in evaluating parent education? What effects should be selected for study? Logically, the criteria should be those with the most validity, namely, those closest to representing an increase in the child's mental health. This suggests that the ideal criteria would be careful appraisals of personal characteristics of the children of parents involved in parent education programs, on an experimental, before-and-after basis. Evaluation studies have only recently begun to recognize this. One step removed from this ideal set of criteria are those characteristics of the parent which theory holds are instrumental to the child's mental health. Outstanding examples of their use have been the St. Louis County Health Department project's (54) conception of mothers' beliefs in the area of causality in human relations; Ojemann's (50) conception of parental attitudes and beliefs in the area of causality in human relations; the research by the Institute of Child Study in Toronto (33), which explores the effects of parent education on lessening the gap between the parent's ideal and real self-image; and a current project by the Child Study Association of America and the Westport-Weston (Connecticut) Mental Health Association, which appraises the improvement in parent decision processes and problem-solving ability as a result of participation in parent discussion groups.

Most studies have been considerably further away from the ideal criteria, and seem almost to have seized the first available test and used it to evaluate the program whether or not the test was relevant to program objectives. Hence, there are a large number of studies using the currently popular attitude test in the year the study is undertaken, with almost no theoretical explanation given as to why this measure, rather than some other, seems appropriate. Where evaluation instruments are chosen on the basis of fadism and availability, rather than their relation to carefully considered objectives, even the discovery of a significant effect of a parent education program leaves us no further advanced in our understanding of parent education, since one cannot interpret the findings.

WHAT ASPECT OF THE PROGRAM SHOULD BE EVALUATED?

In previous chapters we have dealt with three of the fundamental aspects of parent education programs; namely, the techniques used, the content presented, and the clientele addressed. In the discussion of these matters we have indicated repeatedly that there are few data to guide one with respect to any of these three program aspects. It was made clear that the evaluation research available on parent education had only rarely dealt with a comparison of the different methods, that the evaluation of the different kinds of content was negligible, and, finally, that studies of the relative effectiveness of parent education with different types of clientele had been given attention in only one or two research studies. The evaluation research in parent education often has been of the kind which asks the question: Does technique x have any effects? Sometimes the question is even cruder: Is what we are doing in this program having *any* effect?—without the technique itself being defined. The research on the whole has demonstrated that some programs "have effects" and some programs have none, but attention has not been given to the kind of clientele involved, to the content transmitted, and to specification of the technique itself.

Methods

The conceptualization of educational methods has been very crude in evaluation studies. The research has suffered considerably from failure to specify the characteristics of the technique being evaluated. Shapiro's study (56) is a notable exception in that he clearly describes the philosophy and procedure of the group discussion technique he uses. Specification of techniques would make possible moving on to the next stage in evaluating the methods aspect of the program: comparative studies between different techniques as to their effectiveness, such as a comparison of the relative effects of mass media with group discussion procedures. Still further specification in evaluation studies leads to research on the effects of variations within the three broad classes of methods. For example, in the area of group discussion methods, basic research is necessary which compares the effects of lay versus professional leadership, of differences in group size, and many other variations which we have previously discussed in Chapter VII on methodology.

Content

In Chapter VI on the selection of content for educational programs, we pointed out that the several types of content include information about parents, about social, physical, and emotional stages in child development, and many others. Characteristics of presentation include such varied qualities as the generality versus specificity of the ideas presented, whether advice is given as a firm rule, for example, "always works," or as a probability statement, "probably will work." Evaluation of the effects of different types of content demands a clear specification of the differences between them, such as that attempted by Ojemann and his associates (49). In actuality, none of the evaluation studies has given proper attention to the type of content being evaluated.

Clientele

Responses of parents to educational programs are determined in part by the characteristics of the parents themselves as distinct from the educational procedures and content used. It is well to recognize that in studies of personality and in personality theory generally the effort is made to predict the individual's response from knowledge of his personal characteristics, with relatively less emphasis given to the effects of a situation in eliciting this response. In contrast, studies of parent education programs have attempted to appraise the effectiveness of a situation (the parent education program) upon the individual's behavior with almost no reference to the contribution made by the parent's personal characteristics.

The influential personal characteristics of parents might be classified as personality factors, on the one hand, and as factors pertaining to the social setting of the parental role on the other. In respect to the first, only one study (12) has been concerned with the effects of personality characteristics in determining responses to parent education programs. In addition to the types of characteristics considered in that study, for example, dominance, many others should be explored. We would be interested, for example, in finding out whether persons who are generally submissive to authority are more frequently influenced by parent education. Janis and Field (38) report the isolation and identification of a general personality factor of persuasibility, which certainly would be pertinent to the effectiveness of educational programs. It would be especially desirable to study whether the effects of parent education are contingent upon differences between parents in their anxiety about child rearing. Some research in the mass communication field (e.g., 32, 37), while needing to be repeated in the area of parent education to test its validity, implies that moderate anxiety may be associated with a greater acceptance of parent education materials and that both high and low extremes of anxiety render parent education programs ineffective.

We have found no studies concerned with the social setting of the parent role, but a series of very basic questions can be asked which demand research. How, for example, do the effects of parent education programs vary, depending on whether the mother and father jointly participate in the program or only one parent? What are the effects of the program when the parental role is embedded in a broad family social system, for example, when the grandparents live with the parents? How do the community setting and social leaders influence one's receptivity to a program? In other areas these have been shown to have a powerful influence (40). Even the basic characteristics such as family size, age, and sex of family members need to be appraised in their effects upon parent receptivity to educational programs.

Interaction Effects of Different Program Characteristics

One will readily understand that the relative effectiveness of any program variation, for example, the effects of lay versus professional leadership, or of developmental versus home management types of content, will depend on still other characteristics of the program. The many elements of a parent education program combine and interact in such a way as to make the effect of any one of them contingent on the others with which it is combined. The evaluation of the effects of an educational program thus becomes a difficult theoretical and empirical problem. The research available is extremely naive and rudimentary in the attention it gives to the interaction of different program characteristics. Klapper, in writing about the many studies of the effects of mass communication on public opinion, voting behavior, and so on gives an idea of what may lie in store for parent education evaluation research. He says: "Such anomalous findings as have been cited above seemed to us at first to betoken merely the need of more penetrating and rigid research. We shaped insights into hypotheses and eagerly set up research designs in quest of the additional variables which we were sure would bring order out of chaos, and enable us to describe the process of effect with sufficient precision to diagnose and predict. But the variables emerged in such a cataract that we almost drowned. The relatively placid waters of '*who* says *what* to *whom*' were early seen to be muddied by audience predispositions, 'self-selections,' and selective perception. More recent studies, both in the laboratory and social world, have documented the influence of a host of other variables, including various aspects of contextual organization; the audience's image of the source; the simple passage of time; the group orientation of the audience member and the degree to which he values group membership; the activity of opinion leaders; the social aspects of the situation during and after exposure to the media, and the degree to which the audience member is forced to play a role; the personality pattern of the audience member, his social class and the level of his frustration; the nature of the media in a free enterprise system, and the availability of 'social mechanism[s] for implementing action drives.' The list, if not endless, is at least overwhelming, and it continues to grow." (42)

Complicated though the problem is, the solution, of course, does not lie in ignoring the interaction of different characteristics of programs in determining effectiveness, but in so conceptualizing them that a theoretical simplification is achieved. Seemingly unlike elements become classified in common theoretical groups, thus simplifying the evaluation of their interaction. A number of examples of probable interaction effects in parent education come readily to mind. For example, there are studies which find differences between individuals in their "desire for certainty," their "intolerance of ambiguity." One can hypothesize that programs giving "rules" as content would be more successful with those with a high "desire for certainty" and programs where the content is given only a probable validity may require the opposite kind of parent to be effective. As another example, consider the interaction between parents' initial level of anxiety and the type of content where the potential bad outcomes of poor child rearing are reported. On the basis of work by Janis (37) one might hypothesize that low anxiety-producing materials would be most effective with parents already highly anxious, whereas high anxiety-producing materials would have greater effect on those parents initially low in anxiety. For another example, it may be true as is often argued that mass media techniques are among the least expensive and most effective ways of transmitting factual information, whereas group discussion procedures are superior in bringing about change in attitudes. This, then, is a different type of interaction effect: between type of method and type of result.

To summarize, the effects of parent education probably depend on the interaction of a certain method with certain content, clientele, and type of result being considered. Evaluation studies therefore could with profit be as specific as the study of the effect of group discussion (lay leaders), using information on child development stages, directed to mothers only, upon the parents' actual behavior; or as the study of the effect of mass media (pamphlets), giving home management advice, to college graduates, upon the parents' attitudes.

It is hardly possible for any single project or any single program of research to study the effects of variation along all of these dimensions. However, future studies can move considerably beyond the present level in considering the important questions of interaction effects in evaluation. At the very least, it is within the scope of any future study to specify clearly and to strive to control the many factors known to be pertinent to the effects of parent education, so that the results obtained can be attributed conclusively to that factor or factors in the studies which are experimentally varied. Considerable advance must be made in this regard if research evaluating the effects of parent education is to be comparable from one study to the next, and thus have a cumulative impact upon the field.

WHAT EVIDENCE ON EFFECTS SHOULD BE ADMISSIBLE?

We now turn to the question of what a scientific study of effects requires by way of procedure, selection of subjects, and the like. Much of what passes as research in the area of parent education is pseudoscientific both in design and in procedure. For example, one criterion for the effectiveness of parent education which is often used is whether parents like the program and continue to expose themselves to it. Certain studies using this approach have been summarized by Witmer (66, pp. 67–69), and the same point of view is presented in other studies (e.g., 67). Moreover, this approach has been used by State Congresses of Parents and Teachers in evaluating their annual workshops (46).

Evaluation of this kind cannot be considered satisfactory. The fact that some parents say they like and continue to expose themselves to parent education indicates that the programs are having some effect, but what this is specifically and whether it is beneficial or not is unknown. Much parent education is carried on as a commercial enterprise. However, the fact that parents are sufficiently attracted to these educational programs for financial profit to be made does not necessarily mean that they have beneficial effects, any more than does the success of some other profit-making enterprise, such as the sale of cigarettes, salacious litera-ture, and the like, connote good effects. As Borgatta (9) points out in regard to psychotherapy, popularity is not a legitimate criterion of success, since popularity is not demonstrated neces-sarily to be associated with "good." He holds that the same argu-ment favors faith healers, astrologers, and tea-leaf readers.

One could as well argue that the continued popularity of par-ent education is evidence of its evils in that the effects of parent education are to arouse anxiety in parents which in turn creates the demand for further education to reduce the anxiety, with the net result that the mother becomes dependent on continuous educational programs. This is not, of course, advanced seriously; still, Hale has found (28) that counseling parents results in the identification by the parent of more rather than fewer problems (or at least the admission that the parent has them).

Ridenour (52) has pointed out that since people may be at-tracted to programs or materials which are bad for them in the sense noted above, popularity is not a criterion of success unless the content of the program is known to be good. Where the edu-cational program is sound in content and the parents like it as well, these factors constitute informal evidence that the programs are successful, in the sense of having beneficial effects. But this view seems hardly more satisfactory than the first, for one does not know whether the content has been assimilated by the par-ents or not. It could easily be that he comes to the educational program for diverse reasons and takes home with him little or no improvement in information or attitude. A more cogent criticism is that while the content presented in the program may be judged by experts to be good, as finally assimilated by the parent it may be considerably different from what was actually transmitted, once it becomes adapted and fitted into his own current ideas and individual needs. An actual assessment of the change produced by good content in this sense might show that the change effected was undesirable; for example, a carefully handled discussion of children's infantile sexual impulses may be the cause of increasing a parent's apprehension about the possibility of his child showing such behavior and, perhaps without being aware of it, the cause of a greater repression of these impulses in the child by the parent.

We conclude, therefore, that evaluation research must proceed according to the accepted canons of science. The general outline of the design and methodology for evaluation studies of the kind necessary in parent education are given in the standard sources on social research methods (e.g., 22, 36). It is true that much of the research in parent education has been done by persons who have little or no substantial training in evaluation methodology. This accounts in part for the shortcomings of existing research. However, fundamental errors can be avoided by consideration of the elementary research procedures presented in the sources listed above. Perhaps the future will see the development of regional or other types of training workshops in evaluation research for persons in mental health education programs, so that they could within a few weeks acquire the basic knowledge and training for laying out a research design. They then would be equipped to carry on their own internal evaluation research, with a moderate amount of guidance from outside consultants.

There are several fundamental requirements which determine whether an evaluation study is adequate, and its results admissible as evidence of effectiveness. The first of these is the use of a control group design. That is, the sample for an evaluation study should consist of two groups: an experimental group, comprised of persons who are involved in the educational program and a control group, made up of persons who are not. The reason is that the members of the experimental group involved in the education program are being subjected also to a multitude of daily experiences which can easily change them in the same way as the program is alleged to change them, or in a contrary way, possibly canceling out the true effects of the program. The value of the control group is that it also undergoes this extraneous change, and tells the investigator its size and direction. Where the absence of change in the experimental group is attributed to the ineffectiveness of the program, a comparison with a control group may show the educational program kept the experimental group from changing in a negative direction. Conversely, a positive change in the experimental group may be viewed as evidence of the effectiveness of the program, when in fact a comparison with a control group will show that the control group (by virtue of its other experiences) has made equal improvement, and that the proper conclusion is that the educational program is irrelevant. This latter instance occurs dramatically in one outstanding study in the field of parent education made by Balser and his associates (6, 7). In this study, which we review later, a failure to use control groups, as the authors indicate, would have resulted in false conclusions about the effects attributable to the parent education program. Evaluation studies undertaken without the use of a control group are of no value and, moreover, probably do considerable harm through their reporting of invalid and misleading findings.

About a dozen of the studies to be reviewed in this chapter have used control groups in the experimental design. However, the procedure has been to provide education for the experimental groups and to withhold it from the control group, on the assumption that differences between them in the change that occurs is attributable to the educational experience. But there are other events which might have caused change in the experimental group. It might be that any "attention" given to parents, educational or otherwise, produces a beneficial change in child-rearing practices. In medical research the "placebo" effect is well known. Many patients improve when simple attention is given, when they think they are being treated, even though the treatment consists solely of giving plain sugar pills or placebos. So pronounced is this effect that in the evaluation of the effectiveness of a new medicine, the experimental design routinely includes not only a control group receiving nothing but also a control group receiving placebos.

It is now apparent that the same experimental design is necessary in the evaluation of psychotherapy (e.g., 10), and also in parent education. Good evaluation procedure now demands not just the use of a "no treatment" control, but a "placebo treatment" control as well. In parent education studies this means that the experimental group is matched by another group to whose members it is recommended that they spend fifteen minutes a day discussing child care with their spouses, or discuss serious ideas with a friend whenever possible, or think of their life aspirations, or take a daily walk, or the like. It may be that attention of any kind, even being assigned to a control group in a study (as might have been the case in the Balser study cited above), is sufficient stimulus to produce significant changes in the parents; and that any education itself is irrelevant.

Where the control group is characterized by "no treatment," and no placebo group is used, the true value (if any) of education cannot be separated from the effects of such things as registering for a program, or meeting friends in the evening at a "discussion group." It follows that the ideal evaluation research design in parent education involves experimental and control groups, and the control groups must include both a nontreatment and a placebo group; in sum, an experimental group which participates in the educational program, a group which does nothing, and a group which is given some other task or instruction believed to be irrelevant to changing child-care practices.

Borgatta (9) in a provocative discussion of the evaluation of *therapeutic* procedures calls attention to the many kinds of resistance encountered in using control groups in evaluation studies. In particular, he refutes the commonly voiced objections that to establish a control group, the members of which do not receive therapeutic treatment, is to deprive some of the clientele from available services. It must be recognized as factually true that in order to carry out an adequate scientific evaluation some potential clients must have services withheld for a certain period of time. When this procedure is frowned upon, it is evident that the organization lacks a proper climate for carrying on scientific evaluation research, and until such time as there is willingness to withhold services from a selected group of the clientele, it will not be possible to judge whether or not the services provided are worth providing.

A second fundamental point is that the experimental and control groups must be composed of the same kind of people. This is to say that they must be initially the same with respect to the variable to be appraised in the program. Ordinarily this is accomplished either by matching a member of one group with a member of another on relevant characteristics, or better, by randomly assigning individuals to one or another group; for example, assigning every alternate applicant to the experimental or to the control group. Further refinements of the ways of establishing such groups are available in the general sources referred to previously.

A third fundamental point is that the number of persons studied must be large enough to convince one that the results found are valid. This number is always more than one or two cases. Much research has shown that any one person's answers to a given test vary somewhat from one time to the next in a fairly random way. When the effects of an educational program are measured and changes, whether positive or negative, are found there needs to be assurance that these changes are not simply the result of random variation of individuals in their responses. There are solutions to this problem. One is to require that the change be so large that it could hardly be interpreted as a random variation. The other is that the number of subjects be large enough so that even though the change manifested by each may be small, when the changes are all in the same direction one must assume that the changes are attributable to a common cause, namely, their participation in the parent education program, rather than to random variation. Given the information on the size of the change and on the number of people changing, a variety of statistical formulas are available (22, 36) which enable the investigator to conclude whether the change noted in the program resulted from chance variations, or whether the change is significant, that is, the result of the educational program.

One final, fundamental characteristic of a scientific evaluation study is that the instruments used to test the effectiveness of the program must be such that two observers will agree as to the findings. Thus, it is important to use objective, standardized measures of information gain, changes in attitude, descriptions of parent behavior, and appraisals of children's mental health rather than rely on idiosyncratic "clinical" interpretations by the investigator. The contrary argument usually has been that such measures cannot be used because the effects of parent education are so subtle and devious that no objective measure can assess the change. It may be true at present that there are no objective tests of the characteristics the parent educator thinks are produced in a parent by his program. But this does not justify the use of procedures which are unscientific in nature and which may lead to erroneous conclusions as to whether the program is achieving the avowed ends. Instead, efforts should be made to develop tests which do measure the characteristic the educator feels is changed by his program. This requires him, of course, to specify clearly the characteristic so that tests can be developed. Finally, if the educator holds that the effect is immeasurable, then it follows that it is impossible to evaluate whether or not this effect results from his program.

WHAT DOES THE EVIDENCE SHOW?

In the section that follows we will review all the evidence on the effects of parent education programs, even though much of it is poor by the standards set forth above. Throughout we will endeavor to sound a note of caution, recognizing that poor studies may be dangerously misleading. Before we turn to the experimental studies, there are three other approaches to evaluation which require brief mention.

One of these (e.g., 57) is to ask persons responsible for the program for a subjective evaluation of the results which were produced. For example, leaders of child study groups when asked their opinion of a program may report that they think "the effects are good." This commands no attention as a serious research effort, since it involves the obvious problem of bias when one is judging one's own work; vast research literature on the distorting effects of motivation on judgment and perception indicates all too clearly that what people think happened, is happening, or will happen is colored by their own desires.

Second, there are a number of studies employing a case history approach. For example, Kinnis (41) and French and her colleagues (24) present cases in which brief educational counseling of a mother resulted in change in the mother's behavior which was beneficial to the child. Such studies are useful in the same general way that single case studies are ordinarily useful, namely, as a source of insight and suggestion for further theory and research. However, there is no way of estimating whether such results would occur in other similar cases, since the number is too small to justify any estimate of the contribution of random changes. In addition, no controls are present. The extension of such case findings to other cases, not to speak of parent education programs, is an unscientific and misleading procedure.

A third line of investigation which has become pertinent to the effects of parent education makes use of data suggesting historical shifts in child-care practices among American parents. The interpretation of the historical data is complicated and seems to permit no clear conclusion. The major line of argument is that parent education materials over the past two decades have urged the parent toward greater leniency in child care (61, 64); therefore, any shifts in actual parent practice toward greater leniency during the past two decades can be interpreted as the effect of these parent education materials.

Some of the data on historical change come from comparisons of older with younger persons. Other data are from longitudinal studies of parents. Staples and Smith (60), for example, have shown that grandmothers are significantly more strict in child care than their daughters, now mothers themselves. However, in this and other longitudinal studies an equally probable explanation of the stricter attitudes and behavior of older parents is simply that they are older, and perhaps have less patience with children; in other words, this constitutes a maturational effect rather than an effect of the younger group being exposed to a different kind of parent education. Another interpretation of the same data is that there has been a general shift in the United States in all aspects of the society toward a more liberal attitude concerning other individuals, which would show in parent role behavior of younger persons and, indeed, if one wished to go farther, might even account for the changes in the advice transmitted to parents. In any event, the problems of interpretation of age difference data are serious ones.

Still other data on historical change come from the comparison of samples of parents studied at different times during the past two decades in respect to the degree of leniency of their child-rearing practices. Bronfenbrenner (13) has recently completed an analysis of all such studies dating from Anderson's (1), published in 1936, and including a number of recent and still unpublished studies. The author has done a notable service to our understanding of parent behavior. In this review the various subjects in the different samples of parents are classified as to whether they are white- or blue-collar workers in order to make the studies comparable. In reviewing the overall trends of the data he finds that reliance on breast feeding is decreasing while self-demand scheduling is becoming more common. With respect to class differences on the practices of weaning, of bowel and bladder training, and of both breast feeding and self-demand scheduling, he finds that while these were less common among the middle-class or white-collar wives before World War II, the direction has now been reversed and the middle-class mother is relatively more permissive than the lower-class. Bronfenbrenner then points out the relation between these trends and Wolfenstein's (68) analysis of changes in content which we have cited in Chapter VI. The changes in the middle-class mothers parallel quite closely the changes noted in the Children's Bureau publication, *Infant Care*. Bronfenbrenner calls attention to another body of evidence (reviewed in Chapter V) showing that middle-class mothers are more likely to read such publications on child care than are working-class mothers. He concludes, therefore, that his analysis suggests that these mothers not only read *Infant Care* (and other materials) but take them seriously and over time are influenced by them.

Bronfenbrenner's analysis of these historical data thus has the characteristics of an experimental evaluation in which the middle class is the experimental group and the working class is (comparatively speaking) the control group. Continuous appraisals of its self-reports on attitudes and overt behavior over time indicate that the experimental group changes significantly in the direction of attitudes and behavior advocated by parent education programs. While one can readily think of several other explanations of this pattern of results, they tend to be rather complicated and speculative and have neither the simplicity nor the common sense characteristics of Bronfenbrenner's interpretation.

If the interpretation is valid, then implications follow both for parent education and for its evaluation. First, one concludes that parent education has had some measurable effects on the American parent. Second, one surmises that the effects of parent education over any short period of time and for any given group of individuals may be so small as to escape notice in the ordinary experimental evaluation studies to be reviewed subsequently; but that the change over many years and in many people is such that after several decades significant effects are observed. In conclusion, it now appears that the strategy of evaluation research should include periodic appraisals of attitudes and behavior of parents and children, which are then related to data on the information presented and on exposure rates, so that the long term effects of parent education can be analyzed.

Introduction to the Research Studies

As pointed out earlier, only a few of the many studies undertaken in parent education are satisfactory from the standpoint of design and analysis. Unhappily, the majority of them have various characteristics which run the gamut of research deficiencies: no controls, failure to handle loss of subjects, procedures not specified clearly, use of inappropriate tests of significance, and so on. As already indicated, we will mention them all but will distinguish between them according to level of competence.

The studies are classified into three major groups. The first includes all studies evaluating a single method; the second, studies of multiple methods; while the third consists of studies comparing the effectiveness of different methods. Within each, the studies are further subdivided into those with either partially complete, or complete experimental designs. Finally, these subclasses are themselves subdivided according to the dependent variable (the "effect") being studied. The section closes with a brief overview of research in progress.

Table 1 summarizes this classification, and shows the result of each study. This table is helpful as a guide to the survey which

TABLE 1. A CLASSIFICATION OF STUDIES EVALUATING THE EFFECTS OF PARENT EDUCATION[a]

Method evaluated	Effects studied in partially complete design			
	Parent knowledge	Parent attitudes	Parent behavior	Child behavior
Group procedures	31(+) 55(+)	14(+) 20(+) 31(+) 33(?)	34(+)	—
Mass media	—	—	—	—
Individual counseling	—	—	12(?)	12(?)
Combined methods	—	16(−) 65(−)	16(+) 30(+) 43(+) 65(−)	25(+)

Method evaluated	Effects studied in complete design			
	Parent knowledge	Parent attitudes	Parent behavior	Child behavior
Group procedures	51(+)	6(?) 7(?) 51(−) 56(+)	—	—
Mass media	23(+)	—	27(−) 45(?+) 53(+)	—
Individual counseling	—	28(?)	—	17(?+)
Combined methods	2(+)	—	—	—

[a] The figures under the various headings refer to studies listed at the end of Chapter IX. The (+), (−), and (?) *after* the figures indicate, respectively, that the study reports significant improvement, no change, or results which cannot be interpreted clearly.

follows. Note that in the table the few studies (2, 6, 7, 20, 55) comparing the effectiveness of different methods are reported in the rows for the actual methods concerned for the reasons set forth on page 305.

Studies Evaluating the Effectiveness of a Single Method

1. Studies with Partially Complete Experimental Designs (No Control Group). The first set of studies with a partially complete experimental design evaluates the effects of group discussion procedures on increasing parents' knowledge. Studies by Hedrich (31) and Schaus (55) both report significant increases in factual knowledge.

Turning now to attitude as the criterion, Chandler (14) had as subjects 28 mothers exposed to an eight-week reading and group discussion course. He used a "traditional-developmental" measure (21) which was administered to the mothers before and after the study-group program. This test is based on responses to the questions: What are five things a good mother does? and What are five things a good child does? Chandler found that responses to the "good mother" questions were significantly more developmental after participation in the program. (The probability of the change occurring by chance was less than one in a hundred. Henceforth, such statistically relevant findings will be written as follows: <.01). This difference was also true for responses to the "good child" question (<.05, that is, the probability of its chance occurrence was less than five in a hundred).

Another study (33, pp. 80–81), using only mothers who attended a series of six or eight meetings, investigated changes in the mother's ranking of six items, describing what she hoped to gain from the study group. The results show that the mother's preference for a general philosophy of child care and for general knowledge of children increased significantly, while the desire for reassurance about handling the child and for specific information on how to handle difficulties declined (<.10).

Hedrich (31) used as subjects four groups of parents with a total of 48 subjects. Each group met six times. The educational program was centered on teaching positive attitudes and practices for parents toward the development of self-reliance in their children. It was focused specifically on the four areas of eating, sleeping, toileting, and use of clothing. A before-and-after administration of Ojemann's self-reliance scale (47) showed a significant increase in favorable attitudes of the parents toward self-reliance practices. Attitudes also were significantly improved in child-rearing areas other than those dealt with in the groups, for example, play, thus suggesting that the change was generalized.

The largest study which utilized before-and-after measures with an experimental group, but had no control group, is the Davis and McGinnis research (20); the subjects consisted of members of study groups under the auspices of the Institute of Child Welfare in Minnesota. The individual subjects totaled more than 1,000. The attitude instrument consisted of a fifty-item trait list pertaining to children, and the parents were asked to rate the degree of importance or seriousness of each of these traits on a four-point scale. Ratings were made separately for boys and girls, and for the ages five, nine, and fifteen. Comparisons of ratings before and after the study-group series show that there is an average reduction in the degree to which parents conceive the traits as serious. This result holds generally for ratings for all different sexes and ages. Separate analysis considers the shift of particular items into and out of the category of the "ten most serious" traits. Ratings after the study-group program resulted in the inclusion among the ten most serious items several which pertain to withdrawal types of behavior previously not perceived as serious.

Where parents' overt behavior, rather than attitudes, is concerned, only one study exists. This study by Jack (34) used 38 mothers as subjects and used home interviews before and after a study-group series to obtain information on the mothers' child-rearing practices. The items were scored on the basis of expert judgment as to the degree of favorableness of the practice. Comparison of before-and-after scores showed that the group as a whole improved in the direction of experts ($<.10$). Comparisons within the group between the two halves who were initially the low and high scorers show that the initially low scorers made a significant improvement in changing behavior ($.01$), while the latter did not ($.20$). However, this is likely the result of a regression of the extremes toward the average when tested a second time, a phenomenon well known and adequately explained by the theory of sampling.

Turning now to the next type of parent education method, mass media, there seem to be no evaluation studies with a partially complete experimental design which have been concerned with this method. We thus pass on to studies of individual counseling. One study (12) falls into this class and was designed to evaluate the effectiveness of a counseling procedure paralleling that used in numerous well-baby or child health conferences. The study had a before-and-after design with no control group, the focus being on internal comparisons between subjects. While in one sense it might be said the study had its own internal controls since the emphasis was on the relation of change to personality variables, the fact is that, strictly speaking, it is not a complete experimental design. The subjects were 50 mothers attending child health stations in New York City who reported feeding problems. Subjects were selected on the basis of age, birth order, and health of their children, and the fact that the subjects' current behavior in response to the feeding problem was nonpermissive. The mothers were interviewed and counseled individually, with permissive handling of feeding practices described and recommended, and a pamphlet describing this practice was given to each. The mothers' own report of the handling of food refusals was obtained during the initial interview and then again in a second interview of the same type three to four months later. The results showed that 8 of the mothers adopted permissive practices in feeding, 16 tried the practice but rejected it, 26 made no attempt to try it.

Perhaps the unusual aspect of the study is that it attempted to relate the effects of educational counseling to several personality characteristics of the subjects. The results suggest that the differential effects of counseling of this type are in part predictable from knowledge of the mothers' characteristics. Some of the findings are the following: of the subjects who considered previous advice from physicians to be helpful, there were more who tried permissive feeding; more of the mothers who were primarily concerned about the child's diet, in contrast to his size, made attempts and subsequently adopted permissiveness; more of the subjects low in general dominance or authoritarianism in child-rearing practices adopted permissiveness than did subjects who were not. When the recommended practice was supported by other sources of parental education to which the subjects were exposed, subjects would more often both try the practice and adopt it.

2. Studies with Full Experimental Designs. Several studies fall into the category of research which evaluates the effects of group discussion methods. One by Owings (51), reported in Witmer (66), considered the effects of a course of instruction of parents in how to impart sexual knowledge to their children. This study made separate analyses of knowledge items and of attitudes toward sex instruction. Significant differences for the experimental group but not the control group are reported in gains in knowledge items.

Where attitudes are the focus of research, we find that a study by Balser and his colleagues (6, 7) used 12 parents as one of the experimental groups which participated in a series of group-centered, psychiatrically led, seminars concerning child development and parent-child relations. Two of the four control groups also consisted of parents, and we will be concerned here only with the comparison between the experimental parent group and the two parent control groups. Before-and-after measures for all three groups consisted of the Minnesota Multi-phasic Personality Inventory, of a sentence-completion test, and of a scale of parent attitudes (58). The results showed no significant changes in any group in the sentence-completion test. On the attitude scale, the experimental group showed improved scores, the before-and-after difference for this group approaching statistical significance ($<.10$). However, one of the two control groups of parents also showed a significant ($<.01$) and even larger improvement in score on this measure. This finding should be kept in mind when we consider other studies which utilize no controls, because it demonstrates the possible error of attributing special effects to some educational program when actually none has occurred. In this instance, we need not necessarily conclude that the seminar had no effect on the parents, but rather that it had no more effect on them than did whatever miscellaneous experiences the control group was having at the same time. On the MMPI scales the experimental group tended to show an improvement on the family relation scale which was not paralleled by the control group; on the other MMPI scales, it showed no noticeable change.

Another study using both experimental and control groups was made by Shapiro (56). He exposed 25 experimental subjects, carefully matched with control subjects, to a parent education group discussion program consisting of 12 sessions. The group leadership procedures were carefully controlled. The before-and-after measure consisted of five attitude scales based on the work of Shoben (58) and Harris, Gough, and Martin (29), and included measures of authoritarianism, parent-child integration, rigidity, fussiness, and good judgment. They thus parallel to some extent the attitude measures used in the Balser study. The attitude measures were administered both to experimental and control groups in such a way that the subjects did not relate them to the group education program. The results showed the experimental subjects to have improved to a significantly greater degree than the control subjects on the authoritarianism, good judgment, and possessiveness scales, but not on the other two. Moreover, Shapiro found that parents attending four or more meetings changed more than those attending three or fewer; that the change was the result of gains fairly evenly distributed throughout the experimental group; and that those experimental subjects who initially held more desirable attitudes on the scales changed more than those holding less desirable attitudes.

The Owings study (51) referred to above was concerned both with attitudes and with knowledge. In contrast to the Balser and Shapiro studies there were no significant differences on the attitude items in Owings' study.

We turn now to another group of studies, those evaluating the effects of mass media. There are four such studies. The first deals with effectiveness in increasing the knowledge of parents. The other three studies all are concerned with changes in self-reported behavior of parents.

In the first study (23) a pamphlet of the Minnesota Department of Health on *Getting Your Child Ready for School*, which included information on the importance of physical and dental examinations, immunization, safety training, and the like, was given to an experimental group of 21 parents and withheld from a control group of 14. Two days later 10 multiple-choice questions pertaining to the pamphlet were administered to both groups, and the experimental group was found to be superior to a significant degree to the control group in this knowledge.

The remaining three studies are all large-scale studies, and more importantly, they all investigate the effects of the same pamphlet series. The studies are in part comparable, and thus provide us a rare opportunity to consider the similarity of results of similar research. The pamphlet series evaluated was the *Pierre the Pelican* series of the Louisiana Society for Mental Health (53). The series consists of 12 four-page pamphlets, customarily mailed to parents of first children at monthly intervals during the first year of the infant's life. These pamphlets discuss physical and emotional aspects of child care pertinent to the first year of life, and make concrete suggestions concerning parental care.

Of these large-scale studies, one made in New Orleans (53) utilized an experimental group (identified as "Group II" in the report and in Table 2[1]) of 159 mothers whose children at the time of the study were sixteen months old and who had received the pamphlet series in the preceding year; a control group consisted of 227 mothers with children of the same age to whom the pamphlets had not been mailed. Another experimental group (identified as "Group I," omitted from Table 2) had been used earlier, but the children of these mothers were not comparable in age to those of the control group, and the results will not be considered here. Subjects were interviewed in their home on the basis of a sixty-item questionnaire. It is important to note that the interviewers knew prior to the interview which subjects were in the experimental and control groups.

On 54 comparisons the results showed 18 significant differences (critical ratios of 2.0 or more) favoring the experimental group, and on almost all remaining items there was a consistent but not significant difference favoring the experimental group. The items tend to be unrelated, so that their content is difficult to summarize.

[1] See p. 300.

The second of these large-scale studies (27) was conducted in North Carolina and used two experimental groups, whites and nonwhites, with 868 and 288 subjects, respectively, compared with two control groups, whites and nonwhites, of 765 and 278 subjects respectively. Experimental and control subjects were randomly selected from records of registration of first births in randomly selected counties. The experimental groups received through the mail the complete pamphlet series during the subsequent twelve months, while none was sent to the control groups. Carefully trained interviewers visited mothers at their homes after the series was completed. The five key questions all concerned feeding practices (handling of food refusals, degree of concern over food schedules, changes in methods of giving milk, leaving the infant alone with a bottle on his pillow, and encouraging the child to feed himself). The questions were masked so that their evaluative characteristics were not apparent. The interviewers did not know whether a given subject was a member of the experimental or control group. The results show that differences on the five items between the experimental and control group members were not significant in any instance. Only in regard to the last-mentioned item did the difference approach statistical significance between the nonwhite experimental and control groups.

The third (45) in this group of large-scale studies was carried out in Michigan. It utilized experimental and control groups initially composed of 1,000 mothers each. Subjects were selected by sampling from experimental and control counties, based on registration of first births. The pamphlet series was then mailed to the experimental groups but withheld from the control groups. Following exposure to the pamphlets, a forty-three-item questionnaire based on the pamphlet materials was mailed to both groups. Returns (and thus the actual sample sizes) from the experimental group numbered 477, and from the control group 537. A comparison of experimental and control groups showed significant differences ($<.05$) on 10 of the 43 items. Two of these 10 differences favored the control group.

Three other measures of effects were used in that study. One treated all 43 items as if they constituted a test of information, and scored the items as to right answers. The average percentage of correct answers for the experimental group was greater than that for the control, and the difference approached statistical significance ($<.10$). The second considered only "concept items," those involving some understanding beyond simple factual information. These numbered 24 of the 43 items. Again using these as a "test," the average percentage correct for the experimental group was significantly greater ($<.03$) than for the control group. The third compared the effect of 11 background information variables, for example, education of the mother, upon subjects' responses. The results showed that 9 of these 11 background variables had a greater effect upon the answers of the control group than those of the experimental group. This suggests an interesting finding: that the pamphlet series reduced the individual variability in child-care knowledge and attitudes arising from differences in cultural and other background characteristics, by providing a new and common core of knowledge for all experimental subjects.

Another aspect of the Michigan study utilized public health nurse interviews with 30 experimental and 34 control mothers. A twenty-eight-item questionnaire was followed in the interview. Significant differences were found on 11 items, with 10 of these favoring the experimental group.

These three studies clearly show different results for this pamphlet series. In Table 2 we compare the results for those items which are identical or very similar for the studies. The comparisons arc mainly between the Louisiana and Michigan investigations.

With respect to the *survey* results from the Michigan study, Table 2 shows that the studies agree in finding significant differences on one item (item 6) and possibly three others (items 4, 5, and 7). They agree in finding no significant differences on eight items (item 2 and items 17 through 23). The studies disagree in their findings (one study reporting significant differences, another none) on the remaining 11 items. Concerning the data from the

TABLE 2. A COMPARISON OF RESULTS FOR THREE EVALUATION STUDIES OF *PIERRE THE PELICAN* PAMPHLETS

Subject matter identical or similar in all three studies	Louisiana Study (53)[a] (Group II data only)	North Carolina Study (27)[a]	Michigan Study (45)[a] Survey (45)[a]	Michigan Study Nurses' Interview (45)[a]
1. Parents do not leave baby with bottle and pillow.	S[b]	NS	NS	—
2. Parents not concerned over scheduling.	NS	NS	NS	—
3. Parents try later after child's food refusals.	S	NS	—	—
4. Parents promote independence in feeding.	S	NS[c]	—	—
5. Father changes diapers.	NS[d]	—	S	—
6. Parents ask child's permission to use his things for new baby.	S	—	S	S
7. Parents do not spank child reaching for breakables.	NS[e]	—	NS	S
8. Parents do not believe babies are afraid of the dark.	S	—	NS	—
9. The baby goes to sleep in the dark.	S	—	NS	—
10. Parents would take child to guidance center when problems can't be solved.	S	—	NS	S
11. Parents would give child allowance.	S	—	NS	—
12. Parents believe baby should have separate room.	S	—	NS	S
13. Parents tell first child the second is coming.	S	—	NS	S
14. Parents have thought about what to say when child asks where he came from.	S	—	NS	—
15. Parents believe if they tell child where he came from he will be less interested.	S	—	NS	—
16. Make-believe friends indicate loneliness.	S	—	NS	—
17. Use toilet chair for baby.	S	—	NS	—
18. Parents not bothered when children make house disorderly.	NS	—	NS	—
19. Parents do not believe children under two years should borrow from each other.	NS	—	NS	—
20. Child allowed to do things for self.	NS	—	NS	—
21. Have family budget.	NS	—	NS	—
22. Parents know older child should have special attention after new baby.	NS	—	NS	S
23. Parents know children may be jealous of new sibling.	NS	—	NS	—

[a] Reference number as listed at end of chapter.
[b] S and NS refer, respectively, to significant or nonsignificant differences between experimental and control groups in the study.
[c] Has borderline significance, nonwhites only.
[d] All other items in the "father care" complex show significant differences.
[e] Borderline significance.

nurses' interviews in the Michigan study, the studies agree in finding significant differences on three more items (items 10, 12, and 13), but now disagree in their findings where before they had agreed (items 21 and 22).

Rarely in social investigations are studies sufficiently similar to permit a comparison of their results. However, a comparison is very instructive because it makes apparent the limitation of any one study and the need for repetition of evaluation research. For example, if a generalization were made from the findings of either the Michigan or Louisiana study, the predictions would be wrong as to the outcome of the other study on about one-half of the items (approximately the results that would be obtained if a coin had been flipped). Since the disagreements in the results stem mainly from the Louisiana and Michigan comparison, one might consider the differences to arise from the use of an interview in the first study and a questionnaire in the second. However, this is doubtful for several reasons. The comparison of the results of the nurses' interviews in the Michigan study does not reduce the disagreement; the different methods were used in the Michigan and North Carolina studies, yet on the two items where they can be compared the results agree; moreover, the comparison of similar items in the Louisiana and North Carolina studies with interviewers used in both studies, shows disagreement. One more likely possibility is that the interviewers' knowledge of subjects' membership in the experimental or control groups in the Louisiana study may have resulted in some bias entering into the interview procedure. The most likely explanation of all may be that the parents in the separate studies had different kinds of interests, needs, and cultural traditions, producing differential acceptance and rejection of the material in the pamphlets.

Our next group of studies having complete experimental designs deals with the effects of counseling as a parent education procedure. While two studies fall into this category, in each case there is some difficulty in interpreting the nature of the results. In the first, Cooper (17) has evaluated the results of a counseling program attached to a well-baby clinic in Baltimore. Parents were interviewed and counseled on the general situation of the child, and general advice was given. Data on the child and his situation also were given by the counseling staff to pediatricians and general practitioners of the clinic and to nurses making home visits for their use in counseling.

The measure of effectiveness was the change in the behavior of the child of counseled parents. Use was made of the behavior records of 100 children whose parents had been seen at least three times in a year by the counseling service. The record at the last conference was used. These were compared with the behavior records of the *first* counseling session of 81 other children who were used as controls. The 81 control children were matched pair by pair with 81 of the experimental children on age, sex, and race. The behavior ratings were based on data from an interview with the mother and from observation of the child.

Comparisons of the records of the two groups show those of the experimental group to be generally better (more satisfactory behavior) than those of the controls. Also, 96 of the 100 experimental children improved in ratings from earlier to later sessions. While these results are encouraging, the study design does not in fact permit us to attribute the improvement to the counseling received. It may be that any or most undesirable behavior traits of a child run their course and improve with time; the control procedure used in Cooper's study compares records of behavior traits at possibly different stages of inception and thus does not permit us to rule out this possible explanation of changes.

The other study evaluating the results of a counseling program is by Hale (28), who reports that in a comparison of a group of parents who were counseled with three groups who were not, the former indicated subsequent to counseling that they had many more family life problems than the latter. This study design makes interpretation of findings difficult. It may be, as someone suggested, that this simply represents what is commonly found in counseling situations, namely, that an emotionally healthy person is cautious about revealing himself and his problems until he has tested a situation and the people involved in it and is convinced that he can expose his problems without being ridiculed. On the other hand, the results may show that educational counseling increases the number of problems one perceives himself to have and reports.

Studies Evaluating the Effects of Multiple Methods in Parent Education

As we have pointed out above, several studies have evaluated multiple procedures in parent education and so cannot be classified under any of the major methods described. Only one such study has had a complete experimental design. This is a study by Andrew (2) which evaluated the overall effects of an educational workshop upon gains in knowledge. This workshop utilized methods of lectures, films, recordings, and various types of group discussions. Using a control group of college students not exposed to this overall program, the results show that the experimental group composed of a large number of parents made a significant increase in knowledge (<.01) in contrast to the student control group.

All of the other studies which evaluated multiple techniques have only a partially experimental design, in the sense that the use of control subjects is absent. Two of the studies have examined the effects of multiple methods upon the parents' behavior; two more have dealt with changes both in attitudes and behavior of parents; and a fifth has considered the effects upon children's behavior, one of the few to take this as a criterion variable. Considering the first, Hattendorf (30) concentrated on providing a group of mothers with factual information on sex, and on methods of educating children on sexual matters. One hundred and thirteen mothers were exposed to interviews and counseling, lectures, discussion groups, and printed material, as well as careful observation of programs of instruction of their children in their homes. The results suggest that on a before-and-after basis there was an increase in the use of casual incidental instruction of children in sexual matters as recommended by the program.

A report by Klatskin (43) of the effects upon child-care practices of those who had participated in the Yale Rooming-In Program might be viewed as a study of the effects of exposure to an educational program suggesting "flexible care," which uses counseling, reading, and, of course, some supervision during the rooming-in period in the actual care of the child. Two-hundred and twenty-nine mothers reported on their own child-care practices a year or more after the birth of the child. Klatskin used the Davis and Havighurst materials (19) describing child-care practices as the comparison data, on the assumption that the group had not been exposed to this type of educational program. Comparison on five child-care items, including feeding when hungry, beginning bowel training before the child is six months old, and the like shows the 229 subjects to be substantially more flexible and/or more permissive in child care than were the Davis and Havighurst subjects. These differences are open to other interpretations, of course; for example, regional variations. Klatskin also reports in regard to differences between social classes in her sample that the middle- and lower-class subjects are approximately identical in their behavior. Thus, one might make the inference that exposure to educational programs reduces the effects of cultural variation on child care. This parallels the finding of the Michigan study (45) concerning the effects of the *Pierre the Pelican* pamphlet series reported above.

Of the two studies concerned both with attitudes and behavior of parents one (65) is described by Witmer (66, p. 74), in which the evaluation is of an unspecified course of instruction. The study reports that before-and-after interviews and tests of mothers' opinions and behavior regarding sex instruction show no significant differences with respect to their behavior toward their children.

The second and more recent study concerned with parental attitudes and behavior was made by Collins (16). In this study the subjects were 17 mothers attending an annual two-week training program for parents of hearing-handicapped preschool children. The purpose of the program was to promote sound attitudes on child management. The study asked the subjects to report from their own experience examples of what they considered to be good or bad handling of their children during the preceding week at home; examples from this week were again selected during the last part of the workshop. The incidents reported as "good handling" were rated on eight of the Fels Parent Behavior Scales (4). The results showed significant differences between the ratings of incidents reported before and after the training program, on the control-freedom scale, and the free-growth-training scale. The Shoben scale (58) was also used as a before-and-after measure, but no significant changes were found.

The fifth study having only a partial experimental design in evaluating multiple methods is one made some years ago by Giblette and Macrae (25), utilizing as subjects mothers having feeding difficulties with their children. The mothers were exposed to a program of class instruction in nutrition, in child psychology, and to a period of observation of their children at nursery school under the direction of school personnel. The educational program also included individual counseling interviews. Subsequent to the program the children were rated as improving on 20 of 30 traits.

Studies Evaluating the Relative Effectiveness of Different Methods

This last group of studies consists of those which have sought to evaluate the relative effectiveness of two or more major methods, that is, group discussion, mass media, or individual counseling, or studies which have sought to evaluate the relative effectiveness of variations in procedure within each of these major methods.

Some of the studies in this group have employed a complete experimental design, in that control groups are added and the experimental groups are exposed to variations in method. All the studies which have this complete design have been referred to previously, for they have achieved two objectives in one research study. This follows from the fact that the answer to the question of whether or not parent education is effective can be obtained by comparing all experimental groups with the control groups receiving no education. If, in addition, information is obtained on the relative effectiveness of different educational procedures by virtue of having such experimental variations in the study, then one can ask what is the relative effectiveness of the different methods themselves? We now ask this additional question of some of the studies previously reported.

The first class of studies is concerned with comparisons of *major methods*. There is only one of this kind. It compares the effects of group discussion with the effects of lectures. We have pointed out in Chapter VII on methods that although there is a great deal of literature in other areas of social change dealing with the relative effectiveness of group discussion and other methods, the same studies had not been repeated in the area of parent education. The existing study is by Schaus (55). Subjects consisted of members of three lecture groups and three study discussion groups. Each had eight sessions. Mimeographed summaries of the content material, which was the same for both the lecture and study groups, were given to all subjects and a comparison of the before-and-after gains in knowledge of subject matter showed the study group to have learned significantly more (<.01) than the lecture group.

The second class of studies deals with variations within major methods. The first two are expansions of studies reported previously which utilize a complete experimental design. In one of these studies Andrew (2) evaluated the effects of four different types of leadership. Eight groups of seven to ten each participated in discussion programs with the four following types of leadership procedure: group-oriented, authority, question-answer, and leaderless. Each of the four procedures was used with two groups, making eight groups in all. Members of the groups consisted of parents, teachers, and public health nurses. The groups met from two to three times. A thirty-item questionnaire, based on the content of the information discussed, was administered before and after the meetings. Comparisons of the groups on all items showed that all the procedures resulted in gain, but that there was a significantly greater increase *in knowledge* in the two groups which had no leader. The other groups did not differ significantly. Balser and his colleagues (6, 7) used a research design permitting a comparison between study groups using different leadership procedures. One was group-centered and led by a psychiatrist; a second was leadership-centered and led by a psychologist. While, as we have pointed out earlier, changes did occur as a result of the educational program, there were no apparent differences between groups attributable to the use of a psychologist or psychiatrist as leader, or to the leader-centered in contrast to group-centered process of discussion.

Remaining studies of variations within a method used no control groups. That of Davis and McGinnis (20) evaluated the effects of variations in leadership of discussion groups. The evaluation of the effects of different leaders employed a fifty-item list of children's behavior traits which were rated by parents as to seriousness. The parents' ratings were then compared with the ratings of experts, and the degree of agreement found. These ratings were obtained from parents both before and after the discussion groups. The amount of *improvement* in agreement with experts was compared for groups led by "specialists trained in child development and child psychology" and "groups . . . taught by local leaders." The results showed greater improvement for subjects taught by the specialists. The possible effects of other factors, such as education, were controlled. The authors' tentative conclusion is that experts can teach mental hygiene better than nonexperts.

Two reports by Andrew complete this class. Both come from her study (2) evaluating the effect of a workshop in parent education. As one experimental variation, an attempt was made to evaluate the relative effectiveness of four different techniques of presentation of information. This seems to pertain most closely to variations in the effectiveness of different types of mass media. All subjects were exposed to one general session of the following types: a panel discussion by lay persons, a lecture, a film, and two recordings. A thirty-item questionnaire based on the content covered in four general sessions was administered before and after the series of general sessions. The results show that there was significantly greater improvement in knowledge of the content covered in the sessions using the records and the lecture. However, the possible interaction between the type of content presented and the method of presentation makes it impossible to conclude whether the greater improvement results from the technique, or from the associated content being easier to learn.

Using the same general experimental situation, Andrew (3) investigated the effects of a variation which is hard to classify, but seems to pertain more to variation in content of the educational procedure than to method. If it is so construed, it is, of course, the only one like this. The same thirty-item information test was used as in the foregoing research, to test the learning in different groups. It was found that in groups which permitted the expression of individual "cathartic needs," and where subjects did in fact express them, there was a tendency for a greater learning of factual material to take place than in groups where catharsis was not permitted.

Other Studies in Progress

The volume of research activities has increased considerably since 1950. This research activity is an expression in part of the general ferment and movement toward evaluation research in clinical services. It also indicates that the mental health movement has begun to emphasize prevention rather than cure and that large funds are available for research from new sources such as the National Institute of Mental Health. The resurgence of research activities in parent education is now nurtured by these available funds much as earlier research was encouraged by the Laura Spelman Rockefeller Memorial and the Spelman Fund, and it indicates concretely the influence of available research money on the direction and volume of research in this country. In addition to the studies completed and reported on above which evaluate the effects of parent education, it is encouraging to find that several large-scale studies of good experimental design are under way.

Four of these studies seek to evaluate the effects of discussion group procedures. The St. Louis County Health Department (54) is engaged in a study of the effects of discussion groups upon participating mothers and their children. This study uses an experimental sample of more than 1,000 mothers and an equally large control group. The research includes before-and-after measures of change in mothers' beliefs regarding the causal factors in her child's behavior; for example, whether she is involved as a cause or not, and of change in the mothers' feelings of potency or competence to deal with her child. At the same time, before-and-after measures of changes in the child's behavior are obtained from mothers' ratings, ratings by schoolteachers, and ratings by the child's peers. Thus, in the St. Louis study the criterion variables are changes in the attitude and belief system of the mothers and appraisals of the child's behavior itself. The conceptualization of the mothers' beliefs about causality as the factor influenced by parent education clearly seems to be a large step forward in contrast to some of the earlier studies which deal with perhaps superficial attitudes or discrete items of factual knowledge. Even more valuable is the use of clinical appraisals of the child's health as the fundamental criterion variable for assessing the effects of the educational program.

Another significant study of quite similar design is under way in Austin, Texas, under the auspices of the Austin Community Guidance Center. The criterion variables used in this evaluation study also are quite similar to those of the St. Louis study, in that changes in the child's behavior are appraised by sociometric evaluations, teacher ratings, and other means, and the variables pertaining to the parents are assessed through interviews and attitude scales. In both the Austin research study and the St. Louis program the discussion groups are led by "lay leaders" who have attended workshops for the purpose of obtaining greater skill in leadership, but not to become experts in the field of child development.

Still another important study in this area is being carried on under the auspices of the Westport-Weston (Connecticut) Mental Health Association and the Child Study Association of America. This study evaluates the effectiveness of only one parent discussion group but is significant for two reasons. The first is that the control group in this instance is made up of parents applying for membership in the discussion group but assigned to the control group on a random basis, so that both the experimental and control subjects are self-selected and therefore equally motivated. Second, one of the major criterion variables pertains to changes in the parents' problem-solving and decision-making skills, including such variables as an increase in the number of outcomes of actions considered, an increase in the future time orientation of the parent with respect to taking actions in child rearing, and several others. In addition, standard attitude and information inventories are used.

A fourth study is under way at Toronto at the Institute of Child Study (33) which, like the St. Louis project and the Child Study Association project, is notable for its conceptualization of the criterion variable. This study involves before-and-after analyses of the effects of parent education groups in which the effect studied is the relation between the mothers' self-conceptions of what they believe themselves to be and what they would like to be. It is, in other words, an attempt to measure the effects of parent education in terms of reducing the gap between the mother's ideal self-image and her real self-image.

Studies of the effectiveness of other parent education techniques seem almost nonexistent. In the area of counseling a well-known longitudinal study of the effects of parental guidance has been under way for many years at the Institute of Child Welfare at the University of California (44). The results have not yet been fully reported.

The studies described here are presented to exemplify the level of professional competence which is reached by current evaluation research in parent education. They represent a marked advance in the full use of experimental designs and in the attention given to the theoretical problem of specifying the effects to be measured. These examples are not meant to complete an inventory of research in progress. There are others known to be in progress and doubtless there are a sizable number of program evaluations under way which have not yet been widely reported.

WHAT CONCLUSIONS CAN BE DRAWN?

In Table 1 on page 291 we have presented a simple classification of the existing evaluation studies. A brief summary of the nearly two dozen studies leaves little doubt that their results are inconclusive.

With respect to the method of group procedures, consider the studies using a complete experimental design. One of these (51) reports an increase in parent knowledge, and no change in parent attitudes. A more recent and more significant study (56), on the other hand, finds definite improvement in parent attitudes. The third study (6, 7), however, finds no improvement on one attitude measure, a significant improvement on subscales of another, and a change paralleled by change in the control group on still a third.

Five of the six studies evaluating group procedures which use no control groups, and hence have only a partially complete design, report significant change of some kind occurring in the parents involved in the program. One of these studies (34) reports an improvement in parent behavior; of four others concerned with attitudes (14, 20, 31, 33), three indicate a significant improvement; one of these (31) joins another (55) in reporting significant gains in parent knowledge.

At first glance, it would appear that the evidence points toward significant and desirable changes in parents resulting from participation in parent study or discussion groups. However, when the six not truly scientific evaluation studies are removed from the picture, the other three mentioned above present inconclusive results.

Turning to the research on the effects of mass media, all four of the studies in this field have employed control groups in a complete experimental design. One of these, a comparatively small study (23) concerned with improvement in factual information about children's health, reports a favorable change occurring in the parents involved. The other three major studies have all been concerned with changes in parent attitudes. One of these three (27) reports that no changes occurred; the other two (45, 53) report positive effects upon parent attitudes. However, in these two there are certain deficiencies in the selection of the control groups and, in addition, the positive changes reported differ from one study to the other; thus, the findings of each are open to various interpretations.

With respect to the method of individual counseling, there are only three studies in all. One of these (12) shows changes in both parent and child behavior, although the number of persons changing was few, and the study used no controls. Of the other two studies, which used a more complete experimental design, one (28) indicates improvement in children's behavior, but there was a methodological question involving changes due to maturation raised in connection with this study; the other study (17), really in the nature of a minor report, suggests that counseling increases the number of problems one perceives he has or is willing to report.

In the areas of both mass media and counseling, then, as was the case in the area of group procedures, the data delineate no clear conclusions. Nor is the situation better when we consider the studies evaluating the effectiveness of multiple procedures. Only one of these (2) uses an experimental design in the true sense and this study reports parents as increasing their factual information. The remaining studies in this category, of which there are five, all lack controls; and, in addition, present a quite mixed picture of changes. Two of these (16, 65) report no changes in parent attitudes. With respect to behavior, two (16, 30) report positive changes, one (65) no change, and for the other (43) the results are positive but subject to question. A final study (25) reports significant improvement in child behavior but this is a study having little value. Thus, while the one important study here indicates that parents improve in factual knowledge, this is hardly an impressive finding, and the other studies in this area are inconsistent in their results.

The issue of how effective is parent education in changing parents or children therefore remains unresolved at present. In the absence of conclusive evidence, the arguments favoring one side or the other of the issue doubtless will continue. On the one hand, there are those who argue that there is no reason to expect any important aspects of the adult personality to change as a result of parent education. Protagonists of this position would point out that we do not even know if the adult individual ever undergoes any important changes other than changes in factual knowledge even when exposed to educational experiences much more impressive than parent education, such as attending college or doing graduate work in child development over a two or three-year period. Therefore, it is unreasonable to expect that participating one hour a week in a twelve-week seminar, or reading a pamphlet, or being counseled for half an hour during a monthly visit to a pediatrician could influence the parent-child relation.

On the other hand, an argument presented by many is that the educational programs for parents do produce changes but that for several reasons they will continue to escape detection, given the current measurement procedures. The changes which occur are alleged to be too subtle to be captured by other than clinical techniques, or too small to show up in the sparse samples of parents utilized in most evaluation studies; or are delayed in their occurrence so that they are not discernible except through a longitudinal study. The argument that changes occur but are too small to be detected has received support from Bronfenbrenner's review of the historical data on child care previously mentioned in detail. The supposition is that the changes in any given instance are too small to be measurable but that they are cumulative, so that exposure of parents to a variety of educational events, for example, not to just one pamphlet, or one type of counseling, or one study-group session, but to dozens of pamphlets and discussions over time, produces cumulative change in parent behavior.

Since the issue of effectiveness of parent education is still unresolved, one looks forward to future studies. The critic of programs who seeks to demonstrate that the efforts involved have little value, the educator himself who seeks to convince the public and other professionals that education for parents is justified, the independent social scientist interested in a test of theory, all will be involved in major evaluation research. This increased interest must result in a deeper understanding of the significance of this modern social movement.

REFERENCES

1. Anderson, John E., *The Young Child in the Home:* A Survey of Three Thousand American Families. Report of the Committee on the Infant and Preschool Child, White House Conference on Child Health and Protection. D. Appleton-Century Co., New York, 1936.

2. Andrew, Gwen, "A Study of the Effectiveness of a Workshop Method for Mental Health Education," *Mental Hygiene*, vol. 38, 1954, pp. 267–278.

3. Andrew, Gwen, "The Relationship Between Learning and Expression of Self-Orientation Needs at a Mental Health Education Workshop," *Mental Hygiene*, vol. 38, 1954, pp. 627–633.

4. Baldwin, Alfred L., Joan Kalhorn, and Fay H. Breese, "Patterns of Parent Behavior," *Psychological Monographs*, vol. 58, 1945, no. 3.

5. Baldwin, Alfred L., and Harry Levin, "The Appraisal of Parent Behavior," *Psychological Monographs*, vol. 63, 1949, no. 4.

6. Balser, Benjamin H., Fred Brown, Minerva L. Brown, Edward D. Joseph, and Donald K. Phillips, "Preliminary Report of a Controlled Mental Health Workshop in a Public School System," *American Journal of Psychiatry*, vol. 112, 1955, pp. 199–205.

7. Balser, Benjamin H., Fred Brown, Minerva L. Brown, Leon Laski, and Donald K. Phillips, "Further Report on Experimental Evaluation of Mental Hygiene Techniques in School and Community," *American Journal of Psychiatry*, vol. 113, 1957, pp. 733–739.

8. Blood, Robert O., Jr., "The Use of Observational Methods in Family Research," *Marriage and Family Living*, vol. 20, 1958, pp. 47–52.

9. Borgatta, Edgar F., "Research: Pure and Applied," *Group Psychotherapy*, vol. 8, 1955, pp. 263–277.

10. Borgatta, Edgar F. and Leonard C. Cottrell, Jr., "Control-Group Experimentation in Psychotherapy," *Psychiatry*, vol. 22, 1959, pp. 97–100.

11. Bornston, Frieda L., and James C. Coleman, "The Relation Between Certain Parents' Attitudes Toward Child Rearing and the Direction of Aggression of Their Young Adult Offspring," *Journal of Clinical Psychology*, vol. 12, 1956, pp. 41–44.

12. Brim, Orville G., Jr., "The Acceptance of New Behavior in Child Rearing," *Human Relations*, vol. 7, 1954, pp. 473–491.

13. Bronfenbrenner, Urie, "Socialization and Social Class Through Time and Space" in *Readings in Social Psychology*, edited by Theodore M. Newcomb, Eugene L. Hartley, and Eleanor E. Maccoby. 3d ed. Henry Holt and Co., New York, 1958, pp. 400–425.

14. Chandler, Barbara A., "An Exploratory Study of the Professed Parent-Role Concepts and Standards of Child Behavior of Mothers in a Parent Education Project," *Dissertation Abstracts*, vol. 15, 1955, pp. 219–220.

15. Clausen, John A., *Sociology and the Field of Mental Health*. Russell Sage Foundation, New York, 1956.

16. Collins, Marjorie G., "A Study of Parent Attitudes on Child Management Before and After Training, Utilizing the Critical Incident Technique," *Dissertation Abstracts*, vol. 14, 1954, pp. 872–873.

17. Cooper, Marcia M., "Evaluation of the Mother's Advisory Service," *Monographs of the Society for Research in Child Development*, vol. 12, 1947, p. 1.

18. Crawford, Ronald E., "Teacher-Pupil Personality Relationships," *Dissertation Abstracts*, vol. 13, 1953, p. 589.

19. Davis, Allison, and Robert J. Havighurst, "Social Class and Color Differences in Child-Rearing," *American Sociological Review*, vol. 11, 1946, pp. 698–710.

20. Davis, Edith A., and Esther McGinnis, *Parent Education:* A Survey of the Minnesota Program. University of Minnesota Press, Minneapolis, 1939.

21. Duvall, Evelyn M., "Conceptions of Parenthood," *American Journal of Sociology*, vol. 52, 1946, pp. 193–203.

22. Festinger, Leon, and Daniel Katz, editors, *Research Methods in the Behavioral Sciences*. The Dryden Press, New York, 1953.

23. Ford, M., and E. E. Hartman, "Measuring Reader Comprehension of a Preschool Pamphlet," *Public Health Reports*, vol. 69, 1954, pp. 498–502.

24. French, Anne C., M. Levbarg, and H. Michal-Smith, "Parent Counseling as a Means of Improving the Performance of a Mentally Retarded Boy: A Case Study Presentation," *American Journal of Mental Deficiency*, vol. 58, 1953, pp. 13–20.

25. Giblette, C. T., and A. Macrae, "An Experiment in the Treatment of Feeding Problems Through Parental Education," *Mental Hygiene*, vol. 18, 1934, pp. 92–108.

26. Goldhamer, Herbert, and Andrew W. Marshall, *Psychosis and Civilization:* Two Studies in the Frequency of Mental Disease. The Free Press, Glencoe, Ill., 1953.

27. Greenberg, B. G., M. E. Harris, C. F. MacKinnon, and S. S. Chipman, "A Method for Evaluating the Effectiveness of Health Education Literature," *American Journal of Public Health*, vol. 43, 1953, pp. 1147–1155.

28. Hale, Clara B., "Parent Need for Education and Help with Family Problems," *California Journal of Educational Research*, vol. 6, 1955, pp. 38–44.

29. Harris, Dale B., Harrison G. Gough, and William E. Martin, "Children's Ethnic Attitudes: II. Relationship to Parental Beliefs Concerning Child Training," *Child Development*, vol. 21, 1950, pp. 169–181.

30. Hattendorf, Kay W., "A Home Program for Mothers in Sex Education," *University of Iowa Studies in Child Welfare*, vol. 6, 1932, pp. 11–92.

31. Hedrick, Blanche E., "The Effectiveness of a Program of Learning Designed to Change Parental Attitudes Toward Self-Reliance," *University of Iowa Studies in Child Welfare*, vol. 10, 1934, pp. 249–268.

32. Hovland, Carl I., Irving L. Janis, and Harold H. Kelley, *Communication and Persuasion*. Yale University Press, New Haven, 1954.

33. Institute of Child Study, Toronto, *Well Children:* A Progress Report. University of Toronto Press, Canada, 1956.

34. Jack, Lois M., "A Device for the Measurement of Parent Attitudes and Practices," *University of Iowa Studies in Child Welfare*, vol. 6, 1932, pp. 137–149.

35. Jahoda, Marie, *Current Concepts of Positive Mental Health.* Basic Books, New York, 1958.

36. Jahoda, Marie, Morton Deutsch, and Stuart W. Cook, *Research Methods in Social Relations,* With Especial Reference to Prejudice. The Dryden Press, New York, 1951, vols. 1 and 2.

37. Janis, Irving L., "Personality Correlates of Susceptibility to Persuasion," *Journal of Personality,* vol. 22, 1954, pp. 504–518.

38. Janis, Irving L., and Peter B. Field, "A Behavioral Assessment of Persuasibility: Consistency of Individual Differences," *Sociometry,* vol. 19, 1956, pp. 241–259.

39. Kantor, Mildred B., John C. Glidewell, Ivan N. Mensh, Herbert R. Domke, and Margaret C.-L. Gildea, "Socio-Economic Level and Maternal Attitudes Toward Parent-Child Relations," *Human Organization,* vol. 16, 1958, pp. 44–48.

40. Katz, Elihu, and Paul F. Lazarsfeld, *Personal Influence:* The Part Played by People in the Flow of Mass Communication. The Free Press, Glencoe, Ill., 1955.

41. Kinnis, Gladys C., "Emotional Adjustment of the Mother to the Child with a Cleft Palate," *Medical Social Work,* vol. 3, 1954, pp. 67–71.

42. Klapper, Joseph T., "What We Know About the Effects of Mass Communication: The Brink of Hope," *Public Opinion Quarterly,* vol. 21, 1957–1958, pp. 453–474.

43. Klatskin, Ethyln H., "Shifts in Child Care Practices in Three Social Classes under an Infant Care Program of Flexible Methodology," *American Journal of Orthopsychiatry,* vol. 22, 1952, pp. 52–61.

44. Macfarlane, Jean W., Lucile Allen, and Marjorie P. Honzik, *A Developmental Study of the Behavior Problems of Normal Children Between Twenty-One Months and Fourteen Years.* University of California Press, Berkeley, 1954.

45. Michigan State Department of Mental Health, *A Report of Some Aspects of the Effectiveness of the Pierre the Pelican Mental Health Pamphlets.* Lansing, Mich, 1952, mimeographed.

46. Ohio Congress of Parents and Teachers, *Reports and Evaluation of College and University Parent Education Workshops.* The Congress, Columbus, Ohio, 1953.

47. Ojemann, Ralph H., "The Measurement of Attitude Toward Self-Reliance," *University of Iowa Studies in Child Welfare,* vol. 10, 1934, pp. 101–111.

48. Ojemann, Ralph H., "Changing Attitudes in the Classroom," *Children,* vol. 3, 1956, pp. 130–134.

49. Ojemann, Ralph H., and associates, "A Functional Analysis of Child Development Material in Current Newspapers and Magazines," *Child Development,* vol. 19, 1948, pp. 77–92.

50. Ojemann, Ralph H., Eugene E. Levitt, William H. Lyle, Jr., and Maxine F. Whiteside, "The Effects of a 'Casual' Teacher-Training Program and Certain Curricular Changes in Grade School Children," *Journal of Experimental Education,* vol. 24, 1955, pp. 95–114.

51. Owings, Chloe, *The Effectiveness of a Particular Program in Parental Sex Education.* University of Minnesota Press, Minneapolis, 1931.

52. Ridenour, Nina, "Criteria of Effectiveness in Mental Health Education," *American Journal of Orthopsychiatry*, vol. 23, 1953, pp. 271–279.

53. Rowland, Loyd W., *A First Evaluation of the Pierre the Pelican Health Pamphlets.* Louisiana Mental Health Studies, No. 1, Louisiana Society for Mental Health, New Orleans, 1948.

54. St. Louis County Health Department, Mental Health Research Program, *An Evaluation of a Preventive Community Mental Health Program.* Clayton, Mo., 1956, mimeographed.

55. Schaus, Hazel W., "An Experimental Investigation of Methods in Parent Education," *University of Iowa Studies in Child Welfare*, vol. 6, 1932, pp. 117–134.

56. Shapiro, Irving S., "Is Group Parent Education Worthwhile? A Research Report," *Marriage and Family Living*, vol. 18, 1956, pp. 154–161.

57. Shirley, May, *Can Parents Educate One Another?* A Study of Lay Leadership in New York State. National Council of Parent Education, New York, 1938.

58. Shoben, Edward J., Jr., "The Assessment of Parental Attitudes in Relation to Child Adjustment," *Genetic Psychological Monographs*, vol. 39, 1949, pp. 101–148.

59. Sigel, Irving E., Martin L. Hoffman, Albert S. Dreyer, and Irving Torgoff, "Toward a Theory of Influence Techniques: Preliminary Report," *Merrill-Palmer Quarterly*, vol. 1, 1954, pp. 4–17.

60. Staples, Ruth, and June W. Smith, "Attitudes of Grandmothers and Mothers Toward Child-Rearing Practices," *Child Development*, vol. 25, 1954, pp. 91–97.

61. Stendler, Celia B., "Sixty Years of Child-Training Practices," *Journal of Pediatrics*, vol. 36, 1950, pp. 122–134.

62. Strodtbeck, Fred L., "The Family as a Three-Person Group," *American Sociological Review*, vol. 19, 1954, pp. 23–29.

63. University of Illinois, Institute of Communications Research, *The Development and Change of Popular Conceptions About Mental Health:* Summary Report. Urbana, Ill., 1958, mimeographed.

64. Vincent, Clark E., "Trends in Infant Care Ideas," *Child Development*, vol. 22, 1951, pp. 199–209.

65. Witmer, Helen L., *The Attitudes of Mothers Toward Sex Education.* University of Minnesota Press, Minneapolis, 1929.

66. Witmer, Helen L., *The Field of Parent Education:* A Survey from the Point of Research. National Council of Parent Education, New York, 1934.

67. Wolfe, Bee R., "Some Aspects of Psychotherapy in a Counseling Service to Parents of Young Children," *Mental Hygiene*, vol. 38, 1954, pp. 430–446.

68. Wolfenstein, Martha, "Trends in Infant Care," *American Journal of Orthopsychiatry*, vol. 23, 1953, pp. 120–130.

APPENDIX

A HISTORY OF EDUCATION FOR CHILD REARING

A History of Education for Child Rearing

THIS APPENDIX PRESENTS an overview of the development of organized parent education efforts in the United States and a description of current activities. More detailed histories are available to the reader in the following studies of parent education. Sunley, in a recent summary article (43) based on extensive research, describes parent education in the early part of the nineteenth century. The published proceedings of the Committee on the Family and Parent Education of the third White House Conference (46) gives a detailed description up to 1930 and an extensive report on programs current at that time. The article by Bridgman (6) describes the decade of 1920 to 1930 in detail. The report by W. I. and Dorothy S. Thomas (44) is especially good for the latter part of this decade. The important monograph by Helen Witmer (48) describes developments in the early 1930's, and the article by Sidonie Gruenberg (15) covers the decade 1930 to 1940. The section on "Parent Education" in the *Encyclopaedia of Social Sciences* (18) by Mary Fisher Langmuir provides a good overall view. Sections of the *Social Work Year Book* (24) on family life education provide a periodic report on parent education developments going back to the 1930's.

In addition to these, there are several important historical treatments each with a special focus. The valuable survey by Lemo Rockwood (32) of the development of family life education includes throughout materials on parent education. The recent article by Anderson (3) on the history of research in child development also includes parent education materials, and offers a valuable chronological table. The *Twenty-Eighth Year Book* (29) of the National Society for the Study of Education describes the development of preschool and parent education, and covers the development from the early seventeenth century. Recently, Hsi Chi Yu (50) surveyed the development of the parent education movement and presented unique material on the origin of many organizations in the field.

HISTORICAL DEVELOPMENT TO 1950

In this historical overview we are concerned primarily with two themes. The first is the growth in extent and variety of parent education activities in this country. In regard to this, one notes that organized parent education in the United States goes back at least to 1800, and that in spite of the continued increase, and what appears to be a sudden expansion of interest at present, the greatest growth occurred from 1925 to 1935. The second theme might be termed the "professionalization of parent education." We refer by this term to developments in research and training, and to the emergence of professional organizations which serve the functions of setting standards, publishing professional journals, sponsoring national meetings, and the like. These professional problems in parent education are of long duration, and some of the best thinking about them was done a generation ago.

We present the materials primarily by decade, with the discussion for each period subdivided according to the two above-mentioned issues. Since professionalization did not begin until the 1920's, prior to that decade we are concerned solely with the growth in extent and kinds of parent education.

The historical changes in the *aims* of parent education, in the *content* selected for transmission to parents, and in the *methods* of influence are dealt with analytically and in detail in Chapters IV, VI, and VII.

Prior to 1900

In a loose sense it is clear that activities which we might call parent education are as old as human culture. Indeed, many of the classics from Plato's *Republic* to Rousseau's *Emile* give considerable attention to the duties of parents. This is not unexpected, since the child-rearing function ascribed to the parent is fundamental to survival of society, and thus, like the society's economic system, religion, and politics, receives the attention of critical commentators upon the social order in every historical period.

In a stricter sense, limiting parent education to organized educational efforts, such classical writings fall beyond our concern. The organized efforts are more recent. Sunley (43) has shown that prior to 1800 information on child care was disseminated to American mothers through importation from Europe, thus indicating an active program of educating parents abroad at that time. Indeed, two histories of pediatrics (34, 42) show plainly that in the eighteenth century, and even earlier, specific advice on child care was given to mothers in written form, usually pamphlets very similar to those produced in mass quantities today. Soon after 1800 several American publications for parents were established. Sunley points out that *Mothers' Magazine* was first published in 1832, *Mothers' Assistant* in 1841, and *Parents' Magazine* (not to be confused with the current publication of the same name) ran from 1840 to 1850.

Our first record of group meetings of parents dates from 1815, when one such group was active in Portland, Maine. Bridgman (6) reports that this and similar meetings up to 1882 are referred to by a leader who organized mothers' groups in Chicago. Sunley also reports that before 1820 mothers regularly met in study groups to discuss child-rearing problems, with the groups, called "Maternal Associations," occurring in most of the country. Some were established in foreign lands by the wives of missionaries. It is of interest that these early groups were concerned about the religious and moral improvement of their children and discussed techniques for "breaking the will," especially those groups of mothers belonging to the more numerous Calvinist and Protestant sects; and that they relied on wisdom gained in discussing their problems and also on the strength they might get from prayer and biblical texts.

It is true that these early organized activities do not run in an unbroken line from the past to the present, but on the other hand, there is no evidence suggesting any general hiatus in parent education during the nineteenth century. It is more likely that as organized efforts terminated, new ones arose to take their place. The nursery and kindergarten movement which from its inception was interested in parent education (25) emerged during this period. During the middle of the nineteenth century the first day nursery was established in New York City, the first public kindergarten was started in 1873, and in 1889 a training school for kindergarten teachers was established (32). Influential writers such as Spencer (37) continued to direct their attention to the education of parents. In his famous work on education in 1861, Spencer ranks education "to perform parental duties" ahead of such objectives as being a good citizen. While current literature agrees in dating the formal parent education movement from 1888, and while this is an appropriate date to mark the start of parent education organizations which continue without interruption to the present, it should not lead one to overlook the extensive parent education activities during the century prior to this date.

Beginning with the decade 1880 various organizations with important parent education programs were founded. In 1948 Yu (50) sent a questionnaire to 83 organizations in the United States and Canada, initially selected on the basis of mention in various conference reports and publications as carrying on parent education activities. Seventy of these organizations reported, giving their dates of origin. Two organizations were founded in the decade 1881 to 1890. A steady increase occurs from then through the decade 1921 to 1930, in which the greatest number were started. From 1930 on, a marked decline occurs in the number of organizations founded.

One of the organizations founded during the first decade is the American Association of University Women. The other is the Child Study Association of America, founded in 1888 as the Society for the Study of Child Nature. This is the oldest organization in the United States having a continuous parent education program, and today is the only national agency exclusively devoted to parent education. It was founded by five mothers at the suggestion of Dr. Felix Adler and the earliest program consisted in studying the works of "authorities" at that time, namely, Rousseau, Spencer, Froebel, and Montessori. Later, G. Stanley Hall and Havelock Ellis were added to the list.

During the period 1890 to 1900 the National Congress of Parents and Teachers was founded. Originally organized as the Congress of Mothers, the statement of purpose included the education of parents in child development (8). At its first meeting in 1897 G. Stanley Hall, whose exhibit of child development material at the World's Fair in 1893 had stimulated parents' interest in child study, addressed the group on "Some Practical Results of Child Study."

Mass media carrying materials for parents and beginning before the turn of the century included *Good Housekeeping, Ladies' Home Journal,* and *Woman's Home Companion* (41). Such magazines, and others during this decade, were carrying articles on "Night Terrors of Children," "Parents and the Nervous Child," and the like (19).

By the end of the century, these and other programs had expanded so that large numbers of parents were being reached. Lighty and Bowman (19, p. 23) suggest that "mothers of privileged classes were pretty sure to be in touch with one or another of the organizations interested in her conduct toward her children. For the less privileged mothers, there were the settlement houses with groups for mothers and kindergarten mothers' clubs instituted under Froebel's influence."

1900 to 1920

During this twenty-year period the active organizations continued to extend their programs. For example, in 1912 the Child Study Association published, as a service to parents, its first selected list of books for children. This organization also was observing numerous parent study groups, collecting data to be used in the influential *Outlines of Child Study,* which was published in 1921.

Moving beyond the already-existing programs were two major developments in the scope and variety of parent education which occurred from 1900 to 1920. The first was the emergence of federal support for parent education (6, 7, 25, 32, 50). One thus notes that federal support of parent education occurred in the first part of this century, and indeed took place *prior* to the large-scale entrance into parent education activities by private organizations, which was not to occur until after 1920. This is not to say that parent education in this country was not initiated by private organizations, for clearly it was. The development of parent education follows the pattern of other durable social changes, in that private organizations are the innovators, spearheading the change, but have their functions gradually assumed by public organizations. The point here is that parent education was at an early point quickly adopted as part of the program of public organizations, before many private organizations had yet entered the field.

The four key programs of the federal government which can be cited are the following: (1) In 1909 the first White House Conference on child welfare was held—the Conference on the Care of Dependent Children—resulting in the writing of the Child's Charter and in the creation of the Children's Bureau in 1912, which was placed in the Department of Labor in 1913; in 1914 the first edition of *Infant Care* was published, evidencing the interest of the Bureau in parent education from its inception. (2) In 1914 the Smith-Lever Act made provision for 2,000 County Home Demonstration Agents as part of the Department of Agriculture. These agents carried on demonstration projects in homemaking, home management, and child care, among other duties. (3) In 1917 the Smith-Hughes Act defined "homemaking" as a basic vocation for women, and education for homemaking was henceforth included in the various vocational acts administered by the Office of Education. Extension classes, institutes, exhibits, and demonstrations for the teaching of nutrition and child care were developed in various sections of the country. (4) In 1918 the United States Public Health Service began support of programs of parent education, with special emphasis on health of the child.

The second important development of this period was the founding of many types of organizations which, although not developing parent education programs during these two decades, were to play a major role in parent education in the years lying just ahead. Several examples of such organizations can be given to indicate the wide variety of professional backgrounds which contributed to the development of parent education.

The first child study center in America was begun in the State University of Iowa in 1911 under the leadership of Carl E. Seashore. Six years later at Iowa the Child Welfare Research Station was established under a grant from the state legislature, although some of the senators maintained that "love of the mother was all the guidance the child needed" and resented the implication that "Iowa children were in a bad way." (39)

The American Home Economics Association was organized in 1908, its initial program emphasis giving little indication of its future interest in parent education. As Lemo Rockwood says, in its early development the Association was trying to demonstrate that it was a legitimate scientific enterprise: "Consequently the emphasis was upon dietary skill and techniques. When Minnesota introduced a baby into the home management house in 1919, many good home economists were frankly dubious about the advisability of disrupting the smooth running of the house with any such variable element as a baby. Concern for the baby was a secondary consideration. Gradually, however, there has been a transition in emphasis from the merely technological and physical aspects of family living to thinking of the family in terms of intrinsic quality; more emphasis is being placed on values and less on functions, more emphasis on family sufficiency and less on efficiency." (32, p. 33).

In 1909 the National Committee on Mental Hygiene was founded by Clifford Beers, and was primarily concerned with improving treatment and with helping people learn more about mental illness. This organization merged with other groups in 1950 to form the current National Association for Mental Health. As we have indicated, during the past few years certain educational programs for parents designed to promote mental health have been stimulated by this group.

One might give two other examples. First, in 1916 the first cooperative nursery school in the country opened at the University of Chicago. This was a forerunner of the many current cooperative nursery schools which engage in parent education (47). Second, the Committee on Marriage and the Home of the Federal Council of Churches of Christ in America (now the National Council of the Churches of Christ in the United States of America) was organized in 1909 to stimulate churches to develop programs of education for family life. Most of the larger denominations now publish bulletins and many issue periodicals dealing with family life. Many of the major denominations, indeed, are actively engaged in parent education programs.

In sum, by 1920, in addition to the growth of activities continuing from the turn of the century, the federal government was active on many fronts and on a large scale in parent education. In addition, numerous organizations, of which we have given a few important examples, had been launched and were later to play a role in parent education development. Against this background occurred the impressive expansion and professionalization of parent education in the next decade.

1921 to 1930

The substantial growth of parent education during this decade is best indicated by the survey reported in the National Society for the Study of Education *Twenty-Eighth Year Book* (29), which lists over 75 *major* organizations in the late 1920's conducting parent education programs. These include: (1) national organizations such as the Child Study Association of America; (2) university-based and other research centers carrying on programs in parent education, such as the Institute of Child Welfare at the University of Minnesota; (3) teachers colleges and normal schools, such as Teachers College at Columbia University; (4) women's colleges, for example, Vassar; (5) land-grant colleges carrying on work through home economics divisions; (6) state departments of vocational education; (7) state departments of education; (8) public school systems; (9) private schools; (10) nursery schools; (11) social agencies; (12) child guidance agencies; (13) health agencies; and (14) religious organizations. The data presented by Yu (50) indicate that 26 of the important organizations involved in parent education were founded during this decade.

Especially noteworthy developments in the field of parent education during this decade included the following. Programs were initiated in state departments of education in California and New York, thus extending public support of parent education from the federal to the state level. Programs in the newly founded child study centers at California, Cornell, and Minnesota brought together in the same organizations parent education and basic research on child development. Programs were initiated in public and private schools, in large part under the stimulus of the National Congress of Parents and Teachers, making parent education available in an institutional setting which cuts across economic and ethnic lines. Support from the Laura Spelman Rockefeller Memorial, described below, for parent education program development caused the initiation of large-scale efforts in the American Association of University Women; there was a nationwide child study program guided by the Association's headquarters and a special section in its journal for parent groups. Funds from the Memorial and from other foundations helped to launch the publication of *Parents' Magazine* in 1926. This was originally conceived as an outlet for the research carried on at the newly formed child study centers, and was presented under the auspices of several of them, including those at Yale, Minnesota, Iowa, and Teachers College at Columbia. The purpose was to transmit to parents the research findings of the growing study of child development, and at the time of its founding it had almost a clear field with respect to presenting "expert" content. This publication is historically important also because it influenced several of the older home and women's journals to add parent education materials to their content. The magazine is owned and published by Parents' Institute, and is independent of outside auspices.

The development of professional activities is without question primarily attributable to the financial support offered such programs by the Laura Spelman Rockefeller Memorial and the Spelman Fund. The Memorial was established in 1918 and it continued for a decade. In 1928, the Memorial was terminated. Some of the Memorial funds were used to create the Spelman Fund, and the remainder were transferred to the Rockefeller Foundation. The Memorial, during its existence, and the Spelman Fund, until about 1938, had child study and parent education as one of their objectives, and they were the main support of parent education activities for almost two decades.

Their support of parent education and child development activities began in 1923. The Memorial provided the funds for the establishment of child study centers, such as the early St. George Nursery School in Toronto, the Institute for Child Research at Teachers College, the Institutes of Child Welfare at Minnesota and California; and gave substantial funds for expansion to the Child Welfare Research Station in Iowa. It was planned that such institutions would include both research and parent education functions with the aim of transmitting sound research directly to parents.

This activity coincided with other independent developments attesting to the growth of interest in research on the family. During this decade the National Research Council organized its Committee on Child Development and thereby gave official recognition to the scientific status of child development research; other major child study centers were initiated at Yale University and elsewhere; in 1921 the first university course on the family was offered; and in 1924 the first section on the family of the American Sociological Society was organized (3, 32).

Another activity of the Memorial was support of training programs in parent education. A curriculum and numerous fellowships in parent education at Teachers College were provided with this support; funds were contributed for training in home economics departments, and by 1928 more than 20 colleges and universities were training home economics students in nursery school settings to provide experience in home management and child care which could be taught to the parents with whom they would work (32).

A third professional development aided by the Memorial was self-study and appraisal of their role in parent education by numerous national organizations. For example, in 1926 the American Home Economics Association received a grant for the purpose of assessing its role in child development and parent education and three field workers in this area were added to its staff. The result during the next five years was the establishment of a major division of the Association concerned with child development and parent education. The National Congress of Parents and Teachers in 1926 received a grant providing for the nationwide services of a specialist in parent education. The work was directed toward strengthening the resources in each state, coordinating activities, and getting cooperation in starting programs. Major changes took place as a result of this grant, inasmuch as a survey just prior to this period had indicated a relative absence of parent education activities in the National Congress of Parents and Teachers (8).

From the time the Memorial initiated its parent education and child development program in 1923, it maintained a warm relationship with the Child Study Association of America. This relationship led to two events in 1925 which were turning points in the development of parent education. First, the Child Study Association with support from the Memorial held a Conference on Modern Parenthood, which was attended by 1,500 persons from all states. This was of great value in publicizing the parent education and child study movement to the country at large (29).

Secondly, a week-long, national conference of professionals working in parent education was held, the first of its kind in this country. We quote from the mimeographed report of the conference (10): "Inasmuch as several organizations were known to be working on problems related to the education of parents, the Child Study Association of America planned in 1925 to bring together representatives of the various agencies for an informal discussion of their common problems. Through the generosity of the Laura Spelman Rockefeller Memorial, the Association was enabled to finance a round-table conference, in which representatives of thirteen organizations took part." At the close of the conference it was decided to organize a National Council of Parent Education with a permanent secretary, the aims of the organization being the furtherance of the development of the field of parent education. This organization, strongly supported throughout its career first by the Memorial, and later by the Spelman Fund, began in 1925 and was incorporated in 1929. Almost immediately the Council became the national clearing house for parent education activities in the United States for the last part of the decade and during the 1930's.

General support was also provided by the Memorial for the Child Study Association program, enabling the latter to continue its activities as the major resource organization in parent education in the United States. It expanded several of its programs, namely, publications, leadership training, and study groups; initiated the first radio program designed for parents in 1925; and opened an educational counseling service in 1929.

Thus, by the end of this decade, owing primarily to the money provided by the Laura Spelman Rockefeller Memorial and to the professional leadership of the Child Study Association, parent education programs had expanded substantially in both number and variety, training programs were well established, and machinery was available for the national organization and integration of such activities in the form of the National Council of Parent Education. As a fitting climax to the decade of growth and professionalization, the third White House Conference had as one of its major committees the Committee on the Family and Parent Education. The work of this committee resulted in a 350-page volume on parent education (46), constituting the definitive description of activities, and analysis of issues at that time.

1931 to 1940

This decade in the history of parent education brought first a tremendous expansion of program activities and professional research during the first part and then a marked decline in the rate of growth and general interest in the last part of the period, the latter carrying over into the next decade, through the war years. Let us consider these in order.

Expansion in both extent and variety of parent education continued during this decade, evidenced by the fact that in 1935 the U.S. Office of Education catalogued the agencies, public and private which had programs in this field, with the list covering 53 pages (20). Noteworthy expansion occurred in the public schools and in nursery school and preschool settings. Much of the growth in the public school and nursery school settings came from the activities of the Works Progress Administration during the depression. The WPA made available teachers, group leaders, and other trained personnel to interested groups to present basic materials on child behavior (22). During 1933 to 1934 more than 20 state departments of education employed qualified workers to supervise parent education activities in local programs supported in this manner, and in 1936 there were approximately 1,650 WPA nursery schools in operation (1). In most of these states parent education was included in the range of interest for the first time.

In the professional realm, training programs for parent educators also continued to develop. While the National Council of Parent Education, with the support of the Laura Spelman Rockefeller Memorial, was the focal point of training activities, important training programs existed elsewhere. By 1932 courses in parent education were offered in one or more colleges and universities in at least 25 states (5). These training programs were largely concentrated in colleges and universities having child development and child welfare research stations, with accompanying parent education programs. There were important exceptions, however; for example, in 1930 Ernest Groves offered a course in parent education at the Harvard summer school (32).

During this decade the major development was without question in the area of professional research. Research on parent education was carried on primarily by two organizations. At the Child Welfare Research Station of the State University of Iowa, a series of widely influential studies (40) were made under the leadership of Ralph Ojemann. This series included research on the validity of information given to parents, the effectiveness of parent education programs, and the comparative success of different methods, such as lectures versus group discussion.

The other organization with a major research program was the National Council of Parent Education. The Council was the publisher of a professional journal, *Parent Education* (27), for the five years 1934 to 1938. This journal carried authoritative discussions of theoretical and research issues in parent education, and also served as a medium for the exchange of information on professional activities in the United States. These few volumes of *Parent Education* are still available in most large libraries. They remain the primary repository of theoretical writings in the field of parent education, and the articles are as timely for the problems of today as for those of twenty years ago.

The Council supported several research studies which appeared in monograph form. Some remain unique in the field. We mention specifically two of the monographs: Helen Witmer's *The Field of Parent Education:* A Survey from the Viewpoint of Research (48), and May Shirley's *Can Parents Educate One Another?* (36) The first constitutes a critical study of the research data on parent education up to 1934 and suggests research topics which a generation later still require study. The second is one of the earliest attempts to evaluate the relative effectiveness of different parent education methods.

In addition, the Council operated a fellowship program. Between 1926 and 1934 (although mostly in the latter period) 122 fellowships were granted. Twenty-seven were given for research, and 95 were allotted primarily for training; 66 were year-long fellowships. The research and training program was carried out in the main through arrangements with Columbia, Minnesota, Cornell, and Iowa universities, and the Merrill-Palmer School; that is, through those institutions which at that time had both child study and parent education programs (49).

Turning now to the latter part of the decade, we stated above that there occurred a loss of interest in parent education. It appears now that the writings of certain professional students of the family during the early 1930's may have exerted a retarding influence in this area. There is evidence that some were questioning the permanency of traditional family life and the desirability of parental, in contrast to institutional, child rearing. It is hard to recapture the sentiment then held by some, because it is so different from the current professional view, but a quotation from Reuter and Runner's book *The Family*, appearing in 1931, illustrates this point of view. "Numerous organizations operating on a quasi- or pseudoscientific level—child welfare stations, parent education organizations, character education institutes, family research stations, and the like, are motivated by fear of change and a desire to preserve or reinstate the old and familiar arrangements that are apparently crumbling to ruin." (30, p. 6)

Within a decade, this viewpoint itself crumbled under the weight of growing evidence on the durability, universality, and importance of the traditional parent-child socialization pattern. Anthropological research on other cultures, wartime and earlier studies of the effects of institutionalization upon children, the unpredicted upturn in the national birth rate, all served to reaffirm the importance of, and interest in, the traditional family pattern, and invigorated the parent education effort in subsequent years.

An especially significant causal factor in the decline of professional activities in parent education was the termination in 1938 of the Spelman Fund's support of parent education. Without this financial support, and ineffective in its own fund-raising campaigns, the National Council of Parent Education disbanded in 1938. Many of the original members formed a National Committee on Parent Education in an effort to carry on the program. Not only did the National Council disband, but several other private organizations that had received substantial support from the Spelman Fund also either went out of existence or had financial difficulty for some years.

Because parent education programs during this period from 1920 to 1938 had been increasingly supported by public organizations such as state departments of education, public health services, and the like, the termination of the Memorial had no critical effect on the *extent* of parent education programs. The critical effect instead was in the area of professional activities, since the booming parent education movement was left without a national organization which could guide its professional activities and help to coordinate them at a national level.

1941 to 1950

No decline occurred during this decade in the extent of parent education services offered by various organizations. Indeed, in some areas of state-supported programs such as developed in Mississippi, North and South Carolina, and Georgia there was considerable expansion.

The major growth of activity during this decade came from the greater use of parent education by workers in the field of mental health in order to prevent mental illness. As we have pointed out, the working relation between mental health groups and parent education groups had been established for some time prior; as early as 1930 the National Mental Hygiene Committee and the National Congress of Parents and Teachers cooperatively drew up an outline for a course of child study with suggested readings for parents interested in understanding themselves and their children (25, p. 38). The postwar era brought more of this. Spurred on by the data on prevalence of mental illness gained from the mental health screening procedures during the war, the immediate postwar era saw the passage of the National Mental Health Act in 1946. Under this act each state received federal funds to operate community mental health programs, these programs often including parent education. These programs are administered by state health departments, departments of welfare, and other agencies (21). A major example of the new use of parent education by mental health groups is that of the Louisiana Society for Mental Health, which under the direction of Loyd W. Rowland prepares and distributes an educational pamphlet series to all new parents in the state. The pamphlets are designed to promote mental health of children through influencing child-care practices (33).

While parent education services continued at the same or higher levels than before, the decade showed a decline in research and training as professional activities. In some part this decline must be counted an effect of World War II, which decreased the volume of research on most aspects of human behavior. At the same time one must count as contributing factors those mentioned earlier: the loss of interest in the family, the demise of the National Council of Parent Education, the lack of funds for professional activities, and the absence of *Parent Education* as a national medium for publication of materials.

In regard to research, it is to be noted that of some two dozen research studies evaluating the effects of parent education, only two were made during this decade; the remainder are split about evenly between the decade 1930 to 1940 and from 1951 to the present.

In regard to the integration of professional activities at the national level, the National Committee on Parent Education, heir to the role of the National Council, was unable to perform effectively this integrative function. In 1946 an effort was made by Parents' Institute, publishers of *Parents' Magazine*, to fulfill this function by establishing a parent education clearing house. The purpose of the clearing house was to help coordinate the many efforts in the parent education field, to publish a news bulletin, to hold an annual parent education conference, and generally to provide consultative services and to work for improvement in parent education programs. The first national conference was held in 1946, but shortly thereafter the clearing house effort was abandoned. In 1947 the first annual Institute for Workers in Parent Education was held, under joint sponsorship of the National Committee on Parent Education and the Child Study Association of America. At present this Institute is sponsored by the Child Study Association alone, and is the one national annual professional meeting held in the field. While it now regularly attracts from two to three hundred participants, during the period 1947 to 1950 it was neither large nor nationally representative.

THE CURRENT SCENE: 1951 TO 1958

This section describes the current state of parent education activities. The description will continue to focus on the two topics used to guide the historical materials, namely, the extent and variety of programs, and the professional organization and activities of parent education.

Extent and Variety of Parent Education

The proceedings of one national conference have pointed out (16) that as of 1948 no one foundation or agency had ever made a study of all the extra-school opportunities for education. We as well as others find it impossible to indicate in detail the current extent of parent education, because of the large number of programs unreported in even careful surveys. Instead, we report on a sample of representative programs as evidence of the extent and variety of activities. Extensive lists of organizations providing publications and services in family-centered education are available to the interested reader in the work of McGinnis and Pfeiffer (23). Very detailed descriptions of nine important parent education programs are given by Chamberlain and de Schweinitz (9).

The growth of parent education from 1950 on undoubtedly has been aided by the substantial sums available for work in the area of "mental health." These funds stimulate the growth of parent education today much as did the Laura Spelman Rockefeller Memorial and the Spelman Fund during the 1920's and 1930's. The shift in interest in mental health and other areas of human concern from treatment to prevention has been marked in the past decade, and parent education, primarily a preventive technique, has grown in wealth and recognition with this shift of emphasis.

We will discuss first some of the programs which operate at the national level. Among these are the important activities sponsored by governmental agencies. At the national level, of course, these constitute federally supported programs which are engaged in parent education activities. Such programs are concentrated in either the Department of Agriculture or the Department of Health, Education, and Welfare. The program in the Department of Agriculture is a direct continuation of the program begun in 1914 as a result of the Smith-Lever Act. Parent education occurs here in the context of the extension service affiliated in every case with the land-grant colleges in the several states. Some important duties of the extension people at the state level are to produce written materials, to consult with local county groups, and to train county agents for leadership in educational programs. It is the latter who work directly with parents in the county. The program of the Department of Agriculture, perhaps the largest direct contact program of the federal government, reached nearly 1,700,000 families (45) during 1955 with information on child development and guidance, strengthening family relations, recommended play equipment for children, and so on.

Within the Department of Health, Education, and Welfare, established in 1953, several distinct programs are carried on by the Office of Education, the Social Security Administration, and the Public Health Service. Two divisions of the Office of Education are concerned with parent education. First, one aspect of the program of the Division of State and Local School Systems is to improve the counseling of parents by teachers (12). This aim is pursued through writing and publishing relevant materials (13), direct consultation, promoting summer workshops, holding national conferences, and the like. Second, the Home Economics Education branch is responsible for administering certain funds to state departments of education, and acts as consultant. These activities are a direct continuation of the program launched in 1917 under the Smith-Hughes Act. A major emphasis is on parent education, which most frequently takes the form of adult education classes administered by home economists in the departments of education at the state or community level. Today approximately half a million men and women are enrolled in some 4,000 such educational centers (31).

Within the Social Security Administration, to which it was transferred in 1946 from the Department of Agriculture, the Children's Bureau is responsible for parent education activities. All three divisions are active in one way or another. The Research Division carries a specialist in parent education on the staff, and is also responsible for the publications for parents on child care; for example, the famous *Infant Care*. The total distribution of such publications through 1955 is just short of 60 million copies. The Division of Health Services is involved through administration of a grant-in-aid program to the states for maternal and child health programs, which in turn often include parent education programs within the context of local health services. In addition, the Nursing Section of this division is concerned with the professional training of nurses for parent education leadership. The Division of Social Services is linked to the various state departments of welfare through a grant-in-aid program; members of this staff have published materials pertaining to parent education (11).

Within the Public Health Service the most prominent activity is carried out by the National Institute of Mental Health, which with its funds for research in the field of mental health is currently supporting a number of large-scale studies seeking to evaluate the effects of parent education. These studies are reviewed in Chapter IX.

We now consider the nongovernmental organizations or corporations which have a national scope or outreach. Below is a list of three dozen such organizations which include parent education in their program. This list, we stress, is designed to be representative rather than exhaustive.

> American Academy of Pediatrics
> American Association of University Women
> American Heart Association
> American Home Economics Association
> American Library Association
> American National Red Cross
> American Nurses Association
> American Public Health Association
> American Social Hygiene Association
> Associated Baby Services
> Association for Childhood Education, International
> Cerebral Palsy Association
> Child Study Association of America
> Curtis Publishing Company
> General Federation of Women's Clubs
> Gerber Products Company
> Hearst Corporation
> League for Emotionally Disturbed Children
> Mental Health Materials Center

Metropolitan Life Insurance Company
National Association for Mental Health
National Association for Nursery Education
National Association for Retarded Children
National Congress of Parents and Teachers
National Council of the Churches of Christ
National Education Association
National League for Nursing
National Society for Crippled Children and Adults
National Tuberculosis Association
Parent Education Project (University of Chicago)
Parents' Institute
Public Affairs Committee
Science Research Associates
United Cerebral Palsy Association
Woman's Day
Young Men's Christian Associations

We have found no satisfactory single way of classifying these national organizations. Some of the organizations are composed of professional members, for example, the American Public Health Association, which has sponsored preparation of materials for parent educators including one definitive work on educational counseling (2). Some of the organizations consist primarily of nonprofessional members, such as the National Congress of Parents and Teachers. Some organizations are primarily nonprofit in nature, such as the American National Red Cross, whereas others are straightforward commercial enterprises, such as Parents' Institute. Note also that some of the organizations are supported by foundation or other private funds, such as the Parent Education Project of the University of Chicago; others are supported by public donations, such as the Cerebral Palsy Association.

Some organizations carry on a many-faceted program, such as the Child Study Association of America. Other organizations in contrast have programs consisting wholly or almost wholly of mass media presentations of information. The latter category includes groups such as the Public Affairs Committee and commercial organizations such as Associated Baby Services, Gerber

Products Company, Curtis Publishing Company, Science Research Associates, Hearst Corporation, and the like. Commercial book publishers, such as Pocket Books, publisher of the paper-bound editions (38) of Benjamin Spock's famous book (over nine million copies) on child care, would be included also.

Another perspective is gained by noting that some organizations carry on programs with a specific focus on parents of special children, for example, the National Society for Crippled Children and Adults. In contrast, some organizations employ parent education as a method within the context of their specific programs, as with American Library Association or the National Association for Nursery Education. Still other organizations, characterized by general rather than specific interests, are represented by the Child Study Association of America, Parents' Institute, and the National Congress of Parents and Teachers.

One might make other comparisons and the reader will no doubt think of many. However, these may be sufficient to show the complexity which any classification must have. Of the foregoing national organizations, there are a few which deserve a word more because of the special position they hold on the national scene.

The Child Study Association of America is the only noncommercial, national organization devoted solely to parent education. It carries on a program which includes publication of mass media materials for parents, an educational counseling service, and parent discussion groups. It continues to fill the gap left by the passing of the National Committee on Parent Education, by providing professional leadership in parent education through its publications for parent educators (e.g., 14), through its leadership training program, its program advisory service, and through its publication of the *Parent Education Exchange Bulletin*, currently the only national medium of exchange of information among parent educators. It also holds the annual Institute for Workers in Parent Education, which is a national meeting similar to the conventions of other professional organizations.

The National Congress of Parents and Teachers, with more than nine million current members and many thousand parent study groups, is without doubt the largest membership organization concerned with parent education. The Congress operates through its local chapters in more than 38,000 communities. One of the standing committees of the Congress is on parent and family life education. The aims of this committee are threefold. The first is to help parents become more effective through utilization of study discussion groups and of parent education (26). The Congress publishes the *National Parent-Teacher:* The PTA Magazine, consisting mainly of materials for parents on child rearing. In addition to the magazine special materials for parents in the form of topical pamphlets are published.

Parents' Institute is the major commercial organization concerned with parents at a national level. The Institute publishes *Parents' Magazine*, with a circulation of nearly two million. The magazine carries materials on child rearing, complete programs for child study groups, and special discussion outlines available to group leaders. It also publishes materials for parents interested in setting up study groups themselves, including ideas on such matters as leadership techniques. Advisory services are also offered to subscribers.

The Parent Education Project of the University of Chicago differs from other programs in that it has received its financial support from a foundation, the Fund for Adult Education. This program, experimental in nature, is notable for its development of special materials for parent study groups (e.g., 17) and for its stress on lay leadership of the study groups. Currently, several hundred groups per year are connected with this project, and are co-sponsored by a variety of organizations such as schools, parent-teacher associations, colleges, mental health groups, and YMCA's. The Project seeks in the near future to develop course materials for five different age levels from infancy to adolescence so that a complete curriculum will be available.

The Mental Health Materials Center, a nonprofit organization, is almost unique in serving as a national screening and distribution center for mass media materials. The materials prepared by other organizations in this country, whether pamphlets, films, plays, or other media forms, are examined by a select board of experts; the Center then accepts for national promotion and distribution only those passing rigorous standards. It thus provides for many organizations in the country that are local consumers of parent education material a professional service of suggesting the best available current materials and making them readily available through order. It thus has a significant influence in raising the standard of the average material being given to parents.

The National Association for Mental Health deserves mention because it exemplifies the recent interest of mental health personnel in parent education. While the educational interests of this organization clearly are subordinated to its concern with mental illness, training more professional personnel such as psychiatrists, and with improving hospital and other facilities for treatment, nevertheless, its educational activities provide a stimulus at the internal level to its member organizations. The National Association assists its member organizations by emphasizing better program content, staff additions, and so forth. It may undertake to establish new programs, where necessary. It serves in part as a clearing house for information on educational programs and materials for mental health.

Now we consider some of the programs, public and private, at the state level. One finds many of these programs to be simply an extension of national programs, for example, in local chapters of the American National Red Cross, of religious groups, or of the National Congress of Parents and Teachers. But in addition to these one finds a host of organizations that carry on parent education activities that have very loose ties or none at all to national groups.

State governments usually have a department or division which is concerned with parent education and which is supported from state funds. In two states with leading parent education programs, New York and California, the divisions respectively are the Bureau of Child Development and Parent Education and the Bureau of Adult Education. In many others, it is the state health departments with their associated bureaus or divisions of mental health which carry out the state-supported parent education activities.

At the state level must be listed also the numerous college and university activities. Many university programs in parent education are connected with federal programs through the Office of Education or Department of Agriculture; this is true in particular of the land-grant colleges. But in addition, private schools such as Teachers College of Columbia University, the University of Southern California, and Western Reserve University, to name a few, conduct programs for parents. Apart from universities and state-supported bureaus, there is a third group of organizations which are private and voluntary in nature, exemplified by the Michigan Association of Child Study Clubs, an independent state-wide parent education organization.

Turning now to the community level one finds parent education programs, whether public or private, to exist in great number. For example, the St. Louis Mental Health Association has an active parent study group program. Many community-wide health organizations, such as the New York City Board of Health, sponsor parent counseling and parent discussion groups in child health stations (well-baby clinics), and also prepare and distribute printed materials. Public and private colleges at the community level are also involved. A recent study by the National Education Association (28) of the adult education programs of junior colleges in the United States show that some 7 per cent of participation in adult programs is in the area of family life and parent education. The Merrill-Palmer School in Detroit and Cooper Union for the Advancement of Science and Art in New York both carry a parent education curriculum.

In regard to public schools a recent National Education Association sample survey (28) of all urban public schools in the United States with respect to their adult education programs shows that some 32 per cent of these provided classes or groups in parent or family life education. While this reflects the operation of parent-teachers associations at the community level, not all of it can be attributed to this link with a national organization; much of it arises from independent activities of the school system.

Finally, there are a number of independent organizations at the community level with parent education programs or which conduct research. Some are public service or welfare agencies, such as the Family Service Association of Greater Boston, The Guidance Center of New Rochelle, and the St. Louis County Health Department (35). Communitywide private agencies include the Association for Family Living in Chicago and the American Institute of Family Relations in Los Angeles. Foundation-supported programs include the Oregon Developmental Center Project (4) and the Clara Elizabeth Fund for Maternal Health in Flint, Michigan. There are also religious organizations such as the Protestant Council of the City of New York, and independent parent organizations such as the United Parents Association in New York.

REFERENCES

1. Allen, Winifred Y., and Doris Campbell, *The Creative Nursery Center:* A Unified Service to Children and Parents. Family Service Association of America, New York, 1948.

2. American Public Health Association, *Health Supervision of Young Children.* The Association, New York, 1955.

3. Anderson, John E., "Child Development: An Historical Perspective," *Child Development*, vol. 27, 1956, pp. 181–196.

4. Avery, Curtis A., and Lester A. Kirkendall, *Developmental Center Project in Family Life Education.* E. C. Brown Trust, Portland, Ore., 1955.

5. Bossard, James H. S., *The Sociology of Child Development.* Harper and Bros., New York, 1954.

6. Bridgman, Ralph O., "Postwar Progress in Child Welfare," *Annals of the American Academy of Political and Social Science*, vol. 151, 1930, pp. 32–45.

7. Brown, Muriel W., *With Focus on Family Living.* Vocational Division Bulletin 249, Office of Education, Government Printing Office, Washington, 1953.

8. Butterworth, Julian E., *The Parent-Teacher Association and Its Work.* Macmillan Co., New York, 1928.

9. Chamberlain, H. E., and Elizabeth de Schweinitz, "Nine Programs for the Promotion of Mental Health" in *Community Programs for Mental Health*, edited by Ruth Kotinsky and Helen Witmer. Harvard University Press, Cambridge, Mass., 1955, pp. 46–157.

10. Child Study Association of America, *Conference on Parental Education.* The Association, New York, 1925, mimeographed.

11. Davis, Annie L., *Children Living in Their Own Homes*. Children's Bureau, Government Printing Office, Washington, 1953.

12. Gabbard, Hazel F., "Trends in Parent Education," *Understanding the Child*, vol. 22, 1953, pp. 34–37.

13. Gabbard, Hazel F., *Working with Parents:* A Handbook. Bulletin No. 7, Office of Education, Government Printing Office, Washington, 1948.

14. Goller, Gertrude, *When Parents Get Together:* How to Organize a Parent Education Program. Child Study Association of America, New York, 1955.

15. Gruenberg, Sidonie M., "Parent Education 1930–1940," *Annals of the American Academy of Political and Social Science*, 1940, vol. 212, 1940, pp. 81–87.

16. Inter-Agency Committee (U. S.) on Background Materials for the National Conference on Family Life, *The American Family:* Background Report, May 2, 1948. Government Printing Office, Washington, 1948.

17. Kawin, Ethel, *Parenthood in a Free Nation*. Parent Education Project, University of Chicago Press, Chicago, 1954.

18. [Langmuir], Mary Fisher, "Parent Education," *Encyclopaedia of the Social Sciences*. Macmillan Co., New York, 1933, vol. 11, pp. 573–576.

19. Lighty, Margaret, and LeRoy E. Bowman, *Parenthood in a Democracy:* The Origin and History of a Large Urban Federation of Parents and an Interpretive Analysis of Its Objectives and Methods in Education and Organization for Family Life in a Democratic Society. Parents' Institute, Inc., New York, 1939.

20. Lombard, Ellen C., *Parent Education Opportunities*. Bulletin No. 3, Office of Education, Government Printing Office, Washington, 1935.

21. Lowry, James V., "Public Mental Health Agencies, State and National," *Annals of the American Academy of Political and Social Science*, vol. 286, 1953, pp. 100–106.

22. Lowy, Louis, *Adult Education and Group Work*. William Morrow and Co., New York, 1955.

23. McGinnis, Esther, and Marie Pfeiffer, *Family Centered Education:* Annotated Bibliography. American Home Economics Association, Washington, 1953.

24. National Association of Social Workers and Russell Sage Foundation, Sections on "Family Life Education," *Social Work Year Book*. Russell Sage Foundation, New York, 1930–1949, and National Association of Social Workers, New York, 1951–1959.

25. National Congress of Parents and Teachers, *Parent Education:* The First Year Book. The National Congress, Washington, 1930.

26. National Congress of Parents and Teachers, *Parent-Teacher Manual*. The National Congress, Chicago, 1956.

27. National Council of Parent Education, *Parent Education*. The National Council, New York, vols. 1–5, 1934–1938.

28. National Education Association, Division of Adult Education Service, *A Study of Urban Public School Adult Education Programs of the United States.* The Association, Washington, 1952.

29. National Society for the Study of Education, *Twenty-Eighth Year Book:* Parts I and II, Preschool and Parent Education. Public School Publishing, Bloomington, Ill., 1929.

30. Reuter, Edward B., and Jessie R. Runner, *The Family:* Source Materials for the Study of Family and Personality. McGraw-Hill Book Co., New York, 1931.

31. Riner, Elizabeth, *Frontiers in Homemaking Education.* Vocational Division Bulletin 239, Office of Education, Government Printing Office, Washington, 1949.

32. Rockwood, Lemo D., *Origins and Development for the Movement for Education for Marriage, Family Life and Parenthood in the U. S., 1900–1948,* with Major Emphasis on Developments During the Past Twenty-Five Years. Unpublished manuscript, 1948.

33. Rowland, Loyd W., *A First Evaluation of the Pierre the Pelican Health Pamphlets.* Louisiana Mental Health Studies, No. 1, Louisiana Society for Mental Health, New Orleans, 1948.

34. Ruhrah, John, *Pediatrics of the Past.* Paul B. Hoeber, Inc., New York, 1925.

35. St. Louis County Health Department, Mental Health Research Program, *An Evaluation of a Preventive Community Mental Health Program.* Clayton, Mo., 1956, mimeographed.

36. Shirley, May, *Can Parents Educate One Another?* National Council of Parent Education, New York, 1938.

37. Spencer, Herbert, *Education:* Intellectual, Moral, and Physical. Williams and Norgate, London, 1861.

38. Spock, Benjamin, *Dr. Benjamin Shock's Baby and Child Care.* Pocket Books, Inc., New York, 1957. (This book is a new version of *The Pocket Book of Baby and Child Care,* originally published under the title *The Common Sense Book of Baby and Child Care* by Duell, Sloan and Pearce.)

39. State University of Iowa, *Pioneering in Child Welfare.* The University, Iowa City, 1933.

40. State University of Iowa, *University of Iowa Studies in Child Welfare.* The University, Iowa City, vols. 6 and 10, 1932 and 1934.

41. Stendler, Celia B., "Sixty Years of Child Training Practices: Revolution in Nursery," *Journal of Pediatrics,* vol. 36, 1950, pp. 122–134.

42. Still, George F., *The History of Paediatrics:* The Progress of the Study of Diseases of Children Up to the End of the XVIIIth Century. Oxford University Press, London, 1931.

43. Sunley, Robert, "Early Nineteenth Century American Literature on Child Rearing" in *Childhood in Contemporary Cultures*, edited by Margaret Mead and Martha Wolfenstein. University of Chicago Press, Chicago, 1955, pp. 150–167.

44. Thomas, William I., and Dorothy S. Swain, *The Child in America:* Behavior Problems and Programs. Alfred A. Knopf, New York, 1928.

45. United States Department of Agriculture, *Extension Activities and Accomplishments, 1955*. Extension Service Circular No. 509, Government Printing Office, Washington, 1956.

46. White House Conference on Child Health and Protection, Section III: Education and Training, Committee on the Family and Parent Education, *Parent Education:* Types, Content and Method. Century Co., New York, 1932.

47. Whiteside-Taylor, Katharine, "Cooperative Nursery Schools Educate Families," *Teachers College Record*, vol. 54, 1953, pp. 332–339.

48. Witmer, Helen L., *The Field of Parent Education:* A Survey from the Viewpoint of Research. National Council of Parent Education, New York, 1934.

49. Witmer, Helen L., "Analysis of the Fellowship Program of the National Council of Parent Education," *Parent Education*, vol. 2, 1936, pp. 16–19, 43.

50. Yu, Hsi Chi, *Survey of the Parent Education Movement in the United States of America and Canada*. Master's thesis, University of Toronto, Canada, 1948.

INDEX

Index

Aberle, David F., 134, 163
Abrams, Barbara K., 44
Academy of Religion and Mental Health, 254
Ackerley, Lois A., 141, 142
Adler, Felix, 325
Adorno, T. W., 60
Adult education, and parent education, 23–24, 203, 213
Adult Education Association, 24, 261
Advice to parents: as content in the educational program, 166–176; historical changes in, 166–173; relation to research, 170–176; relation to values, 170–173; rules versus suggestions, 174–176; validity of, 170–176
Aims: and choice of methods, 194–196; ethical aspects of, 80–93; of parent education, 21–27; 79–109; of parents in child rearing, 132–135; parent educators' changes in, 91, 93–109; practical aspects of, 93–109; programs with multiple, 108–109; related to choice of program content, 151–153; 176–178; in relation to program personnel, 238–239; scientific issues in the choice of, 93–95
Allen, Lucile, 158, 310
Allen, Winifred Y., 18, 84, 159, 333
Allinsmith, Wesley, 44
Alper, Thelma G., 44
Ambrosino, Salvatore, 12
American Academy of Pediatrics, 340
American Association of University Women, 324, 329, 340
American Heart Association, 340
American Home Economics Association, 327, 331, 340
American Institute of Family Relations, 346
American Library Association, 189, 340, 342
American National Red Cross, 340, 341, 344

American Nurses Association, 340
American Orthopsychiatric Association, 261
American Psychiatric Association, 261
American Psychological Association, 261
American Public Health Association, 47, 96, 197, 212, 218, 251, 340, 341
American Social Hygiene Association, 340
American Sociological Society, 330
American Theater Wing Community Plays, 185
Ames, Louise B., 185
Anderson, John E., 31, 115, 116, 117, 119, 121, 139, 289, 321, 330
Andrew, Gwen, 291, 303, 306, 307, 308, 312
Annual Review of Psychology, 211
Anxiety, caused by parent education, 84–90, 95–99, 106–108. *See also* Unconscious motives
Associated Baby Services, 340, 341
Association for Childhood Education, International, 340
Association for Family Living, 188, 192, 346
Attitude Change Project, 212, 213
Attitudes, versus behavior as influences on child, 39–41, 95–99
Auerbach, Aline, 12, 21, 86, 191, 199, 204, 205, 219, 225, 226, 236, 243, 246, 247, 253, 260, 263
Austin Community Guidance Center, 309
Ausubel, David P., 39, 92, 135
Avery, Curtis A., 346

Bakwin, Harry, 33, 41, 102
Baldwin, Alfred L., 46, 98, 163, 271, 305
Bales, Robert F., 71, 196, 220, 221, 223, 225
Balser, Benjamin H., 284, 285, 291, 295, 296, 306, 311

353